QUESTIONING THE UNIVERSALITY
OF HUMAN RIGHTS

Questioning the Universality of Human Rights

The African Charter on Human and Peoples' Rights
in Botswana, Malawi and Mozambique

LONE LINDHOLT, Ph.D.
Institute of Legal Science sec. B
University of Copenhagen, Denmark

Taylor & Francis Group
LONDON AND NEW YORK

First published 1997 by Dartmouth and Ashgate Publishing

Reissued 2018 by Routledge
2 Park Square, Milton Park, Abingdon, Oxon, OX14 4RN
711 Third Avenue, New York, NY 10017, USA

Routledge is an imprint of the Taylor & Francis Group, an informa business

Copyright © Lone Lindholt 1997

All rights reserved. No part of this book may be reprinted or reproduced or utilised in any form or by any electronic, mechanical, or other means, now known or hereafter invented, including photocopying and recording, or in any information storage or retrieval system, without permission in writing from the publishers.

Notice:
Product or corporate names may be trademarks or registered trademarks, and are used only for identification and explanation without intent to infringe.

Publisher's Note
The publisher has gone to great lengths to ensure the quality of this reprint but points out that some imperfections in the original copies may be apparent.

Disclaimer
The publisher has made every effort to trace copyright holders and welcomes correspondence from those they have been unable to contact.

A Library of Congress record exists under LC control number: 97007872

ISBN 13: 978-0-367-00042-4 (hbk)
ISBN 13: 978-0-367-00047-9 (pbk)
ISBN 13: 978-0-429-44482-1 (ebk)

Contents

Abbreviations ix
Preface xi

Part I: Theoretical issues

1   General introduction   3

       Sources and levels of human rights regulation   3

       A model of global, regional and local human rights
       regulation   4

2   Human rights and constitutionalism in an African context   11

       Introduction   11

       The concept of "law" in an African context   12

       Africa, constitutionalism and democracy   15

       An African concept of human rights ?   17

       Conclusion   21

3   A universal concept of human rights ?   23

       Introduction   23

       The discourse relating to universality of
       human rights   25

       The scope of universal human rights principles   29

	The concept of universality	33
	a. The question of time	34
	b. The question of sources	41
	Conclusion	51

Part II: Context and genesis of the instruments

4 Background to the constitutions of Botswana, Malawi and Mozambique — 57

- Botswana — 57
- Malawi — 60
- Mozambique — 68
- Conclusion — 70

5 The African Charter on Human and Peoples' Rights — 73

- Historical background — 73
- Entry into force — 79
- Signature, ratification and accession — 81
- Conclusion — 84
- The African Charter and national law — 84
- The incorporation of international law in Botswana, Malawi and Mozambique — 87

Part III: Analysis of material human rights provisions in the African Charter on Human and Peoples' Rights and the Constitutions of Botswana, Malawi and Mozambique

6	Individual civil and political rights and freedoms	93
	Introduction	93
	The right to life	93
	The right to personal integrity	100
	Freedom from slavery	109
	The right to a fair trial	113
	The right to personal liberty	131
	The right to property	139
	The right to participate in democracy	144
	Freedom of conscience	152
	Freedom of information and expression	156
	Freedom of association and assembly	161
	Freedom of movement and residence	170
	Freedom from discrimination	184
7	Other provisions	213
	Economic, social and cultural rights	213
	Collective rights	228
	Duties of the individual	238

Part IV: Conclusion

8	General conclusions and perspectives	247

Appendix:

The African Charter (sample)	255
The Constitution of Botswana (sample)	265
The Constitution of Malawi (sample)	277
The Constitution of Mozambique (sample)	285
A "doughnut"-model for regulation of human rights	297

Bibliography   299

Abbreviations

AC	African Charter on Human and Peoples Rights
ACom	African Commission on Human and Peoples Rights
ACRC	African Charter on the Rights and Welfare of the Child
AFORD	Alliance for Democracy
AMCHR	American Convention on Human Rights
AMCourtHR	American Court on Human Rights
BC	Constitution of Botswana
BCC	Botswana Constitutional Conference
BCCC	Botswana Constitutional Conference Committee
BCCom	Botswana Constitutional Committee
BCPEA	Botswana Criminal Procedure and Evidence Act
BEA	Botswana Education Act
BPC	Botswana Penal Code
CSCE	Conference on Security and Cooperation in Europe
ECHR	European Convention on Human Rights
EcomHR	European Commission on Human Rights
ECOSOC	Economic and Social Council
ECourtHR	European Court of Human Rights
HRC	Human Rights Committee
ICCPR	International Covenant on Civil and Political Rights
ICESCR	International Covenant on Economic, Social and Cultural Rights
ICJ	International Court of Justice
ICRC	International Convention on the Rights of the Child
ILO	International Labour Organisation
KCC	Kenya Constitutional Council
KCCC	Kenya Constitutional Council Committee
MAC	Constitution of Malawi (1994)
MAPC	Malawi Penal Code
MIC	Malawi (Independence) Constitution (1964)
MOC	Constitution of Mozambique (1990)
NCC	National Consultative Council
OAU	Organisation of African Unity

OAUCR	OAU Convention Governing the Specific Aspects of Refugee Problems in Africa
ONUMOZ	UN Monitoring Forces in Mozambique
SADCC	Southern African Development Cooperation Conference
UD	Universal Declaration of Human Rights
UMCA	Anglican Universities Mision to Central Africa
UNCAT	UN Convention on Torture
UNCR	UN Convention on Refugees
UNCRP	Protocol to UN Convention on Refugees

Preface

This book was written over a period of several years during my time as a Junior- and Senior Research Fellow at the Institute of Legal Science, sec. B, University of Copenhagen.

The initial analysis of the African Charter on Human and Peoples' Rights in relation to international human rights instruments as well as the Constitution of Botswana was completed in 1994, when I submitted it for my Ph.D at the University. It was published in an A4 offset publication at my Institute, and distributed in a limited number. At that time it also included a chapter discussing various legal theories in relation to human rights, which has been left out in the present edition.

When Dartmouth agreed to publicize my book in 1995, I was asked to provide "a broader African perspective", and I decided to include in my analysis the two new Constitutions of Malawi and Mozambique from 1994 and 1990, as well as an update of the other chapters to include the latest legal developments in Botswana and, in particular, the initiatives of the African Commission. This revision was completed in July 1996, and no further material has been included after that time.

I owe deep thanks to a lot of people, without whose help this book would never have been finished. First and foremost the Institute of Legal Science sec, B, Faculty of Law at the University of Copenhagen which has provided me with working space, a salary and other resources for many years, and where my colleagues, past and present, have helped and supported me in every aspect of my work. Also the staff at the Danish Centre for Human Rights, which is a place where I always feel very welcome, was most supportive, in particular when it came to letting me use their excellent library facilities. The Danish Research Council financed my 3-month stay in Botswana in 1990, and the Ministry of Foreign Affairs provided me with the opportunity to visit Mozambique in 1993 and 1994 on short-term teaching assignments. Finally, my consultancy with the Danish Centre for Human Rights in 1996 allowed me to go to Malawi just before completing the final manuscript.

Other institutions and libraries who have been very helpful are the School of Oriental and African Studies, the Institute of Commonwealth

Studies and the Advanced Legal Studies Library, all in London. Here, Gillian Nevins at Amnesty International also gave me a lot of encouragement and assistance. Members of staff of the Hunger Project Global Office in New York and Dr. Wolfgang Benedek, University of Graz, Austria, have provided both important information and inspiration over the years. The staff at the secretariat of the African Commisison have also been very helpful.

When undertaking such a study as mine, one is very dependent on assistance from people in those countries where one is a visitor. Also in that respect I have been very lucky, and I want to acknowledge the help of Prof. Daniel Nsereko, Faculty of Law, University of Botswana and Emilias Dokali, Dean, Faculty of Law, University of Malawi. The staff of Danish Volunteer Service helped me greatly during my stay in Botswana, providing me with a place to stay as well as personal friends whose hospitality gave me an opportunity to see "the real Africa" for the first time.

I deeply want to thank Anne Stewart, School of Law, University of Warwick, whose humour, friendship and understanding has supported me during the final steps of the process, and who has facilitated my contact with Dartmouth Publishers as editor of the Law and Development series.

Some people have been more directly involved in the production of this manuscript. Law students Annali Kristiansen and Miriam Møller did a huge amount of work on the first and second editions respectively, and so did my secretary Mariann Helbrandt. I also owe profound thanks to translator Eva Ditlevsen, one of my oldest and closest friends, for reading through large parts of the manuscript and correcting some of those errors which must occur when writing in a foreign language. As with everybody else mentioned above, the various mistakes in this book are solely my own responsibility

Finally, I must thank my friends and family, who kept encouraging me to finish this work, because they felt that it could make a difference. Most deeply I thank my husband Henrik, who put up with my travels, mental as well as physical absence, cooked, cleaned and picked up the children, and followed me through ups and downs all along the process, and our two daughters, Lea and Maria, who were born and started their lives during this time. You all helped me grow to be the woman I needed to be in order to finish this book. I love you deeply, and dedicate this book to you.

And to the men, women and children of Africa...

Lone Lindholt, Copenhagen, October 1996

Part I
Theoretical issues

1 General introduction

Sources and levels of human rights regulation

In relation to a discussion of the basic sources of human rights regulation within any system, the starting point will be to clarify the question of terminology.

Generally we speak of two distinctions of law, the first of which is the international law as a denominator for all forms of legal regulation of a trans-national kind, e.g. involving in some way more than one national state. In contrast hereto stands the domestic law, which is a similar phrase covering all aspects of what the individual state may consider to be valid law within its domain.

The key problem relating to this terminology, and structure of perception, is that we experience an increase in laws and regulation cutting across these borders on a regional basis. The most extensive example hereof is the regulation within the European Communities, which in many cases confers direct significant obligations on member states or even in some cases substitutes the domestic law of the member states.

Within the field of human rights we have two well-established regional systems for protection and promotion of human rights, namely the European and American Courts and Commissions on Human Rights, under the European Council and Organization of American States (OAS) respectively. For a long period of time, these were the only two regional human rights arrangements, and these institutions operate alongside the international regulation established by the various bodies of, mainly, the United Nations. In cases where conflict between these two systems exists, a compromise has to be found, since none of them are above the other in a way similar to the relationship bewreen national and international law.

In relation to human rights promotion and protection the regional institutions would often supply the mechanisms of enforcement lacking in the international systems, while they would also at the same time apply the principles adopted on a global scale through such instruments as the Universal Declaration and the two International Covenants. This way the two systems would supplement each other, reducing the aspect of conflict between them to a relative minimum.

These regional institutions operated within systems with a relatively uniform cultural, political and legal background, and did not have wider impact on states outside the structure itself. Furthermore, both regional instruments contain provisions roughly similar to those of the main international instruments, with the institutions operating on similar conceptions and interpretations of law. Therefore the apparent consensus on the existence of a universally applicable code of human rights remained fairly unquestioned for a long period of time.[1]

Over the last decades this situation has changed, mainly due to a growing influence by states from other geographical regions, in particular Africa and Asia, on the international legal arena.

The key factor here has been the growth in regional human rights instruments, expressed by an African convention as well as various declarations and a draft charter for Asia and the Arab world, resulting in an increased recognition that the unquestioned universal applicability of, particularly, a European concept of law and human rights is no longer valid.

This discussion has been further actualized with the increased tendency of including human rights aspects in the development aid. As a consequence hereof we see a so far unprecedented tendency towards exchange of human rights concepts between Europe and North America on one side and Asia, Africa and Latin America on the other side. This again raises the question of the legitimacy of attempting to "export" human rights from one culture to another, particularly when extensive financial and other pressure is involved in the exchange.[2]

A model of global, regional and local human rights regulation

In light hereof, and in order to accommodate these discussions, I have chosen to operate with a terminology of three different levels, to be defined below: the *local*, the *regional* and the *global* level of regulation.

---

1. See chapter 3 on the question of universality of human rights for a more detailed discussion hereof.
2. A similar dissolving of formerly firm foundations and ideas is the growing recognition that what can be considered valid law and its sources also cannot be universally defined, to the extent that various forms of infomal law ranging from customary law in some African states to women's law in Western Europe plays by different rules and definition.

Still, I will continue to apply the terms "national" and "international", but I use them differently in situations where the particular distinctions are of a different nature or without significance. As such, the term international is used as a common denominator for global and regional regulation in general, while the term national refers to all law without distinction within a given national state.

The outer limit to the first level, the local sphere, is still the borders of the national state, following the distinction national-international, but the difference in relation to national law is more internal. By using the term "local", I intend to leave room for the possibility of sub-levels within the state, both in relation to geographical differences, such as the regulation in different states of the federal systems of Germany and USA as well as the variations in the customary laws between different tribes in Botswana. Also, this term implies the possibility of including different informal regulation applied by particular groups within the State, such as places of work particular to women or among ethnic or social groups or sub-cultures. In other words, it will have to be left to the discretion of each state to determine how far to go when setting the limits of the concept of law internally.

The second distinction of regional regulation is also of a geographical nature, including all forms of human rights regulation applicable to several states within a certain geographical area. These regions may vary, usually following the borders of continents and sub-continents such as Asia or Africa and sub-regional systems may be established. Examples hereof are the SADCC-states of Southern Africa, the Arab states of Northern Africa, or the Francophone states of West-Africa, which may form similar enclaves and establish initiatives within the regional framework of the OAU. All such potential initiatives would have to be encompassed by the distinction of regionality, and although (or because) they may seldom result in substantial structures such as the main regional human rights bodies, such potential conflicts of diversity would then have to be handled.

The third and last term, the global level, contains the element which we usually ascribe to the term international, and implies that we have moved beyond geographical borders and instead apply other criteria such as common interest and commitment or recognition of similar needs. In relation to human rights, regulation at a global level is open to adherence by all states regardless of their geographical location, and the most central example hereof is the above mentioned Bill of Rights. Supplementing this the United Nations, as well as other related organisations such as the ILO, have established a wide spectrum of different instruments, enforced by a significantly smaller number of various kinds of monitoring bodies. All of these instruments cover specific principles or concepts of human rights such as instruments regulating protection against torture and the prohibition against discrimination on the basis of culture, race or sex, just to mention a few.

The distinctions of these three different levels are not based on a presumption of hierachy, similar to the structures found in national law, where constitution is above legislation is above court practice is above administrative regulation etc.

The global regulation of human rights does not necessarily have a status superior to the decisions and legal provisions from the regional bodies. When ratifying a regional or global treaty, the national state usually has an obligation to ensure that the provisions contained herein are effectively transformed into its internal legal sphere, often by including them in national and/or local law. It does not, however, mean that it is hereby inferior to the powers of the supra-national structures, and non-compliance with the obligations of implementation can very often not be formally sanctioned.

Rather than a hierarchical perspective, one could look at such a model as governed by a principle of proximity in a "flat" model of circles within circles.

Here, the centre represents universal principles, if such can be identified,[3] while the next levels indicate each of the three levels mentioned above, and in theory the model continues until it reaches the smallest social and legal unit, the individual. Also, it allows for new regions or groupings to separate within each level, so that on the regional level it can easily accommodate a potential Eastern European or Pacific human rights initiative similar to those of the other regions.

In the centre we find the *basic principles* of human rights, expressed as customary supra-regulatory norms and issues considered to be of such a vital importance that they must be protected by international law. Examples hereof are the right to life and sustenance, freedom from violation of one's mental and physical integrity, the availability of opportunities to develop one's personal capacities, and the access to form and maintain relationships with others at both an individual and collective level.

We formulate these principles in terms of rights and freedoms, but in a legal sense it is doubtful whether we can talk about these formulations of

---

3. See chapter 3 on universality of human rights and a minimum definition hereof.

basic issues and needs within the framework of law at all. Rather, at this core level it is a question of identification of basic needs and values, which are then to be protected and normatized at subsequent levels. Their nature is such that they can be concluded as being fundamental and general, insofar as the lack of fulfilment seems incompatible with human existence and well-being regardless of geography or culture.

However, the same lack of cultural adaption also means that on their own they have limited effect as instruments of international law, since their scope and implications are not defined precisely enough to constitute legally enforceable rights and obligations. Their significance lies in the function of defining an overall framework for the actual human rights legislation taking place at the next levels, which derive their legitimacy from these basic principles. The dependency is mutual, because at the same time the core also relies on the outer levels for its fulfilment and legalization.

It is clear that once we leave the non-legal core of human rights principles, there is a quantum leap into the next levels, where we find the general and specialized *global* instruments elaborating and normatizing the issues and principles established in the centre. Examples hereof are the two International Covenants and the conventions relating to particular areas of human rights such as torture, discrimination etc. These provisions confer direct rights on individuals and corresponding obligations on member states to the instruments after a process of ratification and adherence. Following from this, and keeping in mind the discussion on this topic above, it is here we definitely move beyond any notion of absolute universality.

When we move on to the next spheres, of *regional* or sub-regional regulation, we are faced with partial solutions to the problems related to the global regulation, but at the same time other aspects and problems present themselves.

The lack of recognition of the distinction of this level of regulation can to some extent be accredited to the simple fact stated above, that until fairly recently only two regions, the European and the American continents, had fully established general human rights conventions with corresponding institutions of enforcement. The only available international bodies and measures available to individuals as well as states from other regions such as Africa or Asia were the international ones mentioned above.

Now, the situation has changed over the last decade, with the coming into force of the African Charter on Human and Peoples Rights and the establishment of the African Commission in 1986. The picture has further been enhanced with the Asian Declaration of the Basic Duties of Asean

Peoples and Governments from 1983, and the Draft Charter on Human and Peoples' Rights in the Arab World from 1986, neither of which, however, are of a legally binding nature qua their declarational respective provisional status.

A key characteristic of this level is that we find a stronger cultural impact on the formulation of these instruments than at the global level. The overall principles established at the global level are here given substance in a way which reflects the background, circumstances and general context in which they operate.

Such cultural influence is expressed at different levels and different forms, the most direct expressions hereof in individual provisions being the African Charter's art. 29 stating the individual's duty to preserve and strengthen positive African values and to contribute to the promotion and achievement of African unity.

A less expressive but still poignant expression of cultural impact is found in the formulations and systematics of other regional human rights instruments, such as the emphasis of the Asean Declaration on the duties of states rather than on individual rights.

Finally, cultural priorities and values can be expressed in a tacitly, and therefore often unnoticed or unquestioned, way through the limits in scope of an otherwise general human rights instruments. The example hereof is the European Convention on Human Rights, which limits itself to dealing only with the civil and political rights of the individual.

Regardless of the formulation or form, it is at this level we find the closest attempts of balancing the need for adaption to subjective local considerations with an objective supra-national regulation in conformity with internationally recognized principles. This is the case both with respect to material provisions and their formulation, the substance of law, and in relation to procedural structures, how the law is applied in practice. With regards to the latter, it is also at this level we naturally find strong and effective institutions of complaint and enforcement in the form of Commissions and Courts, since they benefit from their supra-national as well as more contextual character.

Moving to the *local level*, we take another quantum leap, since we now deal exclusively with the laws as they are formulated within the borders of the national state.

Using Botswana, Malawi and Mozambique as representatives of this level, we find that the superior law is the Constitution, including a Bill of Rights, which also forms the basis of this study in all three cases. Several provisions herein refer to various parts of the national legislation in the form of statutes. Different forms of sub-national law may also be formally recognized, as is the case with the various forms of tribal customary law in Botswana, indirectly in Malawi, and not at all in Mozambique.

The judicial institutions are strongly represented at this level, by the Magistrate's Courts (and in Botswana also the Customary Courts) at the lower levels, and the High Court and the Court of Appeal on the highest levels.

What is characteristic of this level is the proximity between the individual and the provisions and institutions affecting him. This has two effects, the positive of which is that conflicts needing judicial interference are solved with the authority's local, and sometimes even personal, knowledge of the circumstances surrounding the individual in the given situation. This subjectiveness, however, also means that personal interests of the State may influence decisions and legislative provisions, to the extent that the interests of the individual are set aside.

In relation to human rights protection, this is illustrated by the fact that nothing guarantees the rights and welfare of the individual better than a well-functioning national system based on precisely defined criteria and their effective implementation in practice. If, on the other hand, the national or local system does not sufficiently fulfil these requirements, the individual is left with very few safeguards, except those that stem from the State's adherence to international instruments and procedures. They, on the other hand, must somehow be transformed into national law, in order for them to have direct significance and impact also at this level closest to the sphere of the individual.

Therefore the mutual interdependence between the different levels of regulation reveals itself at this stage also, legitimizing the regulation transformed from the international levels, while at the same time giving substance to it.

As mentioned already, this study takes its starting point in the middle of the model, so to speak, by analyzing the youngest of the regional instruments, the African Charter on Human and Peoples' Rights. Accordingly, the comparison has been made both with the central circle, exemplified by the Universal Declaration and the International Covenant on Civil and Political Rights, with the other regional levels such as the European and American Conventions of Human Rights, and finally with the national level using the Constitutions of Botswana, Malawi and Mozambique. It is therefore possible to see the development from universal principle through international general concept, further contextualized in the regional conventions and, finally and most specifically, in the national constitution and legislation. The movement going in the other direction, expressed as the evaluation of individuals' complaints by the national courts and the regional and international bodies can also be seen throughout the analysis, even though this is not the primary focus of this work.

2 Human rights and constitutionalism in an African context

Introduction

When dealing with a subject such as the African Charter on Human and Peoples Rights and its transformation to national law in its member states, not to speak of its adherence to other non-African international human rights instruments, one of the issues to be confronted is the relevance or even appropriateness of speaking of human rights in an African context.

The reason for this issue to be brought forward lies within the European roots of the human rights concept in its present form, combined with the strong reaction of sensitive post-colonial young states against any undue influence from outside the African continent.

The strongest expression of this would be to reject all international human rights instruments, on the grounds that they represent an attempt of neo-colonialism, being alien to African culture, and that their provisions can therefore be set aside without regard. Indeed, this approach has over the years served as a convenient excuse for massive human rights violations by dictatorial rulers with a higher regard for personal power than for the well-being of their people.

It is, however, a general trend that even those countries who have otherwise expressed an honest dedication and commitment to improving the standard and quality of living for their inhabitants, states with a positive human rights record, have still been hesitant to adopt more than a minimum of the international human rights instruments.[1] The argument for this has been that even if one assumed that these instruments in their formulation as well as their essence might co-exist with the legal tradition and the domestic law of the states, their provisions are still inappropriate to dealing with the economic, social, political and cultural realities of most African states.

Without going into a long discussion on this point, the situation looks different in the last decade since the establishment of the African Charter on Human and Peoples' Rights and the African Commission. For the first

---

1. See ch. 4 with regard to Botswana's, Malawi's and Mozambique's ratification of international instruments.

time, the African states now have a regional general human rights convention, established by themselves, conferring a legally binding obligation of implementation on member states, and with measures of safeguard and a complaint procedure accessible to individuals.

Nguema, in his article putting the African Charter into perspective, summarizes the discussion into two main statements, that human rights did not exist in traditional African societies, and that the policy of human rights promotion and protection is an imported product imposed on Africa from the outside.[2]

Following his example, I have attempted in the following to approach some of these basic questions, but at the same time I have also taken a slightly different approach and draw the distinction between African constitutional law as such on the one hand and an African concept of human rights on the other hand.

The concept of "law" in an African context

First, there is the very basic question of what is implied in term "law", an issue which has been debated extensively over the years by anthropologists and other social scientists. It is, however, a question which is most pressing in relation to an objective definition of law as distinct from custom and other forms of practice, particularly in a cross-cultural perspective and in relation to a European perception.

There is a distinction to be made between custom and law, and it is true that not all custom has the form, and therefore the force, of law,[3] but in relation to this particular study I hold that the significance hereof is less significant. What is important is whether the overall trends of society, including custom as well as law, reflect some of the same concepts and structures we find in present day legal discourse, and whether they were perceived by the people to have a binding force of some kind.

In relation to the term "African law", we must recognize that this is neither a static nor a uniform concept, but subject to even extreme variations in relation to time as well as location.

Illustrating this view is the fact that traditional customary law was and is characterized by its close connection to the identity and intimate internal structure of the society in which it operates and from where it has origi-

---

2. Nguema, 1990, p. 261 - 271.
3. Sinha, 1989.

nated and developed. It is the local law and legitimized by its recognition as such; even though it will often correspond with actual practice, at least in a historical perspective, it can not be taken for granted that it is still an accurate illustration hereof.

Even within African nation states of today we find the co-existence of many different and distinct spheres of customary law pertaining to each tribe. An example hereof is Botswana, which still counts several spheres of material customary law pertaining to the major tribal lineages,[4] even though it is all being treated as one in relation to the procedural framework and review procedure established by the legislation of Botswana.[5]

On a continental scale *Sinha* draws out 13 different African cultures, and proceeds to demonstrate that they do not operate from a concept of law similar to that which we recognize in the European tradition. His examples are interesting from another point, because they clearly illustrate the differences between the traditions of the peoples of Ashanti, Yoruba, Nandi and Tiv in relation to lineage, societal composition, and the establishment and enforcement of law and tradition.[6]

Adding to the complexity are the various stages of development characteristic of each society, where *Nguema* identifies the four stages of a gregarious, a familial and a hierarchical society as well as the society en route to actual statehood. All of the administrative and power-related structures and mechanisms will vary according to the developmental stage of each society, which will have an impact on how the law presents itself in each case.

This diversity remains, if we move from an isolated view of traditional societies and their customary law and towards the colonial and post-colonial societies of modern Africa.

We can distinguish between three major cultural influences, or "mental universes"[7] coexisting in Africa for centuries and in present day, which are the Islamic, the Christian, and the animist religions. Even though their respective dominance varies among the various regions, with a stronger islamic influence in the northern than in the southern part of the continent, all of them are present to some degree in the majority of African states. The

---

4. Isaac Schapera, 1938, revised ed. 1984.
5. (Botswana) Customary Courts Act, S.I. 12, 1977.
6. Sinha, opr. cit.
7. Nguema, opr. cit.

definition of what is law and, accordingly, its structures of enforcement vary, ranging from the natural and ancestral forces of the animist world, via the Sharia and the Sounna of Islam to the predominantly positivistic law of the Christians.[8] It should be kept in mind that regardless of which system of law is predominant in each society, the absolute majority of the people continue to live according to their ancestral customary law, presupposing a notion of cosmic order where a connection between human behaviour and nature is obtained.[9]

Hereby the uniformity of law is further fragmented, since the most common situation is now one in which several legal systems exist at various levels, by coincidence being either in harmony, in direct conflict, or supplementing each other, all of which allow for "forum shopping" and confusion as to what is actually the law to be applied in each case.

If we also add the factor that the various societies furthermore find themselves at various stages of development, and subject to very diverse historical, political, economic and ecological influences, all of which strongly impose administrative and other structures of significance to law, it is clear that we cannot speak of anything close to a uniform African concept of law.

The question remains, however, if it is possible to draw out some characteristics which are representative of the continent as a whole, because they are features which to some degree shine through in the majority of African societies today. While maintaining the notion that Africa is not one society and that diversity exists, it is possible to make certain generalizations in relation to the notions of individualism, rightism and legalism.

These main features can be summarized into the claims that:

"Since the group, not the individual, is of primary importance, the social order proceeds not on the basis of individual rights but, rather, on the basis of obligations. Obligations themselves are not so sharply distinguished between legal and moral as in the West. Justice consists not in enforcing rights but in bringing about harmonious settlement between the disputants so that group cohesion is assured. Peace is achieved through reconciliation",

---

8. All of these systems may again contain sub-groupings of different systems, an important example of which is the differences of legal concepts in the various European traditions of Constitutional and Common Law. This has resulted in separate constitutional legal frameworks among the various African states, depending on whether the colonial power was French, British, German, Portugese etc.

9. Sinha, 1981.

leading to the conclusion that:

> "Individualism, rightism, and legalism of the West do not seem to have permeated extensively in the bloodstream of everyday life of most Africans".[10]

This conclusion, which I will neither attempt to verify or reject at this stage, leads to the next part of this chapter, and to a discussion of the possibility or appropriateness of claiming the existence of a distinct African concept of human rights, and the role of the African Charter on Human and Peoples Rights in this context.

Africa, constitutionalism and democracy

Another aspect of the discussion, which is highly relevant to this study, deals with the more specific implementation of law in the form of constitutionalism and democracy and their relevance in an African context. This is a very comprehensive area, which shall only be touched briefly at this stage for two reasons. The first is that much of what is said relates to the general area of constitutional law and largely passes by the validity of a Bill of Rights as part hereof. The second reason is that this discussion often moves, appropriately, less in the area of law and more in such a field as political science. In this context I will therefore only present a few of the views to the extent that they contribute to the general discussion on human rights law in an African context.

Constitutionalism can be defined as:

> "the principle that the exercise of political power shall be bounded by rules, rules which determine the validity of the legislative and executive action by prescribing the procedure according to which it must be performed or by delimiting its permissive content",[11]

and in the shorter version that

> "fidelity to the principle that the exercise of state power must seek to advance the ends of society".[12]

---

10. Sinha, 1981.
11. de Smith 1987, quoted by Shivji in ed. Shivji, 1991, p. 28.
12. Okoth-Ogendo, p. 20, in ed. Shivji, 1991.

The question which must be asked, then, is whether this must be achieved through one or two models of universal applicability, or whether the attempts to introduce the Western European version in an African context was doomed to fail for practical as well as ideological reasons.[13]

According to *Shivji*, the liberal concept of democracy rests on the two main pillars of limited government and individual rights, around which all the other aspects such as separation of government, periodic elections, rule of law etc. are built. Such a concept was embedded in most independence constitutions, in spite of the fact that it was never part of the colonial political or legal order, which in contrast could be described as despotic. He claims that "The Western liberal democratic form has been tried again and again in Africa and totally failed", listing a number of examples such as South Africa, Uganda, Libya and Ghana.[14]

Based on these experiences, he presents the alternative New Democratic Constitutionalism, which in contrast is based on the other twin pillars of limited government and fundamental freedoms/rights. According to him, "the new concept of constitutionalism should rest on accountable/responsive state and collective rights/freedoms". They could be structured into four different major foundations described as "right of peoples and nations to self-determination", "right to democratic self-governance", "right to organise" and "right to integrity of person". What is new, he claims, is not so much an inventing of new rights, but rather

"(1) attributing a broader and deeper meaning to them based specifically on the historical experience of Africa, (2) seeing them as integral rather than hierarchical and (3) recognising both their programmatic (or ideological) as well as normative (or regulatory) value".[15]

Kobia states that one solution is for Africa to "legitimate democracy for herself by rediscovering the democratic culture within African political philosophy and practice", with the aim that "having rediscovered her rich democratic past, Africa will take its rightful place in the community of nations in deepening and enriching democratic theory and practice". This would make democracy "more authentically African", so that it will be more easily promoted and defended. The author continues to list a number of traditional African societies, such as Kenya, Ghana and Senegal, where indigenous practices of a democratic nature reflect closely the human

---

13. Kobia, 1993, p. 9ff.
14. Shivji, p. 28 and 36f, in ed. Shivji, 1991.
15. Ibid., p. 39f.

rights concepts of modern days. He concludes that the African Charter on Human and Peoples Rights' catalogue of individual duties expresses the traditional African balancing of rights and responsibilities, and so does also the veneration of the elder generation. Finally, he admits that one area where traditional African societies are highly different from modern day human rights ideology, is with respect to the equal rights and inclusion of women in democratic procedures, and this is one area which has grave implications for efforts in this area as well as economic development in general. He concludes by stating that "African symbol systems and values need to be brought into the current democratization debate and experience".

Arat concludes that, in actuality, some of the African states including Botswana, Gambia, Mauritius and Zimbabwe have maintained "highly democratic systems". Other states such as Cameroon, Congo and Lesotho have experienced "brief democratic rule within a mainly authoritarian setting".[16]

Finally, *Sachs* agrees that "the ideas of democracy, peace and respect for human rights does not belong to one continent", and states that the term "Western Democracy" and Eurocentrism is opposed with universalism rather than with any concept of African exceptionalism. He alerts us to the fact that "the term Africa democracy has been used to deny African people their individual rights as citizens and their fundamental freedoms as human beings" and criticizes that "The eminently good African tradition of talking a matter through courteously and reasonably until consensus binding upon all is reached, is turned around to justify the imposed consensus of one-person rule".[17]

These remarks, indicating that democracy is closely related theoretically as well as in practice to human rights, lead us into the next area concerning the question on how these are perceived in an African context.

An African concept of human rights ?

If we want to discuss the possible existence of a distinct African concept of human rights, and bearing in mind the discussion of legal diversity in traditional as well as present day African societies, we must first draw the important distinction between form and essence.

Looking for a traditional concept in the same form as we know it from a European perspective, as a legally enforceable rights-oriented individual concept, we may only find it in very few, if any, traditional African

---

16. Arat, 1991, p. 55f.
17. Sachs, 1991, p. 3.

societies. This is primarily due to the features presented as being at the same time common (for African societies) and distinct (from a European perspective), where the focus is on the group and on obligations rather than on the rights of the individual, contained in the statement that "in African culture it is the community (consisting of unitary, or extended, families) that has priority".[18] Indeed, we may not even find many examples of forms of traditional governments fulfilling the requirements of European democratic ideals, which again rest on the equality, autonomy and ability of representation of each member of the community.

Another problem with applying a traditional European criteria of human rights directly to an African context is that the fabric hereof, the concept of legal personality, as pointed out by Nguema[19] is not static; rather it depends upon various factors such as a person's ethnic status (which in some societies may be changeable through marriage, so that the woman assumes the ethnic identity of her husband), or on societal status (where a person moves through sharply defined levels of society according to age or some other form of merit). It may even transcend the borders of life and death (as in cases where the child born by a widow who has been taken in by her brother-in-law has the parentage of the late husband). Even though a somewhat similar tendency towards a "fluent" concept of legal personality is also known in European law and tradition, for instance when the right to vote is only acquired when the fixed age of majority is reached, from a purely legal point of view the effects hereof are less significant.

If, however, we do look instead to the essence, the spirit, and to the end result of the concept of human rights, instead of the process and the form in which it presents itself, we may find that many of the traditional societies through other means catered to the well-being and balance of the group as well as its members, and that these structures and approaches would often fulfil similar functions as those we attribute to various human rights institutions.[20]

To compare the two directly would be a mistake since, it would be "based on an assumption that confuses human rights with human dignity".[21]

Still, it has been claimed that some human rights concepts can be

---

18. Tévoédjré, 1985, p. 5.
19. Nguema, opr. cit.
20. See quotations in relation to democracy/constitutionalism above.
21. Howard, 1986.

found to be recognized by most traditional societies. These rights would be the right to membership, the freedom of thought, speech, belief, and association, and the right to enjoy property. Their legitimacy and enforcement stems not from a Grundnorm or a constitutional basis, but are "- a set of social values ingrained as a set of basic principles espoused by at least a substantial majority of a given society".[22] Tévoédjré claims that before the European partition of Africa in the late 19th century, "African maintained a set of rights and duties for its peoples which were substantially in tune with the concept of "natural law" and the "dignity of man".[23]

It may be a correct assumption, but at the same time it does not seem possible to establish on this basis the existence of a distinctly African concept of human rights, in the sense that the identification of a common streak of features is not sufficient in itself.[24]

At the same time I would like to point out that this does not mean that we cannot speak of an African contribution to the field of international human rights, but that it takes the form of an African adaption of universal concepts. A result hereof would be that the concrete interpretations hereof might coincide with those of other regions, predominantly Europe, but also that they may not. In the latter case we have a model where human rights at the same time are universal in their essence, but allow for cultural diversity in their form and in their interpretation and practical application.

In this approach there is an inherent opportunity for conflict in situations where these different approaches and interpretations are in competition, such as would often be the case when including the human rights aspect in relation to development aid from Europe to Africa. Here, one will have to use one of the approaches pictured by Nguema, which apply to the international scene of human rights as well as to a multi-legal African society: Either one adopts the approach of synthesis, which has the drawback of being, in his words, insincere to actual circumstances and "- betraying the truth by concealing the differences". Or the solution of unification and assimilation is applied instead, the danger of which is the oppression by the stronger

---

22. Lakshman Marasinghe, ed. Welch/Meltzer, 1984.
23. Tévoédjré, p. 7.
24. A similar warning of caution against adopting a human rights ideology too specific to Africa was presented to the first meeting of the group of experts preparing a Draft African Charter in Dakar in November 1979: "You have to be careful that your Charter may not be a Charter of 'The African Man'. Mankind is one and indivisible and the basic needs are similar everywhere". Benedek, 1983, p. 148.

of the weaker - which, in this case, could mean that a European approach to human rights would be claimed as having universal value and applicability.[25]

The entire discourse of an African concept of human rights has been simplified with the adoption of the African Charter on Human and Peoples Rights in 1981 and its coming into force in 1986. This, in my opinion, leaves us with one final question, namely if we can choose to accept this instrument, with all of its features, as an African expression and interpretation of what the continent as a whole accepts as a valid concept of African human rights law.[26]

Speaking for a cautious acceptance hereof is the point made by Nguema, bearing in mind his status as retired Chairman of the African Commission on Human and Peoples Right established by the Charter, who points out that among the African states themselves, the Charter has received widespread critique. The difficulties relating to its acceptance, at least among more radical post-and anti-colonialists, is its proclaimed status as an offspring of the Universal Declaration and, as such, based on a non-African concept of law as described above. The objections, he claims, are based on ideological prejudices, historical factors, social structures, and deep-rooted conflict regarding logic, visions of the universe as well as the organization of the world.

However, one should bear in mind that the African Charter perhaps more than any other human rights instruments is based on a compromise between a wide-ranging diversity of national legal and cultural backgrounds as described above, further enhanced by the differences of the "imported" legal systems of such colonial powers as France, England and Portugal.

At the same time the Charter also had to conform to the norms and formats already established by other regional and, particularly, the central global human rights instruments, in order to be accepted as a serious legal instrument by representatives of the non-African legal community.

Seen in this light, it is significant that at this relatively early stage of its history, almost all member states of the OAU have ratified the Char-

---

25. Nguema, opr. cit.
26. The main features hereof are the inclusion of a catalogue of individual duties; a series of peoples' rights; and the firm establishment of the family as the basic unit of society rather than the individual. See Benedek, 1983, p. 150ff.
   For an in-depth analysis of the individual provisions of the Charter, see the empirical part of this study.

ter,[27] thus expressing their unanimous support and adherence to the document.

Conclusion

Without neglecting the valid objections referred above, as non-African scholars, we are hereby left with only two options regarding an African concept on Human Rights:

Either we can continue in the same vein as hitherto, basing our conclusion on imperical facts and analysis combined with opinion and statements according to our choices and considerations - with the risk of confusing "ought" with "is", and without any guarantees that such a discussion will, in the end, be productive in the sense of forwarding greater understanding of the nuances pertaining to this complex issue.

Or we can choose to take a seemingly harsh and abrupt approach terminating, at least for the time being, the questioning of an African concept of human rights, by accepting the African Charter as an expression hereof on the basis of what has been stated above. This would be the same as resigning to a compromise rather than searching for a more complex picture and truth, but on the other hand it is, in my opinion, also the only way to take seriously the efforts of the African states in formulating their contribution to the human rights discourse.

---

27. As of 1995, only two "old" OAU member states, Ethiopia and Swaziland, as well as the new member states of South Africa and Eritrea, had not adhered to the African Charter on Human and Peoples Rights.

3 A universal concept of human rights ?

Introduction

One of the questions relating to the universality of human rights is whether an evaluation hereof is based on an ideological presumption that some values must have universal validity, or if it is established through an empirical analysis of the provisions of a number of instruments. In the first case the issue is whether human rights *ought to be* universal, in the second case whether they *are* universal.[1]

The importance of distinguishing between the two lies within the fact that we cannot legitimately deduce from "is" to "ought", since this represents a confusion of two distinct scientific methodologies. This means that just because there seems to be some degree of universal consensus as to basic human needs formulated as rights and freedoms, we cannot extend this to serve as the only legitimation for claiming that human rights, as they develop and express themselves at different times or under different circumstances, must therefore conform to a narrowly defined universal code of human rights.

As to the contrary situation, deducing from the normative to the empirical, it also carries some dubious consequences. An illustration hereof would be to reject certain types or distinctions of rights, because they do not confirm to a normative definition of a universal human rights conception. One might for instance reject the legitimacy of including an extensive catalogue of collective rights as well as individual duties, as we know it in the African Charter,[2] with the argument that a universal code of human rights should encompass only the protection of individual rights and freedoms. In this particular case it would be a serious mistake, since both concepts are found in a basic form in both the two International Covenants

---

1. The first question is dealt with here, the next is the focus of chapters 6 and 7 of this study.
2. Art. 27 through 29 of the African Charter contain a wide catalogue of more or less specific individual duties, discussed in greater detail in chapter 7.

and the Universal Declaration of Human Rights,[3] not to mention several other international instruments.

Generally speaking, a strong ideological position of universality will result in ensuring a certain constancy and general applicability of human rights concepts, which for instance makes individual country performance both easier to evaluate and impact.[4] On the other hand it will also tend to narrow the possibility of adapting human rights policies to actual circumstances, whether they are of a political or a cultural nature. Hereby the price of consistency is lack of flexibility and, eventually, the danger of stagnation and ineffectiveness of human rights instruments to serve as measures of protection and promotion.

The opposite approach, where the universality of human rights is more or less rejected from an ideological point of view, will also have a direct effect on the conclusions made with regards to the empirical analysis of human rights concepts. In case of the example of the African Charter's particular characteristics mentioned above, there would be a greater willingness to accept these features as a reasonable adaptation to the circumstances under which the African Charter has to operate. From this position, one might even go as far as to see seemingly criticizable features of the Charter, such as the absence of an African Court of Human Rights and even the extensive use of "clawback" clauses, as appropriate in this context - a conclusion which is hard to sustain from a more universalistic approach. The most obvious danger such a position is, of course, that even blatant human rights violations are excused with a reference to the "non applicability" of, for instance, the international conventions on discrimination against women and torture.

The tendency in the theoretical discourse of universality of human rights is not to differentiate between the empirical and the ideological aspects of universality, and that includes most of the legal scholars listed below.[5] Some of the quotations reflect a clear empirical approach, while other are more opinionated, but generally they do not reflect clearly the distinction between "is" and "ought". Instead, they tend to reflect cultural diversions instead, where the American tendency is to adopt a relatively

---

3. See art. 1 of both International Covenants on the rights of all peoples to self-determination and free disposal of natural resources, and the Universal Declaration art. 29 stating that everyone has duties towards his or her community.
4. See for instance Tomasevski in Childers (ed.), 1994, p. 98ff.
5. An exception is Sinha, 1984.

strong universalistic stance. The Scandinavian and European views reflect a more moderate approach in balancing the need for some sort of global alignment with the need to take into account the realities in which human rights must operate. Finally the Africans take a position reflecting both empirically and ideologically a tendency toward cultural relativism rather than universality.

In my own attempt to draw up a scientifically motivated rather than an opinionated position, I begin with taking the literal sense of the term "universal", and on the basis hereof draw up the conditions hereof with respect to both the distinction of conception (history) and of application (presence and future). When applying these criteria, I further distinguish between the question of whether human rights must also remain constant over time, and what the sources of a potential universal human rights concept will be, following the criteria of the initial definition.

At this point, however, I should remark that I myself have purposefully departed from the strict diversion between the empirical "is" and the normative "ought", since I have found that the only valid source to determining the extent of the validity of a theoretical concept of universal human rights, is the empiric. It is therefore not a question of deducing from "is" to "ought", but rather of using the empirical material to determine the extent to which the theoretical and normative conclusions can legitimately be applied in practice. Therefore the question of sources to a universal code of human rights is answered by applying the theoretically defined criteria to the scope of various international human rights instruments. In a similar way the issue of constancy of human rights over time is examined through an analysis of the actual developments of human rights concepts and principles as expressed in these same instruments.[6]

The discourse relating to universality of human rights

The question of universality of human rights has been approached by several legal scholars, and it is interesting to note that one may divide these opinions into schools according to geographical and cultural boundaries,

---

6. This procedure reflects the conclusion that "The theory of human rights - provinig a body of doctrine which suggests a standard against which what is, what happens to be, can be judged. Its own claim to be authoritative, and not just another variety "what is", relies on the observation that it stands outside any particular society or culture - and that it endures beyond a single generation". Vincent, 1986, p. 36.

where the tendency towards the more radical universalism can be found among the Americans.

Howard in particular claims, with a particular reference to an African context, that "I believe that human rights ought to be universal", a highly ideological statement. At the same time she does admit that seen in an empirical perspective "cultural variations do indeed affect peoples' perceptions of human rights".[7]

A similar vein is followed by *Nickel*, who states that "claims of universality and inalienability are plausible at least for some specific rights, if not for all of them", but at the same time maintains that "strong claims of universality and inalienability are not valid for many specific human rights".[8]

A slightly different angle is applied by a third American, *Donnelly*, who carries out an in-depth discussion not only of the theoretical principle of universality but also of its counterpart, cultural relativity. His conclusion is that rather than a universal approach, one should apply what he terms as "weak cultural relativism", where culture is an important source without leaving out completely the aspect of universality.[9]

The Scandinavian and other European researchers apply a slightly more moderate approach to the ideological question of universality, where *Tévoédjré* declares that "there exist certain universally accepted norms for the protection of a people's rights that form a fundamental core of human rights".[10]

Rehof and Trier speak empirically about the definition of a core of universally applicable basic principles governing the relationship between a state and its citizens. At the same time, however, they recognize that different human rights are considered important and fundamental at different points in time and under different circumstances.[11]

From an empirical perspective *Zahle* defines human rights as being neither "eternal" nor "self-evident", but debatable and affected by time as well as location.[12]

Finally, *Eide and Alfredsson*, with a particular reference to the Universal Declaration on Human Rights, state that "(these remarks do not mean) that there is universal consensus about human rights", a clearly empirical conclusion.

---

7. Howard, 1986, p. 12f.
8. Nickel, 1987, p. 44f.
9. Donnelly, 1989.
10. Tévoédjré, 1986, p. 2.
11. Rehof and Trier, 1990, p. 57.
12. Zahle in Gulmann, Nordskov Nielsen and Rehof (ed.), 1987, p. 79.

One of the most prominent and serious investigations of the question of human rights' universality is carried out by *Cassese*. He establishes that the Universal Declaration and the two International Covenants do establish human rights rules of a universal scope, but also claims that, since human rights are both conceived and observed differently, "universality is, at least for the present, a myth".[13]

It is therefore interesting to note that while the American approach reflects a strong ideological stance favourable to universality of human rights, the Europeans base their conclusions more on the degree to which the universality is reflected empirically in the various instruments.

The African approach can mainly be divided into two schools, the first of which constitutes the most radical opposition to universalist approach. The main argument here is rooted in the different philosophical basis of Western Europe and Africa, with a particular emphasis on the lack of an individualistically perceived personality in traditional African culture, which would render most human rights principles inapplicable. As such it represents an example of how empirical facts can form the basis of an ideological position. Representatives of this school are *Khushalani, Dunstan Wai* and *Lakshman Marasinghe* among others.[14]

In contrast hereto we find another, and less radical, African approach ideologically closer to that of the Americans and the Europeans, which at least to some degree recognizes the universality of basic human rights.[15]

A representative of this position is *Quashigah*, who concludes that "since societal development has never been universally in *pari materia*, human rights contents which are specific ideas rooted in certain social facts of the particular societies cannot be expected to be universal", while at the same time acknowledging that certain basic human needs are "indisputably universally ascribable to persons of every historical, geographical and cultural background".[16]

To sum up all these approaches they bridge a span ranging from intentions towards an ideal absolute universalism to a purely relativistic view. The majority of the sources, however, adopt an approach which on the one hand recognizes that universality exists to some extent, at least in relation to basic human rights concepts and principles, but that some space must be left open to allow for cultural and other adaptions hereof.

---

13. Cassese, 1990.
14. Shivji, 1989, p. 12, 37.
15. Assanta and Kannyo; Shivji, 1989, p. 11f.
16. Quashigah, 1992.

An indication of a seemingly global consensus on the issue may be drawn from the final document of the UN Conference on Human Rights in Vienna, Austria, in June 1993, bearing the title "Vienna Declaration and Programme of Action".
Paragraph 3 hereof states that:

> "All human rights are universal, indivisible and inter-dependent and inter-related - The international community must treat human rights globally in a fair and equal manner, on the same footing and with the same emphasis. While the significance of national and regional particularities and various historical, cultural and religious backgrounds must be borne in mind, it is the duty of states, regardless of their political, economic and cultural systems, to promote and protect all human rights and fundamental freedoms".

This is a strong and definitive ideological statement, which would seem to conclude the ongoing discussion of the existence of universal human rights. According to this declaration the opinion now seems to be in favour of a strong universalistic approach which, even though it does allow for some degree of cultural and other variations, still subjects them to a universal application.

It is my opinion, however, that such an apparent consensus gives all the stronger reasons for analyzing the concept in detail, and to define more closely the basis for and impact of the concept of universality of human rights. This is particularly so since the empirical conclusions of my own study[17] indicates that such an approach could be problematic in the long run, for reasons given already in the introduction to this chapter. Furthermore, the tensions at the UN Conference over this issue, where particularly the Asian representatives debated this position strongly, also indicates that the ideological consensus is not as clear as the Declaration presents.[18]

My own motivation for venturing into this discussion is, that if an ideological position is taken, it should have at least some foundation in the empirical realities in order to be taken seriously as a contribution to a legal discussion. If we want to operate with a universal concept of human rights, as lawyers we must ask ourselves where do we find such a concept, at which level of law, and with what material scope?

The following part will be used to define more accurately what lies in

---

17. See ch. 6 and 7 of this study.
18. See the Bangkok Governmental Declaration, Asian Regional Meeting in preparation for the World Conference on Human Rights, 1993.

the term Universal Human Rights Law, identifying the ramifications and implications of each component, and drawing up a workable definition of the concept on the basis hereof. This concept is then applied to the scope of international human rights regulation, and on the basis it is determined what the substance of an ideological approach to universal human rights may consist of.

First, however, I will start by outlining the material basis of human rights, and the scope of principles into which this has been elaborated over the years through the various international instruments.

The scope of universal human rights principles

When approaching the concept of human rights from a general perspective, one method is to generalize in broad categories and distinctions on the basis of what is perceived as universal human needs.

One may apply the terminology of requirements for a so-called "good life". This term is to be distinguished from the more basic notion of "a minimally decent life", but this distinction is not sharp, since it is not easily determined which standard a certain violation of rights and freedoms endangers. Subsequently such an instrument as the Universal Declaration does not distinguish clearly between the two, even though it would seem to be directed principally towards establishing minimal standards aimed at the most basic level.[19]

Several other attempts have been made towards breaking down the scope of human rights and freedoms into few and basic categories and principles for the purpose of generalization and operationability. Some of these follow the lines of the central international human rights instruments, and basically distinguish between the three categories of civil and political rights and freedoms, economic, social and cultural rights, and collective rights. This approach is perhaps one of the most basic features of the human rights discourse, to the extent that even those instruments which explicitly adhere to the principle of indivisibility between the various distinctions of human rights still list them separately in groups following one another. One example hereof is the African Charter.

A more scholarly approach, seemingly a paradox, is one of defining human rights concepts according to human needs and basic principles rather than according to their legal form or subjects. Where the effect of the

---

19. Nickel, p. 51f.

approach described above is one of distinction and expansion, this approach has the opposite effect of generalizing and narrowing down the scope of human rights to a handful of essential all-encompassing principles expressing basic human requirements.

One of the first examples hereof are the so-called "Four Freedoms" proclaimed by F.D. Roosevelt already in 1941, which were defined as four essential human freedoms given the following priority: freedom of speech and expression, freedom of worship, freedom from economic want, and freedom from fear expressed as a world-wide reduction of armaments.[20]

This principle has been applied by various jurists working in the academic field, most prominent of which is *Shue*, who establishes the notion of "basic rights" as being essential to the enjoyment of all other rights, and primarily to be contained within the three concepts of security, subsistence and liberty.[21]

A similar approach has been adopted by other scholars, who all to a varying degree include among basic rights the concepts of life, liberty, subsistence and food, and freedom from torture, arbitrary arrest and detention, disappearance, and extrajudicial execution.[22]

Whether this approach to dealing with human rights is productive in the long run, or whether such simplification of the concept does not come in the way of a more in-depth analysis of the problems connected with this issue, will not be given further thought here.

It does, however, serve the notion that what we are dealing with in a universal perspective are very basic concepts and principles, and that the implementation and interpretation hereof is quite a different matter, depending on the actual circumstances under which they operate.

To some degree we can establish the generally applicable definitions of such a concept as torture, and various UN-agencies have defined a minimum standard on consumption of calories per capita per day (depending on age etc.) as a measurement for adequate nutrition. Also, the extent of such rights as to a nationality, to freedom of assembly and association and to limitation of working hours can be generally defined.

Other types of rights are not so easily defined with regard to their precise fulfilment. For instance the general standard of living, climate or

---

20. Eide/Helgesen ed., 1991.
21. ed. Donnelly, 1989.
22. Donnelly, 1989, who lists Shue, Ajami, Bedau, Matthews and Pratt, and Reiter, Zunzenegui and Quiroga.

culture of a particular region may establish different norms for what would be defined as adequate housing, at least beyond the most basic level. Here one solution is to operationalize the concept by establishing a relative measure of a "minimum threshold" based on country-specific thresholds measured by indicators measuring a series of factors such as infant mortality rate, nutrition, life expectancy income, unemployment etc.[23]

A similar example is the concept of the right to a fair trial and the right to have legal defence at one's disposal during the trial. Even though it has been globally recognized, one must bear in mind those states, particularly African, which have incorporated the customary courts and law as part of their national legal system. In these cases it must be taken into consideration that the judges presiding are not legally trained, and it might therefore endanger the "balance" and fairness of the trial if both or one of the parties had legal representation. As a consequence hereof the provisions of the legislation of Botswana explicitly prohibit the use of legal representation at that level.[24] This is a situation which would be regarded as a gross violation of the right to a fair trial in the European or other similarly oriented systems, but one which is an appropriate application of the principle to the actual situation.

These variations exist not only in space, but also in time, since the fulfilment of an acceptable minimum standard is subject to changes in economic and political circumstances as well as the collective consciousness. An example hereof is the development of human rights principles rooted in already existing concepts, but taking into consideration such changes as described below. Examples hereof from the latest years are the emphasis on the rights of the child and on the protecting of the environment.

With regards to the Universal Declaration, established below as being the primary, if not only, source of universal human rights, it should be noted that this instrument limits itself to the establishment of basic principles rather than fully defined and applicable legal provisions.

It aims at the establishment of a "common standard of achievement" for all states, but leaves the actual implementation hereof to other sources, of where the two International Covenants are considered the most immediate, along with the European and the American Conventions on Human Rights.

---

23. See Eide, 1989.
24. See ch. 6 on fair trial.

In other words, the universal character and appropriateness of the Declaration spanning both time and place is achieved at the price of its lack of legal enforceability and its subsequent dependency on other "secondary" sources for its fulfilment in reality.

Finally, one may attempt to define universality of human rights on the basis of the derogation clauses in various instrument, in an attempt to single out those few and most basic rights which cannot be set aside under any circumstances. Here, the effect is different than that following from the other methodologies described above, because this would create a "first class" type of human rights, presumably from the distinction of civil and political individual rights, which would then be more "sacred" than other types of rights and freedoms.

The difficulty in applying this strategy is, in relation to this particular study, that the African Charter in contrast to some of the other instruments[25] does not contain a clause outlining the conditions for derogation, i.e for a limited period of time during a state of emergency and only to the extent that such measures are necessary to maintain public order. Instead, it is necessary to look at the formulation of the individual provisions in AC, and see whether they are absolute, allow for some restricitve and narrowly specified exceptions, or have a broad reference to national law or other similar criteria of a general nature.

When looking at the four international instruments ICCPR, ECHR, AMCHR and AC, we do find some correspondence, since all of them list that a number of rights cannot be set aside. Those are, not surprisingly, life and conditions with respect to the use of death sentences, torture and degrading punishment, slavery. In the same category falls freedom from *ex post facto* laws and punishment, which is perhaps less obvious. With respect to other rights and freedoms, such as fair trial, discrimination, conscience and information, all of the instruments on the other hand show remarkable variations, so that rights which are held to be exempt from derogation in one instrument may be set aside according to another. Interestingly enough, AMCHR and AC are the most restrictive and allow derogation for very few rights only, ICCPR is more liberal, and ECHR is by far the least protective insofar as it only exempts from derogation those first four types of rights and freedoms mentioned above.[26]

The national Constitutions of Botswana, Malawi and Mozambique

---

25. ICCPR art. 4, ECHR art. 15 and AMCHR art. 27.
26. Lindholt, 1995.

show similar variation in their derogation clauses, and hereby support the general conclusion that an indisputably universal concept of human rights, at least beyond the most fundamental principles, cannot be deduced from this basis.[27]

The concept of universality

To begin with, we must start by drawing up some definition of universality, a term we apply so willingly without always checking what it actually means.

The terms "universal" and "universality" can be defined as "of, belonging to, done by, all; affecting all", and a universal rule as one with no exception.[28]

This definition implies two requirements, referring both to the origin and to the present application of a rule or concept, and similarly to all locations within a given sphere as well as all entities within each location.

According to this definition, a rule or concept of human rights law, in order to be defined as universal, would have to have been established by a consensus of all states and must presently apply to all individuals within each of these states.

Accordingly, this is a very strict requirement, which narrows down the scope and sources of potential universal human rights significantly, as will be seen in the following.

Also, in wake hereof two important questions arise, the first of which relates to the question of *time*, and whether such a definition would also imply that human rights are static and do not evolve during the course of time. The second question follows closely at the heels of the first, particularly when this is not answered affirmatively, and relates to the legal

---

27. BC sec. 17 only specifies the conditions for and procedures relating to derogation from rights and freedoms in a case of emergency, but does not single any particular rights out for special protection in these cases, and a similar approach is found in MOC art. 106. In contrast to these two instruments, MAC sec. 45 not only specifies in a very thorough manner the limited conditions as well as the protective safeguards which derogation is subjected to. Sec. 45.3.a also specifically states that derogation may only take place in relation to a particular and limited catalogue of rights, corresponding roughly to those outlined by the international instruments, without applying the exact same scope as any of them. The pattern revealed by these three instruments therefore corresponds to that which is already outlined by the conventions.
28. Oxford Advanced Learners Dictionary of Current English, 1989.

sources on which so-called universal human rights concepts are based. In particular this refers to the issue of which international human rights instruments we presently claim as representative or formative of universal human rights.

a. The question of time

The question to be asked here is whether the definition of universality stated above does or does not allow for a development of the once-defined concepts of human rights over a longer period of time, and an appropriate starting point would be to look briefly at the historic development of human rights.[29]

An example of this historic development is the far more expansive inclusion of concepts and ideas in the Universal Declaration from 1948 than in the national Bills of Rights and Declarations of the previous couple of centuries, exemplified by such instruments as the French Declaration on Human Rights from 1789, and the American Declaration of Independence from 1776. Since the adoption of these early instruments, which focused almost entirely on the civil and political rights and freedoms of the individual, the Universal Declaration elaborates on these basic concepts and transforms them into actual rights, adding a number of important provisions concerning the individual economic, social and cultural needs.

Using the Universal Declaration of 1948 as a starting point for a new phase in history which moved the human rights discourse from a national to an international level, we already here ignore the dynamics of the historical and political developments which led to the evolution of this instrument. It is, however, appropriate to do so, not only because it is *de facto* the first global instrument to clearly define a general catalogue of human rights and freedoms, but because it is also recognized as such in the preambles of most of the subsequent global and regional instruments as well as by most independent states of the world.[30]

The principles of the non-binding Universal Declaration have since then been codified in a series of international human rights instruments, some of the most important hereof being the two International Covenants

---

29. "Human rights date back to the very dawn of human civilization and quite often appear clearly enshrined in the great religions of the world". Nagendra Singh, 1986, p. 1.
30. Sieghart, ed. Blackburn and Taylor, 1991, p. 24ff.

on Civil and Political Rights and on Economic, Social and Cultural Rights, which have now been ratified by a substantial number of states.[31]

Since 1948 more than 60 Conventions, Declarations, General Assembly Resoultions and other instruments have been issued by the United Nations alone, all of them elaborating on the basic principles enumerated in the Universal Declaration. These principles cover such concepts as a peoples' right of self-determination, freedom from war crimes and crimes against humanity, and freedom from discrimination, slavery, and forced labour. Other principles deal with the administration of justice, nationality and employment, political freedoms, family life and social welfare, while a number of instruments are aimed specifically at individuals in need of special protection such as refugees, women and children.[32]

Most of these instruments, and particularly those developed during the 1970's, were fairly non-controversial, in the sense that they operated on a basis of "individual rights vs. state duties" model, and elaborated on the concepts already defined in the International Bill of Rights created by the Universal Declaration and the two Covenants.

On a regional level the European Convention on Human Rights from 1950 followed the same course of adherence to the basic principles of the Universal Declaration. Still, by limiting itself to a narrow scope of civil and political rights and freedoms of the individual, one may question whether it does not in fact stray from the broad conception of human rights expressed in the Declaration.

In the South and Central American region the Organization of American States adopted the American Convention on Human Rights from 1969, based on the American Declaration on the Rights and Duties of Man from 1948. A tendency of narrow adherence to the basic concepts of individual rights is found, similar to that of the European Convention.

Thus the overall picture of human rights remained at the same time both dynamic and relatively stable for several decades, with the main

---

31. The International Covenant on Civil and Political Rights was of 31 December 1995 ratified by a total of 132 states, 15 of which joined it in 1992. Of those only about half of the member states of the OAU have ratified this Covenant, and 14 hereof have also ratified the First Optional Protocol. The International Covenant on Economic, Social and Cultural Rights had at the same date been ratified by 117 states, and with respect to the African countries all of the member states to the Covenant on Civil and Political Rights have all ratified the Covenant on Economic, Social and Cultural Rights, with the addition of Ginea-Bissau, Niger and Uganda.

32. United Nations, 1988.

schism between the Western emphasis on individual freedom and the Eastern claim that social well-being was equally important, underscoring the distinction of so-called 1. - and 2. generation rights.

During the 1980s, however, the international community has seen a significant development on two fronts, both with respect to the growing number of regional initiatives and instruments concerned with the issue of human rights, and in the elaboration and expansion of traditional human rights principles with more controversial concepts.

Regarding the expansion of regional initiatives, the most important of these is the African Charter on Human and Peoples' Rights adopted by the Organization of African Unity in 1981. This convention, which binds its member states to adhere to it and to give effect to it in national law, is presently ratified by almost every African state, thus making it the largest regional human rights instrument in terms of state membership.[33]

These three regional conventions covering the continents of Europe, America and, now, Africa, form the corner stones of regional human rights protection and promotion, since all of them are legally binding instruments with one or another form of implementation mechanism.

They have been supplemented, however, over the last decade with other regional human rights initiatives, the more important of which are the Declaration of the Basic Duties of Asean Peoples and Governments from 1983, and the Draft Arab Charter on Human and Peoples' Rights from 1986. An expression of the same tendency of regionalization of human rights, and the recognition of the importance of the subject, can be seen within Europe, where the EEC has issued a Declaration on Human Rights,[34] and where the CSCE and the Nordic Council have issued resolutions and other instruments and statements relating to human rights.

Looking at all these different instruments, some of which will be dealt with below to the degree of which they concern the question of sources of human rights, the overall tendency is for these instruments to elaborate on, but also in many ways significantly expand, the traditional concepts of human rights. This is particularly true for the non-European instruments, which each in their own way reflects adaptations to basic differences in cultural background as well as economic and political circumstances.

Examples hereof are, for instance, the above mentioned African Charter, the Draft Arab Charter and the Asean Declaration.

---

33. South Africa, Swaziland and Etiopia are not presently parties to the Charter.
34. Declaration on Human Rights, 1986, EEC-Bull. 7/8-86.

Some of the more particular features of the African Charter are the catalogue of Peoples' Rights in art. 19 through 24, including the right to peace, to a satisfactory environment and to development, and the inclusion of a series of individual duties of both a declarational and of a more substantial nature.

Looking now at the actual concepts of human rights in both the international and the regional sphere, we must make a preliminary evaluation of the degree to which these new initiatives do actually alter traditional and once-defined human rights principles, or whether they are merely elaborations hereof and therefore do not give rise to greater controversies.

Under the auspices of the United Nations, some of the most important instruments of the 1980s are the Convention on Torture and other Cruel, Inhuman or Degrading Treatment or Punishment from 1984, the Convention on the Rights of the Child from 1989, and the Declaration on the Right to Development from 1986.

Both of the first instruments are examples of elaborations of already defined principles regarding such special needs, codified as rights, for individuals considered to be in particularly vulnerable circumstances such as children, and the wish to firmly prevent particular forms of violations to human dignity such as torture.

It is thus important to note that both of these conventions are preceded by international declarations, the Declaration on the Rights of the Child from 1959 and the Declaration on the Prevention of Torture from 1975.[35]

Although the formulation and contents of several of the provisions in both conventions express a need not only to codify more clearly but also bring up to date the provisions and specific rights and duties contained herein, these developments do not violate or significantly expand the basic principles already expressed in the Declarations. An expression of the timeliness and appropriateness, combined with the above-mentioned lack of controversy, is the almost unanimous support which particularly the Convention on the Rights of the Child has enjoyed in spite of its short history, which on a smaller scale is also true for the Convention on Torture.[36]

Significantly different is the situation concerning the Declaration on

---

35. UN General Assembly Resolution 1386 (XIV) of 20 November 1959;
    UN General Assembly Resolution 3452 (XXX) of 9 December 1975.

36. As of December 31. 1995 a total of 190 states have ratified the Convention on the Rights of the Child, and 3 states have signed it. The Convention on Torture has been ratified by 93 and signed by 13 states as of the same date.

the Right to Development, which was adopted by the UN General Assembly in 1986,[37] and states the right of all individuals and peoples' right to participate in, contribute to, and enjoy economic, social and cultural development.[38]

The important tendency expressed in the Declaration as well as in the regional instruments described above is one of softening up, balancing, or even rejecting, the purely individualistic approach to human rights, which had so far been the general approach as illustrated in the previous human rights instruments considered to be the most important. Politically, this illustrates the shifting of the basic conflict of approaches and priorities from what had previously been mainly a schism between West and East, as illustrated above, to a confrontation between North and South. This has been exemplified by the reaction from developing countries in Asia, South America and, particularly, Africa against what has sometimes been described as a neo-colonialistic attempt to export values and belief systems.[39] At the same time these legal developments also show the commitment of these regions and cultures to adhering to the principles of human rights in accordance with the growing pressure from the international community, while at the same time attempting to make them appropriate to their own situation.

Now, in light of the superficial account of the historic development of international human rights, a preliminary conclusion will be reached as to what degree basic human rights principles and concepts have been changed and expanded since their initial formulation.

Using the two aspects which have proved to be most controversial, the broadening of the scope of collective rights and individual duties, which is exemplified in the African Charter and to some degree also in the Declaration on the Right to Development, we will have to look and see if a basis for these distinctions exists in previous basic human rights instruments.

The concept of individual duties, we find, is considered an intrinsic principle in relation to human rights, as expressed in the Universal Declaration art. 29.1: "Everyone has duties to the community in which alone the free and full development of his personality is possible", and adding in art. 29.2 that every person shall be subject to limitations of their right solely on the basis of respect for the rights and freedoms of others and "the just

---

37. UN General Assembly Resolution 41/128 of 4 December 1986.
38. See chapter 7 on the collective right to development.
39. See chapter 2 for a discussion hereof.

requirements of morality, public order and the general welfare in a democratic society".

The step taken to an elaboration hereof into legally enforceable individual duties, at least towards one's own community as has been done in art. 27 through 29 of the African Charter, therefore does not seem to violate or even extend beyond a reasonable limit the boundaries of what we could term basic human rights' principles.

Regarding the collective rights, as expressed through the UN Declaration on the Right to Development and the catalogue of Peoples' Rights in the African Charter, there is no such precedence in the Universal Declaration. Indirectly, however, the principle may be interpreted as included under art. 28 which speaks of a social and international order in which other types of rights may be fulfilled.

If we go, however, to what is considered the immediate next level or step in the evolvement of human rights, the two International Covenants on Civil and Political and on Economic, Social and Cultural Rights, we find the principle expressed in art. 1, which is identical in the two instruments. They state in art. 1.1 that: "All peoples have the right to self-determination. By virtue of that right they freely determine their political status and freely pursue their economic, social and cultural development", and in art. 1.2 that: "All peoples may, for their own ends, freely dispose of their natural wealth and resources...".

Whether this overall principle also can encompass the rather extensive rights of a people as stated in the African Charter is a matter that will be looked at more closely at a later stage.

Also the Declaration on the Right to Development must be examined in this light. It must be viewed basically as an elaboration of the above mentioned principles and, insofar as it also states the right to development as an individual right, of the principles of non-discrimination and fulfilment of economic and social needs expressed in the Universal Declaration.

In order to draw up a preliminary conclusion as to whether a universal concept of human rights also includes a requirement that those rights do not change over time, we can to a large extent base it on the historical perspective outlined above. This shows that even though the number of human rights instruments has grown significantly over the last decades on both a global and a regional level, the overall tendency is one of broadening and elaborating on principles already defined at an early stage of human rights history.

A simple answer to the question as to whether human rights can change in time and still remain universal, would be that the human rights evolution so far has allowed for such an answer, and that this would therefore be sufficient basis for future practice as well. In order to avoid the trap of extending empiricism into ideology, one might say that from an ideological perspective it should be with some concern that the principle of unlimited expansion of the scope of human rights concepts is accepted. The danger hereof is that we might risk a situation of cultural fragmentation, the "watering down" of what are now substantive protective and promotional measures, and the risk that human rights will not be taken seriously as a discipline of international law. Still, when viewing the empiric material as outlined above, we can see that the actual development has in fact proceeded far more cautiously, and that practically all of the additions to the family of human rights are in fact elaborations on already recognized concepts. Therefore one should be more willing to accept a position allowing for a dynamic conception of human rights than if the empirics showed a tendency towards the more negative trend as outlined above.

This discussion may be greatly facilitated by making a distinction between the *essence* of a human rights concept or principle on the one hand, and its *elaboration and interpretation* through various instruments and practices on the other hand.

With regard to the first distinction, it encompasses basic concepts which do little more than establish an overall framework and thus have limited legal contents even though they may be significant in other ways. Examples hereof are the right to a fair trial and freedom from torture or the principle of non-discrimination, and we can draw up a definition of potentially universal human rights as those which have been included in such instruments as can be identified as sources of universality. The identification of such instruments will be dealt with below, as it relates to the question of sources rather than time, and bearing in mind the definition of the term as stated above with respect to universality of origin as well as present applicability.

Similarly, the issues relating to the second distinction regarding the filling out or interpretations of these basic concepts, is also closely related to the discussion of sources rather than time.

We can, however, line up a suggestion for a preliminary first requirement as to the potential universality of human rights based on the empirical realities. This would be expressed as the principle that a "new" human rights principle must somehow reflect or be an expression of a basic concept already defined as universal in order to fall within the accepted regime of human rights. This would not prevent, or in fact require, that the provisions in various instruments contribute to a closer definition of what these overall principles actually entail.

An example hereof is the International Covenant on Civil and Political Rights and Freedoms, which for instance transforms such a generally formulated principle as the right to liberty in UD art. 4 into a substantial number of enforceable rights and freedoms related to personal freedom, freedom from arbitrary arrest or detention and measures of safeguards for persons who have been arrested or held in detention (ICCPR art. 9, 10 and 11). A similar example is the right to life, UD art. 4, and its corresponding provision in ICCPR art. 6, which introduces provisions relating to the concept of genocide and death penalties.

Hereby we have a mutual interdependence between the two distinctions:

The overall concepts lend credibility to and links together a number of human rights provisions, and establish certain outer limits as to how far the development of human rights can go without disintegrating as one recognized legal system. At the same time the individual human rights provision found in younger global or regional instruments give legal meaning and contents to important but lofty and vaguely formulated principles, and allow for implementation mechanisms to operate with them.

All of this does, however, raise the question as to which instruments we can then accept as authoritative in defining human rights principles, which brings us into the next part on sources of human rights.

b. *The question of sources*

Coming back to the definition of the term universal, as stated above to be both "of, belonging to, done by all" referring to its origin and "affecting all" applying to its present application, a number of human rights instruments or distinctions hereof naturally fail to comply with these requirements.

Regional instruments do not qualify as sources of universality, for the obvious reasons that neither have they been developed or accepted by, nor do they apply to, states outside their geographical region.

Firstly, this would rule out the scope of regional human rights instruments, such as the European Convention on Human Rights, the American Declaration and Convention on Human Rights, and the African Charter on Human and Peoples' Rights, as well as all other regional initiatives of a more or less binding nature as stated above.

This is a point which has increased significance in relation to such issues as, for instance, the linking of human rights and development aid. Here the West European and North American donor communities will have to take into consideration that their interpretation of basic human rights concepts on a closer scrutiny might not always correspond to those of, for instance, African states receiving development assistance. This potential conflict to some degree can be solved by using global instruments, both of an overall and of a more specific nature, as basis, particularly if both states are parties hereto. Another solution, which might require a greater willingness to compromise from the donor states, would be to use as basis the regional instrument of the developing region, in this case the African Charter on Human and Peoples' Rights.

All this does not mean that these initiatives are not significant; in fact, they might even be considered "universal" within their own region, if they fulfil the requirements on this level.[40]

Also, these instruments will, for a number of reasons which will not be dealt with further at this point, very often be the most appropriate way of ensuring human rights protection and promotion on a national level. The reason for this is mainly their ability to define more closely and give legal meaning to the overall universal concepts by including an appropriate adaptation to cultural and other factors. Furthermore, they have the advantage of being closer to the national law and citizens of its member states, which will also be significant in relation to their implementation mechanisms, particularly in those cases where the instruments and their corresponding institutions of safeguard allow for individual and not just inter-state complaints.[41]

---

40. The African Charter on Human and Peoples' Rights was adopted by the General Assembly of the Organization for African Unity in 1981. Speaking for such an evaluation would be the fact that the Charter has been ratified, within few years, by all excluding only a few states on the entire continent.
Similarly, the European Convention on Human Rights was adopted by all of the member states; with the expansion of Europe over the last couple of years since the fall of socialism in Eastern Europe, it is questionable whether such a viewpoint can still be upheld, since these states may have different backgrounds and interpretations of concepts and principles.

41. For a discussion on universalism versus regionalization, see Robertson and Merrills, 1989, p. 222f. They state that not only is the establishment of regional human rights systems fully compatible with art. 33 and 52 of the Charter of the United Nations,

Global Conventions Secondly, most global human rights conventions would also be excluded as sources of universality, because they (as a general rule) contain provisions which obligate the state parties to effectively enact their contents as enforceable rights and duties in accordance with the provisions of the Vienna Convention on the Law of Treaties. They are mutual legal agreements, but their effect on non-member states is limited, because they are not bound by the provisions, and consequently not by the interpretations stated herein.[42] Due to their wide-reaching consequences on member states, they will often enjoy limited accession, being ratified only by those countries which find themselves both willing and able to comply with their provisions.[43]

Therefore, as a general rule, most human rights conventions cannot be described as universal, since they have neither been elaborated and accepted, nor given legal effect on all states in accordance with the definition of universality given in the beginning of this chapter.

It can be questioned, however, whether this rule is without exception, or if a few of these human rights conventions can claim to have some form of universal character.

In the following, I will discuss two different examples of such possible exceptions, which each in their own way seems to have universal traits.

The first examples hereof are the International Covenant on Civil and Political Rights and the International Covenant on Economic, Social and Cultural Rights, which at first glance seem to have all the characteristics of a non-universal instrument as outlined above. Both of them are legally binding documents open for signature, ratification and accession by any member States of the United Nations or its specialized agencies (ICCPR art. 48, ICESCR art. 26), and enters into force for each new member state three months after the date of deposit of its instrument of accession or ratification (ICCPR art. 49, ICESCR art. 27). They constitute an agreement between member states, as can be read from the formulation of both instruments'

---

they are simply more practical with respect to communication and mutual understanding, and are easier implemented because "given the diversity of the modern State system, it is natural that regional systems of enforcement should be more readily accepted than universal arrangements".

42. See Rehof/Trier ed., 1990, p. 67ff; Henkin, 1981, p. 34ff.; Cassese 1990 p. 48, in relation to the two international Covenants.

43. See note 29 on the number of ratifications to the two International Covenants.

preamble: "The State Parties to the present Covenant ... agree upon the following articles...". They obligate Member States to respect and ensure to all individuals within their jurisdiction the enjoyment of the rights contained in the Covenant (ICCPR and ICESCR art. 2.1), to enact legislative or other measures necessary to give effect to them in national law (art. 2.2), and to ensure access to effective remedy of violations hereof (art. 2.3).

All of these are characteristics typical of a convention, with the specific and limited legal effect on member and non-member states as outlined above, and indicating that as legal instruments the two Covenants cannot be regarded as universal.

However, by referring directly, in their preamble, to the Charter of the United Nations as a fulfilment of the obligation herein for all states to recognize the dignity, rights and freedom of all people, both instruments stand out as embodiments of such principles. They hereby draw on the universal character of the UN Charter, which applies to all states and all individuals herein, and could therefore be seen as merely an elaboration of the general principles in the Charter, which could justify their universality.[44]

In my opinion, however, this is an accurate example of the confusion created by a lack of distinction between overall and basic principles relating to human needs and the aspirations of an international community on the one hand, and specific provisions relating to human rights and freedom in international legal instruments with an implementation- and enforcement mechanism on the other.

While the former can be said to be of a universal nature and hereby outlining a framework for further developments of the principles listed herein, the latter will seldom fulfil the requirements of universality, since they have neither been agreed upon nor given legal effect on all states.

In relation to the two Covenants, this position is strengthened by the historical fact relating to the development and adoption hereof, resulting in a splitting up of the principles placed side by side in the Universal Declaration into two different instruments. It should also at this point be kept in mind that the contents of the two instruments are different, in the sense that ICCPR contains directly enforceable rights, while ICESCR is formulated along more promotional lines without giving individuals the same legal position as the ICCPR.

---

44. This is a point made by Pechota with particular regard to the ICCPR, ed. Henkin, 1981, p. 32.

Finally, one may look at the status of ratification of the two instruments, noting a significant absence of developing states as members to the ICCPR, and the traditional emphasis given to the instruments in an East-West and North-South perspective.

In my opinion all of this speaks against accepting the two Covenants as universal instruments according to the definition of the term used here.

In favour of this viewpoint see *Nickel*, who dismisses the Covenant(s) as universal, and to some degree also the Universal Declaration, on the basis that for instance political rights are not universal, because they do not apply to children, persons with severely limited mental capacities and non-citizens.[45]

Following the same vein is *Cassese*, who operates with the distinction between basic principles on the one hand and their interpretation in practice on the other hand. He maintains that while the latter hardly shows any signs of universality (not even within such a relatively homogenous group as the states of Western Europe), the former might allow for the concept of universality.[46] On this he concludes that "a restricted core of values and criteria universally accepted by all the states is gradually emerging", based on the convergence of states in accepting the Universal Declaration and the two Covenants as basis hereof.[47]

The second example of a human rights convention, which despite of its character fits the characteristics of a potentially universal instrument as outlined above, is the Convention on the Rights of the Child from 1989.[48]

This instrument is important in the sense that it transforms the principles of the Declaration of the Rights of the Child from 1959[49] into legally binding and enforceable rights, while updating and strengthening the scope hereof.

As a side-remark one might question whether such a catalogue of rights related to children falls beyond the framework established by, for instance, the Universal Declaration, which has no mention of children as accredited with special rights. We might therefore see it as an exception from the argument stated above that the scope of human rights has not been

---

45. Nickel, 1987, p. 45 ff.
46. Cassese, 1990, p. 50.
47. Ibid p. 64.
48. Convention adopted by the UN General Assembly on 20 November 1989.
49. United Nations General Assembly Resoultion 1386 (XIV) of 20 November 1959.

broadened over the last decades but that all developments are merely elaborations of basic concepts already defined at an early stage.

On the other hand one might also apply the more appropriate argument that the Convention on the Rights of the Child is an example of how the intentions and spirit, if not the direct formulation, of the principles of the Universal Declaration is what matters, and that there is a subsequent broad limit to development of human rights provisions in accordance herewith.

If one might wish to do so, it could also be argued that protection of the special needs of children is included in a number of provisions of the Universal Declaration. Examples hereof are art. 1, stating that all humans are born free and equal in dignity and rights, art. 6 on the right for everyone to recognition everywhere as a person before law, and art. 16.3 stating the family as being the natural and fundamental group unit of society and entitled to protection by society and the State. In any case it is an example of how the definition of "human" in terms of a subject worthy of protection of his (or her !) rights has developed since the early national instruments in the last centuries.

Within the discourse on universality of human rights, this instrument is significant for a different reason, namely the widespread and almost unanimous support it has gained at its adoption and in the few years of its existence.[50]

This massive support indicates that the instrument has attained a state of what I would term *factual universality*, since the principles herein now in varying degrees apply to a vast majority of the world's states.

As such the status of factual universality is, in principle, a position available to every global instrument, even though few if any instruments up to now in practice have succeeded in reaching it.

The important point I want to make by introducing this distinction is that the provisions of the Convention still only bind those member states who have already ratified it or are in the process of doing so. Non-member states, few as they may be, are on the other hand not legally bound by them, except to the degree of which they can also be said as constituting principles of customary international law, which is a much different ques-

---

50. The Convention on the Rights of the Child was adopted - unanimously - by the United Nations General Assembly on 20 November 1989. As of 30 December 1995, the Convention had been ratified by a total of 190 states, where the number was 154 just two years earlier. UN, 1995 and 1993.

tion to be dealt with further below.

The Convention on the Rights of the Child therefore does not formally comply with the requirement of "true" universality, insofar as it does not apply universally, even though its adoption may come close to fulfilling the requirement hereof.

"Soft law" Thirdly, there is the question of declarations, recommendations and resolutions as sources of human rights law.

This group of instruments covers a wide range of initiatives and statements issued by regional and global agencies such as the various bodies of the United Nations and the European Council.

Contrary to conventions and covenants, as dealt with above, these instruments are characterized by being one-sided statements instead of mutual agreements, and as such they do not have the legally binding quality of the instruments mentioned above. They do, however, serve as moral obligations on those states which have signed them, and in those cases where the states do not live up to or fulfil the contents of the Declaration, other states as well as the international community in general will take note hereof and react accordingly.

The importance of these instruments lies in other areas, namely in serving as formulations of general principles and statements in a given area, often as forerunners of binding conventions, or as instruments of interpretation and clarification of already existing conventions.

One example hereof is the above mentioned Declaration on the Rights of the Child from 1959 followed by the Convention on the Rights of the Child from 1989. Another example is a series of Recommendations spanning over a period since 1977 on various issues relating to refugees and asylum seekers, supplementing the Convention Relating to the Status of Refugees from 1951 and the Protocol attached to it in 1967.[51]

With respect to the question of these instruments as sources of universality, as defined above, they will sometimes always have the support from a majority of states. Furthermore, the elaboration and adoption process of these instruments with some degree of state participation and -adherence to the principles does not have the specific character of the ratification process related to conventions. This means that the two requirements relating to universality are not fulfilled, since we can neither determine whether they

---

51. Recommendations nr. 8, 15, 22, 24, 30 and 44 from 1977 through 1986, from the Executive Committee of the High Commissioners Programme.

in fact have been elaborated by or are representative of a more than significant majority of states, or whether they do apply to all states with a legally binding effect.

There is, however, one exception from the general rule of instruments of a declaratory nature, namely the Universal Declaration of Human Rights adopted by the United Nations General Assembly on 10 December 1948.[52]

The Declaration is considered the most basic and well-known of all human rights instruments, and has served as a source of inspiration as well as legitimization of subsequent international human rights regulation.[53] It must be seen as the first international attempt to implement the obligation in Article 55 and 56 of the Charter of the United Nations for all states to take joint and separate steps in cooperation with the United Nations to achieve respect for human rights.

The drafting of the Declaration was done by a small body of prominent individuals, representing predominantly Western Europe and USA, but including participants from such states as China, Chile, Lebanon, India and the Soviet Union, as well as Egypt as the sole African representative.[54] Even though this seems a fairly limited representation of what is today considered the world of developing countries,[55] one must keep in mind the

---

52. General Assembly Resolution 217 (III), part A. Part B of the Resolution dealt with the "Right of Petition", and Part C with the "Fate of Minorities", thus underscoring the importance of these two issues. Part D was entitled "Publicity to be Given to the Universal Declaration of Human Rights", and finally Part D took the final step of implementation in accordance with its title, "Preparation of a Draft Covenant on Human Rights and Draft Measures of Implementation". All these other parts, however abstained from making specific provisions on these issues, and referred them to the future work of the Human Rights Commission. This has now resulted in a selection of implementation mechanisms, as well as provisions regarding the rights of minorities included in several instruments such as the International Covenant on Civil and Political Rights and Freedoms and other instruments of similar importance (Eide ed., 1992, p. 13).

53. See for instance the Preambles of the two International Covenants, the UN Convention on Torture and the European Convention on Human Rights, all of which refer directly to the Universal Declaration. The preamble of the African Charter contains a general reference to "the declarations, conventions and other instruments adopted by - the United Nations".

54. The Universal Declaration; Eide ed., 1992, p. 11.

55. See also Espiell in ed. Ramcharan, 1979, p. 61, which also points out that they did, however, participate in the drafting of the two Covenants and in the Third Committee of the General Assembly in 1966, where particularly the economic, social and cultural

fact that, particularly in Africa, almost none of today's independent states were at that time free from colonial rule. It is true that the universality of the Declaration must be evaluated in light of the subsequent unanimous support and recognition accredited to the Declaration both at the time of its conception[56] and in later years. Still, it would not be correct to conclude that the Declaration fulfils the first of the two requirements of universality defined above, in the sense that it cannot be said to have been "done by all".[57]

Progressing to the second requirement, that it should "apply to all", a different indication exists since the provisions of the Universal Declaration are as widely recognized as mentioned above. Most other human rights instruments refer directly to them, and they serve as basis for some of the most important work in the field of human rights within different bodies under the United Nations. Also, the Universal Declaration serves as a solid instrumental basis for organizations such as Amnesty International concerned with country performance in human rights and, in particular, violations hereof.[58] Finally, an important point is that most of the African states have also repeatedly endorsed it.[59]

One must keep in mind, however, that the Declaration was not conceived as law, but as "a common standard of achievement".[60] The effect hereof is that it does not directly seem to confer enforceable legal obligations of implementation on states, but rather establish a set of principles and aspirations which states may have a moral obligation to strive towards.

The legal effects of the Declaration have been disputed, since it has

---

rights were given priority.

56. The consensus on the Declaration was to some degree threatened by the political disunion of the United Nations, and although no states voted against the adoption of the Declaration, 8 abstained from voting. Those were Byelorussia, Czechoslovakia, Poland, Saudi Arabia, South Africa, Ukraine, the USSR and Yoguslavia; Sieghart in ed. Blackburn and Taylor, 1991, p. 27.

57. Tévoédjré, 1985, p. 4f, stating that "the Universal Declaration of Human Rights cannot be considered as truly "universal" since the values therein enshrined appear to have been derived from the concepts and values of only a section of our planet".

58. Examples hereof are the procedures of communication and investigation established by Resolution 1503 of the Economic and Social Council (ECOSOC) and to some degree also the deliberations of the Special Rapporteurs of the Commission on Human Rights (UD, Eide red., p. 7).

59. Hopkinson, 1992, p. 15.

60. Henkin, 1981, p. 9, and the Preamble of the Declaration.

been claimed that the principles of the Universal Declaration and their importance have now been so widely recognized that they form part of customary international law.[61] The consequence hereof would be that states had an obligation to respect and adhere to them beyond the limits of a usual declaration and similar to those following the adherence to or ratification of a treaty.

This discussion is one which, however, will not be entered further into at this stage for a number of reasons.

Firstly, because it is one on which the international community differs in opinion, and because it is difficult to define, since it is hard to tell whether states adhere to certain principles for legal or for other reasons. Secondly, and most important, it is a discussion which to a large degree is made superfluous due to the significant expansion in legally enforceable human rights instruments on a global and regional level, all of which rely more or less directly and expressly on the Universal Declaration. Therefore, the discussion hereof can stop at this point, with the recognition of the significance of the Universal Declaration as an instrument endowed with a legal as well as a moral and political significance beyond that which is generally attributed to any other declaration (or other instrument, for that matter) in the field of human rights.

It would seem from all that is stated above that the Universal Declaration is the instrument which comes closest to being regarded as a source of universal human rights, even though it was, technically speaking, not conceived on a universal foundation. On the other hand it was created in a space of universal support and recognition, and continues to be regarded as such during the course of time.

In order to eliminate as much resistance as possible among the states of the United Nations, the drafters of the Declaration limited themselves to defining broadly termed and basic principles. This decision can to a large degree be attributed to the lack of consensus on the definition of human rights, which became even more clear during the attempts to complete the Bill of Rights and resulting in two different international Covenants.[62] Even today diversions exist with regard to the interpretations, limitations and attribution of relative importance to various principles of human rights. The main difference between now and then is that the conflict now resides more between North and South, the industrialized states and the developing

---

61. Henkin, 1981, p. 38.
62. Henkin, 1981, p. 37f; p. 9f.

world, while the predominant differences at the time of its inception were between East and West, socialism and capitalism.

Whether or not we can attribute the format of the Declaration to the brilliant foresight and understanding of its capable drafters, or to the more pragmatic recognition of the state of the world at that point in time, the result is an instrument which more than any other is of a universal nature.

A further strength of the Declaration is the balancing of the nature of the principles in it, not only between civil and political rights and economic, social and cultural rights, but also between the individual and the group, and between rights and duties. This is a tendency which we now, more than 40 years later, see returning, expressed in such instruments as the African Charter on Human and Peoples' Rights, and in relation to an issue of growing importance such as the balancing of the individual's free exercise of certain rights and freedoms with the protection of the environment.

Based on all which has been stated above, it can be accepted, as a preliminary conclusion, that the Universal Declaration, and to a limited extent some of the features of the International Covenant, act as the sole legal sources of universal human rights principles. The next step is then to analyze the provisions herein in order to determine more accurately what the extent and implications hereof are.

Conclusion

From an empirical perspective, the conclusion to the question asked in this chapter as to the universality of human rights must be given both negatively and affirmatively in accordance with everything stated above.

The answer is positive in the sense that by, albeit only partly, accepting the Universal Declaration as a source of universal human rights principles, we can also accept that the provisions contained herein may be of a universal nature, at least to the extent that they are broadly formulated.

Such basic principles, to be found in articles 1 through 27 of the Universal Declaration, cover the following: freedom from discrimination, slavery and torture; the right to life, personal integrity, privacy and personal honour and integrity; the right to be recognized as a legal entity, to have access to the courts, and to be given a fair trial; freedom of movement; the right to a nationality, to family life, and freedom of thought, expression, assembly and association; the right to participate in the political and cultural life of one's community, to work and leisure, to education and to an adequate standard of living.

In addition hereto the universality of the principle of collective rights and freedom can be deduced from a combination of the provisions relating to self-determination of all peoples in the Charter of the United Nations as well as article 1 of the two International Covenants, and article 28 of the Universal Declaration which states the right of everyone to a social and international order in which the rights and freedoms mentioned above can be realized.Finally, the principles of individual duties balancing the enjoyment of rights and freedoms can be extracted from article 29 of the Universal Declaration and recognized as a basic and universal principle in line with human rights and freedoms.

While concluding this, however, it must also be established, from what has been stated above, that the extent of universality of human rights principles stops at this point, covering only the basic principles but leaving out the closer definition hereof.

There is, for instance, a universal agreement on the principle of the right to a fair trial, but the actual meaning and extent hereof, and accordingly the legally enforceable claims of rights based upon it, are subject to potential variations based on a principle of cultural relativity. This does not mean that such differences in interpretation in fact have to occur, or to which degree they can be accepted within the framework of the general principle itself. Upon researching, one may indeed find that there exists a de-facto global consensus as to the implications and interpretations of a certain provision. It does mean, however, that such consensus necessarily is of a permanent nature, whereby it must be recognized that changes herein and divergences, for instance as a result of rulings and statements from regional human rights organs such as the European Court or the African Commission, must be accepted.

Therefore the question of universality of human rights must be answered with a "Yes" as well as a "No", keeping in mind the distinction between the basic principle on the one hand, and its interpretation and application on the other hand.

With respect to an ideologically based conclusion on the universality of human rights, I have already pointed out that it cannot be derived directly from the empirical level of analysis.

I do hold, however, that the empirical findings outlined in this chapter, as well as illustrated by the in-depth analysis of rights and freedoms in the African Charter and three African Constitutions in chapter 6 and 7, substantiate my own position in the matter, namely that we must somehow find a balance between the two extremes of absolute universality versus radical cultural relativity.

On the one hand we wish to keep the international system of human rights promotion and protection as effective as possible, and in order to do that we cannot allow the material concepts to develop totally independently within each region, not to mention state. The ultimate consequence hereof would be that the strength, and to some extent also the legitimacy, of having an international apparatus in this area is lost, when it is no longer able to operate with generally definable standards.

On the other hand it is important that the intrinsic dynamic nature of human rights, which has indeed been one of its most characteristic features through the history, is not lost in favour of a formalistic and rigid approach. That will also seriously put at risk the ability of human rights law to effectively impact and improve the lives of people all over the world.

Therefore my conclusion to the question of the legitimacy of maintaining a universal approach to human rights follows the distinction between essence and detailed formulation. While we uphold that human rights must in their essence conform to the framework already defined and established, at the same time we must accept, and even appreciate, cultural diversity which serves to adopt human rights effectively to the circumstances under which they operate. Only that way can human rights remain a viable discipline under international law.

Part II
Context and genesis of the instruments

4 Background to the constitutions of Botswana, Malawi and Mozambique

The purpose of this chapter is to give a short overview of the historical background, on which the human rights provisions of the Constitution of Botswana, Malawi and Mozambique must be viewed.[1]

Botswana

At the end of the last century the British Government annexed the territory under the name of Bechuanaland Protectorate, and the Resident Commissioner governed it through various Acts and Proclamations.[2] Even though this was contested by some of the chiefs, the Bechuanaland Special Court upheld the Proclamations[3] and confirmed the unlimited authority of the British Government over the Territory and its inhabitants despite its status as a protectorate. Both Proclamations were enforced by repeated Proclamations in 1943,[4] which further delineated the relationship between the Protectorate administration and the African population. While the authority of local administration officers was strengthened, the Proclamations also officially recognized some of the traditional institutions.

In 1920 a Native Advisory Council and a European Advisory Council had been established, and in 1951 they were supplemented by the establishment of a Joint Advisory Council consisting of 16 members. The European and the African Advisory Councils each elected six members to this new Council, while the remaining four were selected by the Resident Commis-

---

1. In the following see Botswana Chronology, 1989; ed. Morton/Ramsay, 1987; Information Branch of the Bechuanaland Protectorate Government, 1961.
2. Examples hereof were the Native Administrations Proclamation No. 74, and the Native Tribunals Proclamation No. 75, both of 1934, which attempted to subject the chiefs and tribal governments to the control of the Protectorate administration for the first time.
3. Tshekedi Khama and Another vs. The High Commissioner, 1926-53 High Commission Territories Law Rep. 9.
4. Native Administration Proclamation, No. 32 of 1943, and the Native Courts Proclamation, No. 34 of 1943.

sioner.

The various fractions of the Joint Advisory Council now agreed that the time had come to update the government of the Protectorate through the formation of, among other institutions, a Legislative Council.

In order to facilitate this procedure the Joint Advisory Council established in April 1959 a Constitutional Committee, which consisted of the Resident Commissioner as Chairman, four Government Officials, four African non-officials, and four European non-officials. The Committee met several times during the year, its final report was approved by the Joint Advisory Council in October 1960, and after the Law Officers had put the recommendations into precise legal form, the Queen of England conferred a new Constitution on the Protectorate by Order in Council signed on 21 December 1960.[5]

The next step was achieved when the protectorate achieved the status of internal self-government through the Bechuanaland Protectorate (Constitution) Order in Council 1965,[6] which contained a judicially enforceable Declaration of Fundamental Rights.

Before this was achieved, the Bechuanaland Constitutional Conference during its 1963 discussions had decided on the elaboration of a Code of Human Rights built closely upon the similar section in the recently adopted Constitution of Uganda. In order to facilitate a smoother and more effective procedure than could be accomplished by the entire Conference, it was decided to set up a Committee under the chairmanship of the Assistant Attorney General. The Committee, which consisted of seven members including the present President Masire, would return with its recommendations, and the Conference would then examine the question and determine whether

---

5. It should be noted that the Committee apparently fuctioned both effectively and in an atmosphere of positive spirit, an example of which is the fact that it achieved unanimity in all its decisions. Also, their work was greatly facilitated by the high degree of goodwill and cooperation between Africans and Europeans, which had always been a characteristic of both the Joint Advisory Council and of life in general in the Protectorate. How the Committee saw their mandate is reflected in the following quote from the last paragraph of the introduction to its report to the Joint Advisory Council, on "the need to formulate proposals which are progressive yet are not of such a nature as to be likely to prejudice or break down anything of value in the present harmonious life in the Territory". Information Branch of the Bechuanaland Government, 1961.

6. Statutory Instruments 1965, No. 134.

or not to accept them, which they eventually did.[7]

The final step in the procedure was taken the following year, when on 30 September 1966 Botswana became an independent state following the Botswana Independence Act and the Botswana Independence Order.[8] A Constitution, Schedule 2 to the Order, established a republican government with executive power vested in a president elected by the legislature, a unicameral body elected by universal adult suffrage. This Independence Constitution preserved the consultative House of Chiefs and the Declaration of Fundamental Rights, the latter of which now encompasses Chapter II, sec. 3 through 19 of the Constitution.

As a source of inspiration and a model for the code of human rights was chosen the relevant provision in the recently established code of human rights in the Constitution of Uganda from 1962.[9] It was then the task of the Committee to adapt it to Botswana by making the necessary changes, and during this work they were also to take into consideration the recommendations of the Committee of a Bill of Rights set up by the Kenya Constitutional Conference in 1962. Furthermore, the Committee also took inspiration from the provisions of the Constitution of Nyasaland (now Malawi), adopted in 1964, which in a similar fashion was an adaptation of the Uganda provisions.

It is interesting to note that the Uganda Constitution, which thus served as a model for Kenya, Nyasaland, Botswana and other states, is also itself an adaptation of a former British colonial constitution, namely the Nigerian Constitution's Code of Human Rights from 1959, which again was modelled closely upon the provisions of the European Convention on Human Rights.

Only minor adaptions differ from one Constitution to the other, and the catalogue of human rights herein resembles that of other international and UN instruments, such as the Universal Declaration and the International Covenant of Civil and Political Rights.

The catalogues in the constitutions of Botswana and Malawi are very

---

7. Bechuanaland Protectorate Constitutional Conference Discussions, 1963, Paper No. 11 with annexes, BNB 5407.
8. SI 1966, No. 1171.
9. SI 1962 / 405.

similar,[10] containing almost identical articles listed in the same order and with minor adaptations only. The rights established by these constitutions are the right to life and personal liberty, freedom from slavery, forced labour and inhuman treatment; the right to privacy of home and other property and freedom from deprivation hereof; the right to secure protection of law; freedom of conscience, expression, assembly and association and freedom of movement, and finally freedom from discrimination on the grounds of race etc.

Concluding the Bill of Rights, all these constitutions contain articles regarding public emergencies, enforcement of protective provisions and interpretation and savings.

Malawi

Similar to Botswana, and in contrast to Mozambique, Malawi was always dominated by British rule, which began with the various missions establishing European settlement from the latter part of the 19th century. Those include the Anglican Universities Mission to Central Africa (UMCA) in the Shire Highlands around Blantyre in 1861, and the Church of Scotland's formation of the Blantyre Mission. The Free Church of Scotland established the Livingstonia Mission in the North in 1875, and its members were behind the formation of the commercial African Lakes Company in 1878. Even the Dutch Reformed Church of South Africa established a mission in the Central region in 1889.[11] Even though there was pressure from the Portugese and the Roman Catholic missionaries in Mozambique to include Malawi in its territory, and similar efforts from Cecil Rhodes' British South Africa Company, the Church of Scotland managed to help securing Malawi on British hands. Consequently, a Protectorate was established in 1891, with an administration directly answerable to the Foreign Office in London.[12]

European settlement grew around the turn of the century, with the

---

10. The Constitutional provisions on a Bill of Rights in Kenya follow the same outline, with the above mentioned Recommendations on a Bill of Rights for Kenya from 1962 referring to both the already existing Bill of Rights for Kenya from 1960 (which was based closely upon the model of the Nigerian Constitution from 1957 and, subsequently, the European Convention on Human Rights), and the Uganda Constitution from 1962.
11. Pretorius p. 365ff, in Pachai, 1972.
12. Here and in the following see CIIR Comment, p.6ff.

establishment of plantations utilizing cheap African labour in a situation amounting practically to serfdom.[13] After the Chilembwe-rising in 1915, which was based on the vision of Malawi as a free and independent African state in spite of its quick suppression, a national body, the Nyasaland African Congress based on the Native Associations, was formed in the 1940s.

Similar to the relatively peaceful process of independence enjoyed by Botswana, one might have imagined that a similar transition could have been the case in Malawi. This is particularly so since the country lacked mineral resources and other economic assets attractive to the colonial power, serving primarily as a reserve of unskilled manpower for the country's own plantations as well as the South African mines.[14] Still, a brief federation with Rhodesia imposed by the British in 1953, causing bitter resentment among the leaders of the Congress, only fuelled their attempts to become a self-governing nation, and the exiled Hastings Kamuzu Banda was asked to serve as leader of the struggle. After all the Congress leaders had been imprisoned under the Emergency regulations in 1959, to be viewed as a token of their increased level of importance, they were released one year later, and finally in 1964 Britain formalized the independence of Malawi.[15]

The Constitution was established by the Independence Order in Council enacted by the British Parliament in June, and entered into force on July 6 1964.[16] Its Bill of Rights was almost identical to that of Botswana, as seen above, but because of the political events following independence it was only to be in force for a short period, following an even briefer revival at a much later stage.

Already in 1961 general elections were held for the Congress,[17] and the winning Malawi Congress Party headed by Banda continued to maintain a united front, despite the political rivalry among its leaders, which became

---

13. European population reached its peak after World War One, but at that time it still stayed below 1,500. In contrast, nearly 3 3/4 million acres of land was held by European planters in 1920. Wills, 1985, p. 277f.
14. This migration did, however, act as a source of income as well, since compulsory savings, taxes and remittance to families went back to Malawi. In 1960, it was estimated that these amounts ran up to a total value of more than £1,5 mio. McMaster, 1974, p. 36.
15. Ibid.
16. Kaunda, 1994, p. 14; Pachai, 1973, p. 244.
17. See Mair, 1962, for a detailed description of the elections.

evident right after independence was achieved. However, Banda quickly established himself as the one and only master, totally dominating not only the Party but also political life in general. During a Cabinet crisis just after independence, he ousted all opposition, and transformed Malawi into a Republic with himself as President on 6 July 1966.[18]

The new Constitution was drawn up by a Constitutional Committee, and submitted to the National Convention of the MCP in October 1965, and this body, which was later described as a "Parliament no. 1" with the National Assembly reduced to serve as a "rubber Stamp" on all decisions, accepted the proposal unanimously. It should be noted that this was the state of affairs even before the actual introduction of the one-party state, which was formalized by the Republic Constitution of 1966.[19]

In contrast to the Independence Constitution, the Republic Constitution which was to be the supreme law the country for more than 25 years had no catalogue of human rights. It merely contained the short statement in sec. 2.1.iii that

> "The Government and the people of Malawi shall continue to recognize the sanctity of the personal liberties enshrined in the United Nations Universal Declaration of Human Rights, and of adherence to the Law of Nations."

The following sub-sections of this article added that no person may be deprived of their property without payment of fair compensation and when required by public interest, and that all persons should enjoy equal rights regardless of colour, creed or race. The general nature of these provisions was, however, firmly established by the human rights practices of the next decades, which revealed a systematic pattern of human rights abuses totally neglecting the principles in the Universal Declaration.[20]

To enable the Government to justify its actions, a provision was added to the Constitution in 1968, the formulation of which resembles closely those used both in AC and in the national Constitutions of Botswana and Mozambique as seen below.

It was hereby stated in sec. 2.2 that:

---

18. Kaunda, 1994, p. 15ff; CIIR Comment, p. 14ff.
19. Kaunda, 1994, p. 17ff.
20. See, among other sources, the reports of Amnesty International for a documentation hereof.

> "Nothing contained in or done under the authority of any law shall be held to be inconsistent with or in contravention of sub-section 1 to the extent that the law in question is reasonably required in the interests of defence, public safety, public order or the national economy".

The human rights protection in Malawi therefore depended on the enforceability, or rather lack hereof, of the Universal Declaration, and what could be determined as forming customary international human rights law.[21] This was particularly the case since the African Charter had not yet come into being and Malawi was not then a party to the ICCPR.[22]

Some attempt to remedy the situation was made by the Judiciary in 1982, when Chief Justice Richard Banda of the Malawi Supreme Court of Appeal decided that

> "We accept that the UNO Universal Declaration of Human Rights is part of the Law of Malawi and that the freedoms which that Declaration guarantees must be respected and can be enforced in these courts".

He excluded the African Charter on Human and Peoples' Rights on the basis, firstly, that Malawi had a dualist system of incorporation of international law[23] and that the reference in the Constitution applied only to the Universal Declaration, and, secondly, that Malawi had not adopted the African Charter but only signed it.[24]

It should be noted, however, that this part of the decision may no longer be valid, because Malawi has now not only signed but also ratified the Charter, which furthermore entered into force as well. There exists now a legal obligation, albeit of a somewhat different nature in respect of the dualist system, on Malawi to respect and to implement the Charter in

---

21. See chapter 3 for a more in-depth discussion of the question of sources of a potential universal conception of human rights, where it is concluded that it cannot be said with unquestionable certainty that the Universal Declaration has acheived this status even today.
22. Dokali, 1993, p. 3, who raises the question whether the two Covenants would not have had a binding effect as law in Malawi. This is, however, a dispute which has merely a historic relevance in relation to the ICCPR, since Malawi is now a party to this instrument, UN 1995.
23. See chapter 5 on the incorporation of international instruments in Botswana, Malawi and Mozambique.
24. Chafukwa Tom Chihana vs. The Republic, M.S.C.A. Criminal Appeal No. 9 of 1982. Kaunda 94 p. 23.

accordance with art. 1 hereof, and the situation must therefore be viewed differently from that of 1982.

Banda continued to rule in an increasingly autocratic manner, suppressing political or any other form of perceived opposition with all means. With respect to foreign policy he also alienated Malawi to its neighbouring countries and the international community by establishing formal diplomatic relations with South Africa in 1967 as well as supporting the colonial government in Mozambique. Allegedly, Malawi also provided supply, rest and training camps to Renamo during the civil war following independence in Mozambique.[25]

It is an accurate, but tragic, reflection of the state of affairs that this situation was allowed to persist and that extensive human rights violations domestically as well as abroad was deemed by the West to be a small price to pay for the relative economic stability of the country and for the sake of having a strategic ally in a region at the height of the Cold War.

The international climate changed, however, around the beginning of the 1990s, as a result of several factors working in the same direction.

One factor was the internal situation, where Banda's personal health and vigour was seen to decline and where political influence fell more and more to people like John Tembo and others, who continued to utilize the powers of the presidential office.[26] While the people of Malawi might have a high degree of tolerance and reverence for Banda because of his status as "Saviour" of their independent state, they would have been less likely to accept a continued oppression instigated by other representatives of the government. This opened up the opportunity for the underground organisation's campaign for multi-party democracy and general political change, led by the United Democratic Front and the Alliance for Democracy.

Another factor was the external political climate, where the end of the Cold War and the abolition of apartheid in South Africa, including the release of Nelson Mandela from jail in February 1990, did no longer necessitate that the Western donors put up with the situation. Simultaneously, concern for human rights was increasingly linked to the development policy of several countries,[27] and in May 1992 the fourth Consultative Group of Aid Donors meeting in Paris suspended all human aid except that

---

25. CIIR Comment, p. 19.
26. ibid., p. 20f.
27. See ed. Rehof and Gulmann, 1989.

which was purely humanitarian. This was done for a period of six months and would be lifted only if and when Malawi made progress on political reform and observance of human rights standards. As described below, the elections for a multi-party democracy were in fact announced within that period.

A third factor came from a somewhat surprising angle, namely in the form of a letter from the Catholic Bishops published on 8 March 1992 entitled "Living the Faith", and issuing a harsh and unequivocal critique of the Government's treatment of the people. It was all the more surprising since the attitude of the Church had so far seemed to be able to exist in a "working relationship",[28] and had refrained, at least in public, from making any political statements against Banda or his government.

The claim of the Church is that although such a policy had been maintained, the letter expressed what members of the public had been felt for years; according to one of its representatives, "there was pressure from all sectors on the bishops to free themselves and the Church from the silence of compromise and acceptance".[29]

The letter was publicized unofficially all over the country, and in spite of the government's harsh reaction the effect apparently was like setting a match to dry hay, as the public supported the letter and its inherent devastating critique.[30]

The Presbyterian Church followed the initiative by issuing a similar critique in June 1992, calling for the establishment of a body to review structural reforms to the political system as well as for immediate steps in a number of human rights area to stop violations from continuing.[31]

On 18 October 1992 the Government took the first irrevocable step towards ending the one-party regime of Banda, by announcing a public referendum on the introduction of multi-part democracy. At the same time, however, the human rights situation continued to look very bad, and a

---

28. An example hereof was the visit of the Pope to Malawi in 1989, which was treated as a state occasion. CIIR Comment, p. 22.
29. Mgr. John Roche of St. Patrick's Missionary Society, 1993.
30. Two days later, the Bishops were subject to interrogation for eight hours, and the letter was banned. Human Rights Watch 1993, p. 26.
31. CIIR Comment, p. 23f. An example of such a body was the National Consultative Council (NCC), which was charged with the responsibility of drafting the new Constitution and Bill of Rights.

symbol hereof was the death of Orton Chirwa[32] in prison on 20 October. In November, the Government declared the Alliance for Democracy (AFORD) illegal and arrested hundreds of its supporters.[33]

The referendum was scheduled for and held on 14 June 1993, and despite a campaign fraught with suppression and human rights violations[34] as well as the obvious lack of equality between the 30-year old ruling party and the newly established democratic coalition, the elections resulted in a 63 per cent vote in favour of democracy.[35] This promise was later fulfilled when the general elections were held in May 1994, cementing Banda's defeat to the new President Bakili Muluzi.[36]

It was recognized that some form of legal steps would have to be taken to cater for human rights and democratic interests during the transition period until general elections could be held and a new Constitution created. The Government and the National Consultative Council (NCC) therefore decided to include *in toto* Chapter II of the 1964 Independence Constitution which contained the original Bill of Rights.

It is debatable whether or not this proved to be a wise decision in the long run, even though it was heavily criticized both locally[37] and by foreign experts.[38] Among those are Amnesty International, which recommended that it "should be given full scrutiny and amended as soon as possible to make it fully compatible with international standards of human rights". The organization further referred critique from the UN Centre for Human Rights, focusing on its "extensive restrictions and limitations" on many human rights provisions including its measure for derogation.[39]

---

32. Described as perhaps the most prominent politician in Malawi and a former Minister of Justice, Orton Chirwa was sentenced to death in 1983 along with his wife Vera. The sentence was issued by a traditional court on charges of treason, and commuted to life imprisonment in 1984. Kamminga, 1992, p. 21f.
33. Human Rights Watch, 1993, p. 26.
34. Amnesty International, May 1993.
35. Ibid., p. 25.
36. Africa Research Bulletin, May 1994.
37. Dokali, February 1994.
38. Amnesty International, February 1994.
39. It is interesting to note that no similar critique has been raised internationally against the Constitution of Botswana, almost totally identical to the Bill of Rights as it was re-introduced in Malawi, which has been in force for more than 30 years without any indication of substantial amendment or replacement. The assumption might therefore

In any case, the NCC continued to work on the drafting of a new Bill of Rights to be included in a new Constitution, which had to balance the rope between the twin towers of addressing the concrete context of Malawi as well as adhering to international standards.

The former was ensured by including popular participation in the various stages of the process through a series of Constitutional Conferences,[40] in which individuals and organizations from all sections of the community participated.[41]

The latter was seen as particularly important since Malawi had acceded to the ICCPR and the ICESCR in December 1993, and it was therefore natural for the drafters to seek advice from the UN Human Rights Centre.[42] However, attention should perhaps also have been paid to the fact that Malawi had become a party to the AC already in February 1990,[43] and that similar assistance could have been provided by the African Commission in accordance with its mandate under art. 45. Apart from the availability of technical assistance in itself, the inherent statement signifies that the new Constitution of Malawi should be local and international in scope, while compliance with the African Charter would not be sought in particular.[44]

As will be seen in chapters 6 and 7 of this study, it is interesting to note that the final version of the Constitution of Malawi does not follow a blueprint established by either the UD, ICCPR or AC, but includes extracts from all of these in addition to national considerations, which in the end may have played the dominant role.

---

    be that the demands for protectional mechanisms are increased proportionally to the implied danger that human rights violations might occur, or in other words that nobody wishes to rock the boat as long as it is sailing along relatively peacefully as in Botswana.

40. February 1994 in Blantyre and Kwacha, and February 1995 in Lilongwe, among others.
41. Kaunda, 1994, p. 61.
42. Amnesty International, September 1993.
43. Status of Ratification, Annex to the Annual Activity Reports of the African Commission on Human and Peoples' Rights.
44. This goes against the recommendations issued by a delegation to Malawi from the Council of the Bar of England and Wales and the Scottish Faculty of Advocates, which, following a visit to Malawi in October 1993, stated that a new Bill of Rights should be "consistent with the provisions of the Universal Declaration of Human Rights and the African Charter on Human and Peoples' Rights". Report of the delegation, 1993.

Several drafts later, the new Constitution of Malawi was finally adopted by the Parliament to enter provisionally into force on 18 May 1994. Since then, several provisions have been amended,[45] but with one minor exception in relation to sec. 40 regarding financial support to political parties, there have been no changes in the Bill of Rights, and finally the Constitution was brought definitely into force on 18 November 1995.[46]

Mozambique

The main difference between the colonial history of Mozambique and that of Botswana and Malawi, is that the former was under Portuguese and not British domination,[47] and during that time the legal system was totally colonial in nature and application. The law was based on Portuguese codes and statutes derived from a historical and cultural background alien to Africa, and traditional law was reduced from a pre-colonial refined and well-functioning system of oral law, to the status of "uses and customs".[48]

Mozambique did not undergo a similar process of peaceful transition to independence in the early 1960s as did Botswana and Malawi, but only achieved this on 25 June 1975 after more than ten years of long and violent war. One of the results hereof was that the legal system had to be completely rebuilt, a process further impeded by the fact that all of the Portuguese judges and prosecutors left, leaving a few trained lawyers along with half a dozen Mocambican law students who returned from Portugal to take up the challenge of building the new State.[49]

All of this means that no similar procedure of adaption and development of a constitutional Bill of Rights with a European-liberalistic view similar to that of the Commonwealth states took place.

Instead, the Central Committee of the ruling Frelimo party[50] proclaimed the Independence Constitution on 25 June 1975, which had more the character of a programme for action than regulatory law, laying down

---

45. Act no. 30 of 1994, and Act no. 6 of 1995.
46. Republic of Malawi (Constitution) Bill, Act no. 7 of 1995.
47. The Portuguese presence in Mozambique dates back five centuries, and already during the 17th century they established a considerable amount of settlement along the Zambezi river as feudal landlords under the crown of Portugal. Timmins 1963, p. 12.
48. Sachs 1988, p. 3f.
49. Ibid.
50. A few years later Frelimo became a Marxist-Leninist party.

the general principles of popular participation and power as well as the administrative functions of the various organs of the State. Amendments to these provisions were made in accordance with the political developments over the next ten years,[51] but still this Constitution did not at any time contain a catalogue of individual human rights.[52]

During the years following independence, a bloody and violent civil war between the ruling Frelimo and the opposing Renamo, the latter supported first by Rhodesia and later directly by the apartheid-regime of South Africa, dominated the entire country.

In spite hereof efforts continued to develop the institutional foundation and democratic structures in Mozambique, and even though the second general elections in 1986 were interrupted because of the war,[53] work progressed from then on towards the development of a new Constitution under the leadership of President Chissano.

A draft Constitution within the overall framework of socialism was approved by the Peoples' Assembly in 1987, but apparently not to the satisfaction of the President, who returned it to the Commission for Revising the Constitution with the request that it should reflect more closely a Western liberal ideology.[54] Also, one cannot rule out entirely the possibility that inspiration for these changes was also found in the African Charter, which by that time had entered into force and with a Commission in function, so that Mozambique would more easily be able to ratify and comply with this instrument.

In 1989, a revised draft Constitution was prepared unanimously by the Frelimo, since peace negotiations with Renamo had not yet proceeded to a stage where cooperation in the procedure could take place. It was published on 9 January 1990,[55] and during the spring and summer of 1990 was distributed widely across the country. Apart from a number of substantive changes in the judicial and democratic procedure, it added a substantive catalogue of human rights provisions. This is particularly important to note, because no similar protection of individual rights and freedoms had been in force in Mozambique until the adoption hereof and the ratification of such

---

51. One of the examples hereof was the Law of Judicial Organization adopted by the Peoples' Assembly in 1978, following a National Conference on Justice.
52. Hall and Young, 1991, p. 3f.
53. Ibid., p. 13.
54. Ibid., p. 107.
55. Mozambique Information Office Dossier no. 3, January 1990.

general human rights instruments as ICCPR and AC.

A contributing factor to the positive peace negotiations between Renamo and Frelimo was undoubtedly the decision by the latter to support the establishment of a multi-party system in Mozambique in August 1990, which was allowed for but not demanded in the draft Constitution. Incorporating this decision into the re-draft along with other changes, the Peoples' Assembly unanimously adopted the new Constitution on 2 November 1990, and it entered into force on 30 November the same year.[56]

The status of human rights in Mozambique was further improved when, on 4 October 1994, the General Peace Agreement between the Government and Renamo was adopted. It ended the civil war and provided the monitoring force, ONUMOZ, with the opportunity to send more than 1,000 UN civilian police observers into the country to help stabilize the situation.[57] This agreement obligated both parties to guarantee the exercise of fundamental human rights and freedoms, and even though its mechanisms were critized for not being sufficient enough to investigate human rights violations in the future,[58] there is no doubt that it has served to ensure the legal recognition and protection of human rights in Mozambique even further.

Conclusion

The development of the constitutions of the former British colonies, which gained independence during the 1960s, reveals two interesting factors:

First, it is clear that very little original creation and adaptation to local conditions was used when drawing up the respective constitutions of the new African states.

We may divide the early colonial constitutions in two groups according to their time of conception:

- a "first generation" dating back to the Indian Constitution from 1949 and the European Convention on Human Rights from 1953, comprising the Bill of Rights for Nigeria from 1959 and the first Bill of Rights for Kenya from 1960, and

- a "second generation", where the drafting was done on a more independent and creative level, starting with the Bill of Rights for Uganda

---

56. Art. 207.
57. Amnesty International, June 1994.
58. Amnesty International, January 1993.

The Constitutions of Botswana, Malawi and Mozambique 71

from 1962, which again served as the primary source of inspiration for the Second Bill of Rights for Kenya from 1962 as well as the Bill of Rights for Nyasaland from 1963, and the Bill of Rights in the Constitution of Botswana from 1965.

The difference between these two generations is, however, mainly systematic, with the same scope of rights and freedoms established in the various constitutions as listed above, with the important exception that the later constitutions, for instance those of Uganda, Malawi and Botswana, include freedom from interference with correspondence under the concept of freedom of expression, a provision which is not included in the constitution of Nigeria or the first Bill of Rights for Kenya.

Finally, one may categorize the Constitutions of Malawi and Mozambique as falling within a "third generation", comprising these and other post-Cold War Constitutions particularly from Eastern Europe and Africa. They may also be subject to some form of influence from Western Europe and other areas, albeit in a different form, since the background is not traditional colonial bonds but rather the inclusion of constructive human rights projects as part of development cooperation.[59] With respect to Malawi and Mozambique, on the other hand, it is evident that the drafting hereof took place in the context of the country itself and that they may appropriately be regarded as being "indigenous" in nature in spite of inspiration from other international and national sources.

---

59. Examples of states which have included concern for human right in their development policies in later years are USA, Canada, Holland, Norway and Denmark. Rehof p. 7ff, in ed. Rehof and Gulmann 1989.

5 The African Charter on Human and Peoples' Rights

Historical background

We can roughly divide the time preceding the adoption of the African Charter into three periods, the first of which is the pre- and colonial period, which to some extent has been dealt with already in chapter 2 regarding human rights law in an African context. This, therefore, leaves two periods, the first of which covers the political and legal developments on the African continent in the 1960s and 1970s. The second period concerns those years when the Charter was actually conceived and drafted, up to 1981 when the African Charter came into existence.[1]

Beginning with the first period, it is interesting to note that the first step of the process was not really the establishment of the politically oriented Organization of African Unity and its Charter in 1963.

Rather than giving protection to human rights specifically, the primary aim of the OAU was the total de-colonialization of the African continent, and the Charter does not contain any specific catalogue of human rights. On the other hand it speaks in its preamble of such human rights notions as "the inalienable right of all people to control their own destiny", freedom, equality, justice and dignity; it makes references to human progress and to "the aspirations of our peoples for brotherhood and solidarity".

Instead it was the African Conference on the Rule of Law, held in 1961, in Lagos, Nigeria, which took steps to carry out the intentions of the International Commission of Jurists (ICJ) to ensure the global adherence to the principle of Rule of Law. Here, the Conference proclaimed the Law of Lagos, which stated, among other things:

> "That in order to give full effect to the Universal Declaration of Human Rights of 1948, this Conference invites the African Governments to study the possibility of

---

1. The following is largely based on the following sources: Kunig, 1982, p. 141-150; Welch, 1981, p. 401-420; Bello, 1985, p. 289-291 and 1987, p. 23-31; Naldi 1989, p. 108-112.

adopting an African Convention of Human Rights ".[2]

Interestingly enough the Conference also proposed the establishment of an African Court of Human Rights, which was temporarily abandoned at the conception of the African Charter in favour of a more promotionally oriented Commission. The idea, however, still lives among scholars, and in fact is now looked upon as a much greater probability of coming into viable existence than ten years ago when the African Charter was in its first youth.

At the Third Afro-Americo-European Conference on "Regional Systems of Human Rights Protection in Africa, America and Europe" in Strasbourg in June 1992, the issue of regional human rights courts was discussed. Here, Prof. Umozurike of the African Commission took the view that an African Court was also a matter of timing. Given the desperate shortage of funds for the work of the Commission, it seemed unwise to establish another institution now. There was also the issue to determine which rights in the Charter were justiciable and could be taken to a Court. Without underestimating the importance of a Court, in view of the existing constraints, it would be better to strengthen the Commission and come back to the issue of a Court in a few years time.[3]

This stage was reached when, at the 16. Ordinary Session in October-November 1994, the African Commission took note of the decision by the OAU[4] to work towards the establishment of an African Court, and elaborated a draft to be reviewed and, eventually, adopted by the General Assembly. The draft takes the form of an Additional protocol, and would therefore be subject to ratification by each member state in order to have effect. It will therefore be some years before an African Court on Human and Peoples' Rights is functional or even in existence, but the significant and decisive first steps have been taken.[5]

We hereby see how the groundwork for a separation between the two areas, the political and the legal, were established and continued to show itself up to the present day, and often the two developments have taken curiously opposite directions at the same time. This is illustrated by the apparent contradiction that on the one hand the political scene during the 1970s saw extensive and widespread human rights violations by African

---

2. Law of Lagos, 1961.
3. Benedek and Heinz ed., 1992, p. 24.
4. Resolution 230 XXX of the Assembly of Heads of State and Government of the OAU.
5. Secretariat of the African Commission, 1996.

governments, to some degree facilitated by the marked policy of non-interference in internal affairs upheld by the OAU. Examples hereof are the Hutu-Tutsi murders in Burundi, which received no comments from the OAU, and other violaters of human rights of the period accounting such rulers as Amin in Uganda, Nguema in Equatorial Guinea and Bokassa in the Central African Empire.[6]

At the same time, however, the process of establishing positive measures in specific areas of human rights continued with the establishment of such an instrument as the OAU Convention Governing Particular Aspects of the Refugee Problems in Africa from 1969. It has been joined by numerous resolutions and other initiatives in such areas as the self-determination of peoples, non-discrimination, economic, social and cultural rights, education, science and technology, and the settlement of disputes.[7] One of the most recent expressions of this positive trend is adoption of the African Charter on the Rights and Welfare of the Child by the OAU in 1990,[8] which has so far not yet entered into force.

During the 1960s and 1970s the process towards the creation of a legal framework of human rights in Africa, begun with the Law of Lagos, continued, expressed through a series of conferences and seminars.

Some of the most important milestones of this process were the United Nations Human Rights Commission's seminar in Cairo in 1967 pressing for the establishment of an African human rights commission, which in 1971 was followed up by a seminar in Addis Ababa in conjunction with the United Nations Economic Commission for Africa adopting this proposal. Another significant event was the International Commission of Jurists' seminar on "Human Rights in a One-Party State", co-hosted with the Government of Tanzania in 1976, which drew up the important conclusions that human rights included both "individual and collective rights", and stated that "the establishment of civil and political rights must go hand in hand with the promotion of economic, social and cultural rights".[9]

These statements were to represent some of the most characteristic aspects of the African Charter on Human and Peoples' Rights. Later seminars following in its wake took place in 1978 in Butare, Rwanda, and in

---

6. Welch, 1981, p. 405ff; Kunig, 1982, p. 141f; Naldi, 1989, p. 108f.
7. Bello, 1985, p. 287.
8. Reproduced in African Journal on International and Comparative Law (AJICL) 1991 vol. 3, p. 173ff.
9. Bello, 1985, p. 25.

Dakar, Senegal, both under the heading "Human Rights and Economic Development in Francophone Africa". Also in 1978 the third general meeting of the African Bar Association in Freetown, Sierra Leone, affirmed that individual human rights were fundamental in Africa, at the same time as the United Nations Human Rights Commission decided to review the human rights situation in several African countries. Finally, the Commission also adopted a resolution moved by Nigeria, which requested the assistance of the United Nations in establishing regional human rights institutions.[10]

The seminar in Dakar was particularly important, since it succeeded in drafting concrete proposals for a human rights document. Here, President Senghor of Senegal agreed to sponsor a draft resolution which would provide for an African human rights commission at the next OAU Assembly meeting. Furthermore, he delegated Keba Mbaye, President of the Supreme Court of Senegal and a judge at the International Court of Justice, to draft a text on human rights, which was later to form the basis of the present African Charter on Human and Peoples' Rights.[11]

In more than one respect the road had now been paved for the initiation of the process resulting in the elaboration and adoption of the African Charter. The founding principles had already been laid out, as shown in the quotes above, and even more significant was perhaps the OAU's constructive change of policy towards more direct interference against the massive human rights violations in some African states. Significant in this respect was the establishment of the Bokassa inquiry in May 1979, where an independent OAU commission of five judges from the Ivory Coast, Liberia, Rwanda, Senegal and Togo publicized its findings of substantive violations of human rights.[12]

The major breakthrough happened shortly thereafter, in July 1979, when President Senghor moved a resolution, during the Assembly of African Heads of State and Government, that a group of highly qualified experts should be called upon to prepare a preliminary draft of an African Charter on Human and Peoples' Rights. The resolution was unanimously adopted,[13] and this marked a distinct difference in attitude on behalf of the

---

10. Bello, 1985, p. 25f.; Kunig, 1982, p. 142.
11. Naldi, 1989, p. 110.
12. Bello, 1985, p. 290.
13. The famous resolution is referred to as "Decision 115 (XVI) of the Assembly of Heads of State and Government at its Sixteenth Ordinary Session held in Monrovia, Liberia, from 17 to 20 July 1979 on the preparation of a preliminary draft on an Af-

OAU, from active resistance and lack of cooperation to direct endorsement and support, without which it is hard to imagine that the Charter could have been brought viably into existence.

In addition hereto the United Nations Secretary-General organized a seminar in September 1979, also in Monrovia, where thirty African governments attended, concluding that an African Commission should be established.

Now the actual drafting procedure of the Charter began with the first meeting of experts in Dakar, in November and December 1979, which produced a draft specifically suited to cater for the special problems relating to human rights in Africa. The forceful accentuation of the need to take into consideration specific African culture can to some degree be seen in view of the fact that the expert group, to their surprise, discovered that the Secretariat of the OAU had already prepared a preliminary draft based primarily on the European and American Conventions on Human Rights.[14] The meeting rejected this draft accordingly, and outlined their own draft Charter, which had the same basic characteristics as the final Charter, even though it underwent several amendments.[15]

The next step was for the Ministers of Justice of the OAU Member States to review the project, and the first meeting hereof in March 1980 in Addis Ababa failed to materialize, mainly due to various political circumstances. The Council of Ministers proceeded to meet two times in Banjul, Gambia, and also the first of these sessions in June 1980 was unsuccessful, resulting in the drafting of only 11 articles at the end of the session. The basis for these difficulties was found mainly in the lack of consensus and a general atmosphere of suspicion among some delegations, and a prevailing tendency to maintain a cautious attitude towards on the subject.[16]

Fortunately enough, the climate shifted remarkably at the second meeting of ministers in January 1981, also in Banjul, and in only two weeks the delegates succeeding in fully revising and adopting the text of the Char-

---

rican Charter on Human and Peoples' Rights providing, inter alia, for the establishment of bodies to promote and protect human and peoples' rights". Bello 1985, p. 28.

14. Bello, 1985, p. 28.
15. An example hereof is the preambular statement that the "conception of an individual who is utterly free and utterly irresponsible and opposed to society is not consonant with African philosophy", which was deleted from the final draft of the Charter. Aluko, p. 235.
16. Bello, 1985, p. 30.

ter. This was done in sufficient time for it to be presented before the 18. Assembly of Heads of State and Government of the OAU on 17 June 1981 in Nairobi, Kenya. Here the African Charter on Human and Peoples' Rights was formally approved and adopted *in toto*.

A note should be made on the extensive amendments to the original draft, which were made by the Council of Ministers during their sessions in 1980 and 1981.[17] Some of these amendment unfortunately served to weaken the protective material provisions of the Charter, and particularly two examples should be mentioned here.

The first is art. 10.2, on the negative freedom of association, where the original Dakar draft made this right unconditional. The Banjul text, however, made art. 10.2 subject to art. 29.2, on the individual's "duties of solidarity", in effect making art. 10.2 without any legal content, since the duties are formulated so broadly that they cover almost any given situation.

The second example is art. 12.5 on freedom from mass-expulsion, which the Dakar-draft did not only state as being unconditional, but further enforced by adding the statement that neither political nor economic nor any other reasons whatsoever could justify measures of this kind. This statement was deleted in the Banjul-text, and in addition hereto the term "aimed at" was inserted, indicating that only those expulsions directly intended to affect a particular ethnic minority were included under art. 12.5., ruling out all cases where this could be considered in any way unintentional.

Another amendment which had significantly weakening effects concerns art. 18. 3 and 4, when the Dakar draft contained a right of children to protection "as stipulated in international declarations and conventions", while providing for the additional enactment of "special measures of protection in accordance with the requirements of their physical and intellectual well-being". Now the provision simply refers to international provisions for both women and children, without any specific considerations or elaborations.

Counterbalancing these negative results, one should see also the increases in levels of protection which were introduced during the Council of Ministers' drafting procedure.

One example hereof is art. 5, which was expanded to embrace "all forms of exploitation and degradation of man" instead of just the particular references to slavery, slave trade and torture in the Dakar draft. Another example was the inclusion of art. 14 guaranteeing the right to property as

---

17. For the following, see Kunig, 1982, p. 146ff and Naldi, 1989, p. 111.

an independent basic right, where the Dakar draft made it subject to provisions in national law and excluded restrictions hereof in those cases where the State legislation already guaranteed this right.

Another example is art. 9.1, which was made to refer to information without the qualification that it be "objective", and similarly in art. 12.2. on the right to freedom of movement the restrictions were limited to specific reasons following the insertion of the term "only".

Finally, in art. 21.2, on peoples rights to free disposal of their natural resources, a right to recovery and adequate compensation was added in the event of spoliation of such resources.

In its final form, the African Charter on Human and Peoples' Rights is divided into three parts (where only the first shall be discussed here as it relates to this particular study), following a Preamble, in which its ground of being, fundamental principles and viewpoints, and its relation to the OAU as well as to other international human rights instruments are stated.

Part I, covering articles 1 to 29, is again divided into two chapters, where the duties for states as well as for individuals are contained separately in Chapter 2, article 27, 28 and 29.

Chapter 1 contains the full scope of human and peoples' rights, without specific distinctions other than the systematic, which places first the civil and political rights of individuals in art. 2 to 14, the individual economic, social and cultural rights in art. 14 to 17, and finally the collective rights of the family in art. 18 and peoples' rights in art. 19 to 24.

Complementing this, we find the corresponding duties of states in art. 1, 16, 18, 21, 22, 23, 25 and 26.

This makes it fairly clear to get an overview of the rights and freedoms of the Charter, still in keeping with the natural relation between individual rights and freedoms and the duties of states, separating individual duties as an underscoring of their distinct nature.

Entry into force

According to art. 63.3., the Charter comes into force 3 months after a simple majority of the member states of the OAU have ratified or acceded to the Charter.

The number of member states of the OAU was at that time, in 1981,

50,[18] and a simple majority therefore meant that 26 states would have to ratify the Charter in accordance with the provisions of art. 63.1. and 2. in order for it to come into force.

This caused great concern and doubt among those who wanted to see the Charter come into effect, because they feared that lack of sufficient commitment among the African states would leave the Charter as one more well-intended but powerless instrument never to come into effect. Indeed the process was slow, with only one state ratifying it in 1981, five countries in 1982 and in 1983, and four in 1984. In 1985 the process seemed to have come to a halt, when no countries at all ratified the Charter, giving way to grave speculations and widespread scepticism about the future of the Charter. Then in 1986, however, as many as 13 states ratified it, and suddenly the Charter was a reality with a status similar to the European and the American Conventions on Human Rights.

It happened on 21 October 1986, when on 21 July 1986 Niger as the 26. country deposited its instrument of ratification, and as such tipped the crucial balance of the Charter coming into force. Once this was a reality, several more countries undertook steps to adopt the Charter, and subsequently 49 out of 53[19] states have now completed, or are in the process of completing, the adoption of the Charter.

This would ensure that the future of the Charter is secured, and eliminate the question whether an increase of the member states of the OAU, without those states adopting the Charter, would cause less than the required simple majority of support for the Charter, thereby rendering it effectless.

The period of five years from the adoption of the Charter to its coming into force was not unduly long, considering the fact that the UN Covenants took eleven years to accomplish the same. Compared to the other regional instruments, where the European Convention took only three years and the American Convention nine years, the African Charter stands out proudly, given the political, social and financial circumstance in which it was born. This is particularly noteworthy since most of the countries were less than one generation old as independent states.

---

18. The Sahrawi Arab Democratic Republic (SADR) became a member of the OAU on February 22, 1982, after long political deliberations, making the number of member states a total of 51. Amate, 1986, p. 347ff.

19. These states which have not done so are Eritrea, Ethiopia, South Africa and Swaziland. 8. Annual Activity Report of the African Commission 1994-1995.

Still, why did it take 5 years for the Charter to come into effect once the initial struggle of drafting and adopting it had been completed?

Apart from concern held by governments, who were clearly unwilling to give up too fast their chosen policy of violating human and peoples' rights for fear of losing comfortable privileges and positions, it should be noted that a substantial numbers of African leaders since the days of independence in the mid-sixties have regarded almost all jurisdictional bodies, particular of an international nature, with suspicion, and therefore were hesitant, at best, to accept supra-national provisions regarding human and peoples' rights.[20] The increase in the number of states having ratified or signed the Charter since 1986, however, indicates the growing commitment and willingness of African states to improve the states of human and peoples' rights on the continent, and the drafters, individuals and organizations, who for years have been keeping a steady pressure on the OAU and its member states to have such an instrument be a reality, can clearly count the entry into force of the Charter as a victory and an important milestone in the work of human rights.

Signature, ratification and accession

The African Charter deals with three of the most common means of acceptance of a treaty, namely signature, ratification and adherence (art. 63).[21]

Regarding signature, the interpretation of the implications hereof must be found in the text itself, but the Charter contains no more explicit statements on this.

If we then turn to the Vienna Convention, art. 18 states that:

> "A state is obliged to refrain from acts which would defeat the object and purpose of a treaty when - it has signed the treaty - until it shall have made its intention clear not to become a party to the treaty - or it has expressed its consent to be bound by the treaty, pending the entry into force of the treaty and provided that such entry into force is not unduly delayed".

This means that the signature of the state prevents it from making any steps, legislative as well as any other way, which do not correspond with the protection of rights and freedoms as stipulated in the charter.

---

20. Bello, 1985, p. 135.
21. Other terms used more often instead of "adherence" are "accession" or "adhesion", but the meaning and legal effect is the same. Brownlie, 1966, p. 490.

What can happen, though, is that a state signs the charter, thereby restricting its free exercise of power, and then suffers under various political turmoil, where neither a majority for or against the ratification of the charter can be reached, and a legislative vacuum then arises.

A question also appearing is whether a state would be allowed first to sign the Charter, then after a period decide that it does not wish to be bound by it, and then at a later date decide to sign it again.

Still, these questions are somewhat theoretical, given that art. 18 states that the entry into force must not be unduly delayed, implicating that if a state cannot "make up its mind", or has other problems in accepting to be bound by the Charter, the assumption then is for the state to need to resort to one of the other methods of acceptance.

When a state has signed the Charter, and wishes to be bound by it, the next step is the ratification, by which the state becomes fully bound by the Charter (unless reservations are made).[22]

The ratification takes place through the depositing of the instruments of ratification with the Secretary-General of the OAU (art. 63.2 of the Charter), and it will then take effect for the state three months after the date of deposit (art. 65).

Adherence is a process very similar to signature, and only differs from it in the sense that it doesn't require the process of signature first. This method of consent is generally used when a treaty already has come into force through the ratification of a given number of states, and other states wish to join it.

In this case, the states who have not yet taken any steps to adopt the Charter, or have not yet so far been in a position to do so, might use the process of adhesion instead of the longer and more complicated method of signature and ratification.

The Charter encompasses all three ways of acceptance, stating in art. 63 that "The present Charter shall be open to signature, ratification, or adherence of the member states of the Organization of African Unity".

So far 49 countries have ratified the Charter, out of where 28 states signed the Charter first. The period between the date of signature and that of ratification varies greatly, the longest being Gabon and Sudan with 4 and 3 1/2 years respectively, and the shortest being Niger, 6 days, and Zaire with 5 days. The latter is also the fastest country to accept the Charter, ratifying the Charter on 20 July 1987, signing it 3 days later and depositing

---

22. See Bello, 1985, p. 135ff, for examples.

its instrument of ratification on 28 July 1987. Most other countries take between 1 month and 1 year to complete this step.[23]

After the ratification itself, the instrument of ratification or adherence shall be deposited with the Secretary-General of the OAU, in accordance with art. 63.2, and the Secretary-General must inform member states of the organization about all such deposits, regardless of whether those states themselves have accepted the Charter, according to art. 67.

The time between the ratification itself, as an act of the individual state in accordance with its constitutional procedures, and the deposit of the instrument also varies a great deal, the longest being 7 1/2 months for Somalia and 4 months for Sierra Leone and Equatorial Guinea, and the shortest being 5 and 6 days for Gambia and Niger.

This specific act is important for two reasons, the first one being the demand in art. 63.3 regarding the need for a simple majority of the member states to have delivered their instruments of ratification to the Secretary-General of the OAU in order for the Charter to come into force. Since this has already happened,[24] the more important aspect lies with art. 65, which states that the Charter will take effect 3 months after the date of deposit for states ratifying or adhering to the Charter after it has come into force.

This means that, according to the Charter, the actual act of ratification is important only in the sense that it is being followed up by the deposit of the instrument, and not in itself constitutes legal obligations between the states as mentioned earlier in this chapter.

A campaign to have all OAU member states accept the Charter has been carried out successfully, and while being respectful to the sovereignty and individual development of states, this is an area in which pressure can be applied from the individual community. Now Africa can be seen as a continent reflecting unanimous commitment to improving the state of human and peoples' rights - at least on paper!

The adoption of the Charter in particular is impressive when noting that the African countries in general do not have an impressive record of the adoption of international conventions and instruments.[25]

---

23. Final Communique of the 12th session of the African Commission on Human and Peoples' Rights, Banjul, October 1992.
24. On 21 October 1986.
25. See chapter 3 on sources to a universal concept of human rights, when this is discussed.

In contrast to these instruments which have been heavily influenced by a European cultural influence, the African Charter has been created and established by the Africans themselves, and therefore countries must be expected to tolerate greater pressure from the international community towards adopting the Charter, than with regards to the international human rights instruments.

Conclusion

Generally concluding, we can see that the African Charter underwent a long process of formulation and adoption, which was nonetheless acheived with remarkable speed and consistency, seen in light of the turbulent circumstances on the continent during the years of its genesis. It should be noted, also, that even though the process received massive support from international non-African bodies such as the United Nations and the International Commission of Jurists, it is in fact an entirely African instrument. Once the OAU decided to endorse it, the drafting procedure proceeded in a purely African context, and the expressions hereof can be seen throughout the Charter, which at the same time manages to adhere largely to the basic human rights principles already established by other international instruments. Therefore it should also be seen as a unique document, not only for the African continent, but also in the context of an expanding number of regional human rights instruments adapted to the particular needs and interests of the region in which they operate. In that respect the African Charter truly represents a breakthrough.

The African Charter and national law

With respect to the general issue of how to make international treaties part of national law, a distinction is drawn between two schools of thought.[26]

One is the dualist view, also known as the doctrine of transformation, where international and national law are seen as two distinct and separate legal systems. From a national perspective international law is seen as inferior to and weaker than domestic law. This is based in a perception that the two types of law regulate different subjects, where national law operates with individual subjects while the international law has the states as its

---

26. See in the following Brownlie, 1966 p. 29f., Dixon, 1990 p. 40ff., and Sieghart, 1983 p. 40ff.

subjects. This school of thought is closely related to a positivistic approach to the concept of law, acknowledging only few specific sources to determining the concept of what is valid law.

The other is the monist view, the doctrine of incorporation, according to which there is only one system of law, of which the national and the international law are aspects. Seeing the state as a collection of individuals, the problem of different subject-matter is avoided, and both aspects are seen as manifestations of one single concept of law. Here the international law is superior and stronger than national law, and can be directly applied to the effect that national law must yield in case of conflict.

It is up to each individual state to determine which of the two schools it adheres to, and to a large extent it can be deduced from looking at the state's practice with respect to different international instruments.

Looking to the instrument in question, the African Charter itself has taken into consideration that its member states may subscribe to different practices of implementation as listed above by including one article regarding its transformation. This provision is art. 1 which states that

> "The Member States - shall recognize the rights, duties, and freedoms enshrined in this Charter, and shall undertake to adopt legislative or other measures to give effect to them".

On the one hand the Charter has hereby recognized the dualist theory mentioned above, making the national application of the provisions dependent on legislative or other measures giving effect to them.[27] It is also a clear indicating that the drafters wanted to emphasize its character as a legal instrument binding on states.[28]

On the other hand the term "or other measures" also gives a certain amount of leeway for the states to apply that particular method of implementation which they find to be most appropriate. Still, this can only apply to those states who subscribe to a monist perception of the relationship between international and national law, since those states applying a dualist view are necessitated to make some kind of incorporation through legislation.

In view of the rules established above, it would apply that States founded on a dualistic view will need to implement the Charter through

---

27. Kunig, 1982, p. 151.
28. D'sa, 1989, p. 102.

provisions in national legislation. This could be done either through an Act declaring the Charter in its entirety part of national law, or by expressly re-enacting the provisions of the Charter in its own legal system in such a way that the rights and freedoms are guaranteed to the same extent, or better, than in the Charter.

Other States, who recognize expressly or tacitly international instruments as part of their internal legal system, may not need to undertake legislative steps to give effect to the Charter. Still, they will need to uphold the provisions of the Charter in court procedures, administrative practice and provisions etc., referring to the term "other measures" in art. 1. They will also have to face the job of constantly ensuring that their national legislation is in accordance with the provisions and interpretations of the African Charter by the Commission or other bodies.

Failure to do either of the above mentioned constitutes a breach on the provisions of the Charter, and the State will be responsible towards other States for the violation of an international legal instrument.

Given the procedure of communications, such a violation of State duties can be brought forward by other State parties as well as individuals, NGO's and other entities according to the provisions of articles 47 to 59 and the Rules of Procedure mentioned earlier.

On the one hand art. 1, expressed through its wording and position within the framework of the Charter, also applies to the obligations pending exclusively between States. Examples hereof are art. 23.1. "The principles of solidarity and friendly relations implicitly affirmed by the Charter of the United Nations and reaffirmed by that of the Organization of African Unity shall govern relations between States", and art. 21.4. "State parties to the present Charter shall individually and collectively exercise the right to free disposal of their wealth and natural resources with a view to strengthening African unity and solidarity".

On the other hand art. 1 only applies to those provisions in Part I of the Charter which require national measures to make them effective, an exception of which might be art. 17.3, stating that "The promotion and protection of morals and traditional values recognized by the community shall be duty of the State".

In order to support art. 1, and to make sure that the States in reality do adopt the necessary measures to give effect to the Charter, art. 62 obligates each state party to submit every two years a report on its legislative or other measures "with a view to giving effect to the rights and freedoms recognized and guaranteed by the Charter".[29]

The incorporation of international law in Botswana, Malawi and Mozambique

The basic question here is whether AC is directly admissible in for instance Botswana court of law, or whether it has to be transformed into domestic law by some act of incorporation in accordance with the procedures outlined above.

As mentioned here, this can be done either by directly including the document in the laws of the country through an act of Parliament or other applicable procedures, or by indirectly transforming the provisions of the convention into the relevant areas of national law. The important thing is that it is ensured that national law corresponds to the international obligations and, if necessary, is adapted or changed accordingly.

In line with the most common practice of incorporation among states within the Commonwealth,[30] Botswana has so far adapted the policy of implementation of multilateral international conventions through explicit procedure. This is reflected through the incorporation of the Vienna Convention on Diplomatic Relations[31] and the Geneva Conventions of 1948.[32]

Malawi's policy is reflected in the decision taken already in 1965 to incorporate a specific reference to the Universal Declaration in the Republican Constitution, and was confirmed in 1982 by the Malawi Supreme Court of Appeal.[33]

Botswana and Malawi have ratified only a few international human rights conventions. Those are, apart from the OAU African Charter on Human and Peoples' Rights, the UN Convention relating to the Status of Refugees from 1951 and its Optional Protocol from 1967, the International Convention on the Elimination of All Forms of Racial Discrimination from

---

29. As of March 1995, only 14 member States have submitted even their initial reports, and those include Mozambique but neither Botswana nor Malawi. Only three of these (Gambia, Senegal and Tunisia) have also submitted their second periodic reports. African Commission, 1995.
30. Brownlie, 1966, p. 43f.
31. Implemented through the (Botswana) Diplomatic Immunities and Privileges Act of 1969.
32. Implemented through the (Botswana) Geneva Conventions Act of 1970.
33. See chapter 4 on the background for the 1994 Constitution of Malawi.

1965, and most recently the Convention on the Rights of the Child from 1989.

The most important difference between the status of ratifications of these two states, is that Malawi is also party to some of the most important and fundamental human rights conventions. These include the ICESCR, the ICCPR and its Optional Protocol, all from 1966, and the Convention against Torture and other Cruel, Inhuman or Degrading Treatment or Punishment from 1984.

In addition to those mentioned first, Botswana has also ratified the UN Convention relating to the Status of Stateless Persons from 1954, but none of the other instruments to which Malawi is a party, and this would seem to be an unnecessarily restrictive practice.

Mozambique are party to some of the same instruments as Botswana and Malawi, such as the ICCPR, the International Convention on Racial Discrimination, the Convention on the Rights of the Child, and the Convention relating to the Status of Refugees and its Protocol. In addition, however, it is also party to the Second Optional Protocol to the ICCPR aiming at the Abolition of Death Penalty[34], to the International Convention on the Suppression and Punishment of the Crime of Apartheid (now less significant since the democratic changes in South Africa), and to the Convention on the Prevention and Punishment of the Crime of Genocide.

To the extent that none of these instruments have been given effect in national law through an act of government as prescribed above, we must therefore conclude that they cannot be considered as being an integral part of the national law of each state.

This implies that in a given case regarding a question which has not been dealt with in the Constitution or any other national legislation, such as the question regarding freedom of information, the provisions of for instance the African Charter art. 9 do not constitute independently an individual right which can be disputed in the national courts. In other words, as long as a given provision of international human rights law has not been incorporated in national law, the individual cannot apply it as a basis for complaints against the State's violation of his or her rights and freedoms before the national courts.

The only possibility here would then be for the individual or group to file a communication with the African Commission claiming that the State

---

34. See chapter 6 on the right to life, where Mozambique is the only one of the three states to have abolished the death penalty.

in question is remiss in its obligation after art. 1 of the African Charter to recognize the rights and duties of the Charter and "undertake to adopt legislative or other measures to give effect to them".

Given this state of affairs, it is necessary to review the constitutional and in some cases also other legal regulation and practice, to determine the extent to which Botswana, Malawi and Mozambique actually do comply with the obligations binding upon them in accordance with AC. This is the theme of the next two chapters.

Part III
Analysis of material human rights provisions in the African Charter on Human and Peoples' Rights and the Constitutions of Botswana, Malawi and Mozambique

6 Individual civil and political rights and freedoms

Introduction

In the following an analysis is carried out of material human rights provisions as found in the African Charter on Human and Peoples' Rights. While this chapter takes as its focus the individual civil and political rights, chapter 7 deals with other aspects hereof such as the economic, social and cultural rights, collective rights, and individual duties.

In the first part of each section the provision in the Charter is dicussed and related to other human rights instruments of a similar nature. At the global level of the United Nations, these instruments are the Universal Declaration (UD) and the International Covenant on Civil and Political Rights (ICCPR), and from the regional level are included the European Convention on Human Rights and the Inter-American Convention on Human Rights established by the European Council and the OAS respectively.

In the second half of each section the correspondence between AC and the national Constitutions of Botswana, Malawi and Mozambique is analysed, in order to evaluate to which extent the provisions herein adequately reflect those of AC, or to what extent they go beyond it. Also, the aim is to draw up a detailed picture of the universality of human rights expressed on a particular level of law, since it will be shown that the provisions correspond in the main outline and yet are contextual and therefore different in their specific formulation and scope.

The right to life

AC art. 4

AC's article 4 states the fundamental principle that human beings are inviolable, and that every human being has the right to respect for his or her life and personal integrity.

The formulation of this article was originally conceived differently, using the term "sacred" instead of inviolable, but the meaning hereof should in any case be understood as "that which must not be profaned; that which no one is allowed to dishonour or injure".[1]

Traditionally, this principle has been considered highly important in Africa, which is also indicated by the extensive, if rather lyric, inclusion hereof in the African Charter. This duality and the apparent schism between the significance of the concept on the one hand and the extensive violations hereof committed by a number of member states on the other hand, may well have resulted in the lack of use of the term "African" and its substitution with the less obliging and more general "human being" in AC art. 4.[2]

The corresponding duty for the state has in the European context been interpreted such that not only must the state itself abstain from violating the provisions, the so-called "passive" respect. It also has the obligation to protect more actively a residents' right to life, for instance when it is threatened by acts committed by other states, individuals or entities, or by accidents of nature.[3]

In relation to African societies in general, it could be claimed that AC art. 4 also included the duty of the state to ensure the life of its people by securing minimum standards of living through food, medical attention etc. Such a rule would apply particularly in cases of disaster or famine, and a minimum requirement of the State would be that, as a minimum, it does not hinder that emergency aid from the outside world reaches the people in need. Still, such an interpretation of an inherent obligation for member States to ensure a satisfactory level of nutrition for its citizens is weakened by the fact, that although AC contains a fairly extensive catalogue on individual economic, social and cultural rights, this does not include the right to food or nutrition.[4]

---

1. Rapporteur's Rapport, CAB/67/draft Rapt. rpt.(11), Rev.4, p. 8, in Bello, 1985, p. 151f.
2. Ibid.
3. European Commission, No. 6040/73, Coll. 44, s. 121.
4. AC art. 15 on the right to work, AC art. 17.1 on the right to education, and AC art. 17.2 on freedom to take part in the cultural life of one's community. The only provision which to some degree could include an individual right to, at least, the most basic sustenance is AC art. 16.1, which states the right to enjoy "the best attainable state of physical and mental health". Similarly, AC art. 16.2 states that State parties to AC shall take "- the necessary measures to protect the health of their people", apart from ensuring that they recieve medical attention when they are sick.
See chapter 7 on the individual economic, social and cultural rights in the African Charter.

It is noteworthy that AC art. 4, contrary to most of the other articles on rights and freedoms as dealt with above, is of an absolute nature, and does not contain any references to national law or other clawback clauses. This is, however, in line with the recognition of the absolute nature of this right, which cannot be subject to derogation in any of the other international human rights instruments either.[5]

The article does, however, underline that "No one may be arbitrarily[6] deprived of - the right to respect for his life and his person". The formulation hereby suggests that a decision by a court, in accordance with national as well as international law, including capital punishment is acceptable according to the Charter. A sentence to death or imprisonment must, however, not be found to be an undue violation of the respect for the integrity of the person or his life, and as such certain obligations for the state to maintain the Rule of Law are stressed.

Looking to the other general human rights instruments, we find that they adopt different approaches to the question of death sentencing. The UD art. 3 is silent, stating the absolute right to life only, while ICCPR art. 6.2 specifies that it must only be applied for the most serious crimes in accordance with the law. Provisions of a less restrictive nature is AMCHR art. 4.2, according to which the use of death sentences must not extend beyond those crimes to which it already applies. Finally there is ECHR art. 2, which only requires that a death sentence must follow the decision of a Court of Law taken in accordance with the law, and which is consequently, this is the interpretation which is closest to that of the African Charter.

A question which has neither been clearly answered in the Charter nor in the European system is whether the provisions apply to children yet unborn, and as such constitute a prohibition against provoked abortions.

The European Commission has pointed to two possible ways of interpretation, either that the embryo is not included in the protective sphere, or at least only with some limitations.[7] It is hard to reach a conclusion as to the appropriate interpretation of the African Charter on this point, since religious and cultural beliefs and patterns still emphasize the importance of many children being born. This should be seen in light of the fact that the IMR for the continent as a whole is well over 100, meaning that a sub-

---

5. Lindholt, 1995.
6. The accentuation is mine.
7. European Commission, no. 8416/79, DR. 19, p. 244.

stantive number of infants die within the first months or years of birth.[8]

In any case it must be accepted that an abortion can be made on medical grounds and from a proportional point of view, when the pregnancy is threatening the life or welfare of the mother, possibly also including pregnancies following from a case of rape.

BC sec. 4, MOC art. 70, and MAC sec. 16

The right to life is found in all of the three constitutions, but with differences in formulation which indicate, more or less specifically, that their scope may be different, particularly with respect to the use and application of death penalty. Given the rather summaric nature of AC art. 4, it is not surprising to see that none of the three national states' constitutional or legislative provisions can be seen as violating this article. Rather, they broaden and specify the scope of protection of the right to life beyond AC, even though their interpretations are so different that they do not establish a unanimous contribution to the interpretation hereof.

The first issue to be discussed is whether the bearer of this right was intended to be the same in the various instruments, since the formulations differ to such an extent as is the case.

While BC and MAC both speak of "person", AC uses the term "human being", and the former therefore suggest that the right in itself is not embedded in the very fabric of humanity. It is likely to depend on the granting of the status of personality, rather than having the universal and inherent character as suggested in AC, and implied in the first paragraph of the article stating that "Human beings are inviolable". Here, the provision of AC art. 3 should be used as a reference for the interpretation hereof, should the case arise, according to which every individual has the right to respect of the dignity inherent in a human being and to recognition of his legal status. Since the member states of AC are supposed to prescribe to the concept of Rule of Law, and since other provisions of the Charter speak of

---

8. The Infant Mortality Rate is a term used to define the number of deaths among children under the age of one per thousand live births. This means, that the higher the IMR, the lower the standard of living in a given society, and an IMR above 50 in a given society indicates that hunger exists as a persistent society-wide issue. (The Hunger Project, p. 384ff). The latest IMR for Africa is 64, compared to 70 for the world and 10 for Europe. More than half of the African States have IMR's above 100. Some of the highest being Guinea (149), Gambia (138) and Malawi (138).
1993 World Population Data Sheet, Population Reference Bureau (Washington, USA).

"legal personality", it is unlikely that the use of declaring somebody a "non-person" should have much practical significance in a modern society.

Giving rise to much more acute concerns, however, is MOC, which throughout its provisions uses the term "citizen", indicating that the constitutional protection is only directed towards them. Here, we may see a conflict with the general international law of human rights, according to which a state has the obligation to protect the human rights of all citizens under its jurisdiction, including aliens legitimately residing within the boundaries of its territory.[9]

Death penalty Regarding the use of death penalty, BC sec. 4 states that every individual has a basic right to respect for his or her life, and that the deprivation of this right shall be exercised only under some form of restraint.

MOC art. 70 sec. 1 states that "All citizens shall have the right to life", with sec. 2 continuing to state that "In the Republic of Mozambique there shall be no death penalty".

Finally, MAC sec. 16 states that every person has the right to life and no person shall be arbitrarily deprived of his or her right. The provision continues to define what is implied in the term "arbitrarily", namely the execution of a death sentence imposed by a competent court in respect of a person found guilty of a criminal offence under the laws of Malawi.

With a general reference to the delimitations of the right to life, AC merely states that deprivation hereof must not be "arbitrary". It does not proceed to state that it also has to be in accordance with the law, but so does BC, indirectly, in the sense that the deprivation of life must happen in accordance with the procedures described by the law. BC sec. 4.1 limits this to execution of the sentence of an offence under the law in force in Botswana, or as a result of the use of force (BC sec. 4.2) to such extent and in such circumstances as are permitted by law.

An additional requirement is that such measures must be considered reasonably justifiable for a number of reasons, all of which centre upon the maintaining of public peace and order and the ensuring of the rights of other individuals or the community. This allows for a relatively flexible interpretation of the state's right to take the life of its citizens, since BC sec. 4.2 also would include such cases as, for instance, unintentional deaths

---

9. General Comment No 24 of the Human Rights Committee, November 1994, in ed. Steiner and Alston, 1996, p. 774ff.

caused by rough treatment by the police in case of arrest or when dispersing a riot.

Regarding Malawi, the Malawi Independence Constitution (MIC) contained a similar clause, referring to such "justifiable" causes as the defence of any person from violence or for the defence of property, in order to effect a lawful arrest or to prevent the escape of a person lawfully detained, for the purpose of suppressing a riot, insurrection or mutiny, in order to prevent the commission by that person of a criminal offence, or if the person dies as the result of a lawful act of war.[10]

In contrast hereto stands MAC sec. 16, which only allows for deprivation of life in accordance with the execution of a death sentence but has no clause similar to BC sec. 4.2. Finally, MOC art. 70 leads the way, even moving beyond the level of protection afforded by AC, by stating an absolute prohibition against the use of death penalty.

The basic difference between AC on the one hand and BC and MAC on the other hand with respect to the use of death sentence, is that AC is silent with respect to qualifications and competence of the institution by requiring that it be handed down by a judge or tribunal. This would seem to make acceptable the execution of a death sentence by a chief or other institution of power not acting in accordance with legal provisions (either because such provisions do not exist or because they leave the matter to the hands of the relevant institution), but on the basis of tradition or other well-established custom or practice.

This is, however, an abstract situation, and in the case of Botswana this problem has been foreseen and taken care of by a provision stating that no person shall be charged with a criminal offence unless such an offence is created by the Penal Code or some other written law. Furthermore, the most serious offences including murder have been restricted from the jurisdiction of the Customary Courts.[11] Consequently, a violation of the right to life may be found to occur under different circumstances according to the two provisions, although BC provides the strongest protection, as shown above.

In actual practice, the Penal Code of Botswana authorizes the use of death penalties along with other types of penalty (sec. 27 and 28), but it only applies in cases where a person is found to be guilty of murder without extenuating circumstances (sec. 208).

---

10. 1964, sec. 2.
11. The Customary Courts Act, S.I. 12, 1977, sec. 11 and 12.

In contrast hereto stands the Penal Code of Malawi sec. 25, which authorizes the use of death penalty without any stipulation on the degree or type of offence for which it can be applied. The only criteria, as stated in sec. 26, relate to the personal aspects of the offender, stipulating that a death sentence may not be applied to a person who was under the age of 18 years when the offence was committed (sub-sec. 2). Instead the offender may be detained "during the President's pleasure", an indeterminate period which may, or may not, be equivalent to a life sentence, with the added emotional pressure of uncertainty. In contrast hereto sub-sec. 4 states that when a woman otherwise eligible to receive a death sentence after having been found guilty of an offence punishable with death, is found to be pregnant, the sentence shall instead be one of imprisonment for life.

The fact that Malawi has maintained the death sentence has been criticized by Amnesty International, particularly because these cases along with all types of political cases, were formerly heard only in the traditional courts, where no guarantees of fair trial existed. One of the most prominent examples hereof was former Minister of Justice Orton Chirwa and his wife Vera Chirwa, who were both convicted and condemned to death in 1983 following a blatantly unfair trial in a traditional court. Even though the sentence was later commuted to life imprisonment, Orton Chirwa died in 1992, so for him the sentence became, in effect, a capital one.[12]

A communication was lodged with the African Commission by Amnesty International regarding the treatment of the Chirwa's as well as other members of the public. The Commisison held that the State of Malawi had violated sec. 4 as well as sec. 5, 6 and 7.1 (a), (d) and (e), and stated their hopes that "a new era of respect for the human rights of Malawi's citizens had begun". They also decided that "the change of government in Malawi does not extinguish the present claim before the Commission. Although the present government of Malawi did not commit the human rights abuses complained of, it is responsible for the reparation of these abuses", based on the international principles of state succession.[13]

Genocide Another aspect of the right to life, found in MAC sec. 17, should be mentioned here, the provision stating that "Acts of genocide are prohibited and shall be prevented and punished". Here we see the collective

---

12. Amnesty International, September 1993, p. 4f.
13. Communication 68/92 and 78/92, the African Commission on Human and Peoples' Rights, 1995.

aspect of human rights, which is so strongly expressed in the African Charter in contrast to the national instruments, has been reflected in relation to the right to life for the group in addition to that of the individual. Neither Botswana's nor Mozambique's constitutions include such a provision.

Abortion In relation to the concept on right to life, so to speak at the other end of the line, we must address not only the termination but also the beginning of life. With respect to the question of abortion, the Botswana Penal Code sec. 160 and 161 explicitly forbids it without reservation, authorizing a prison sentence up to 7 years (sec. 160), or 3 years if it is self-administered (sec. 161). A similar provision is found in the Malawi Penal Code sec. 149 and sec. 150, with the significant difference that the maximum punishment for a person intending to procure an abortion on a woman is 14 years, while a woman attempting or succeeding in aborting her foetus may be liable for imprisonment for 7 years.

The child becomes "a person capable of being killed" from the moment it has left its mothers body, whether it has breathed or not (BPC sec. 215, MAPC sec. 216). From that moment and up to the age of twelve months, the mother may be found guilty of infanticide instead of murder in accordance with PC sec. 213 and MAPC sec. 208.

In addition, MAPC sec. 231 states that a person who prevents a child from being born alive in such a manner that he or she would have been deemed as having killed the child if it had been born alive, is liable to imprisonment for life.

The right to personal integrity

AC art. 5

AC art. 5 deals with various aspects of the right to personal integrity, a provision which follows closely at the heels of the right to life, and in this way reflects the need for securing a certain level of quality hereof.

The first section hereof states that "Every individual shall have the right to respect of the dignity inherent in a human being and to recognition of his legal status".

The independent scope of this principle is hard to determine, and it is more logical to see it as an aspect of the other more substantial rights and freedoms in this as well as the other provisions on civil and political rights in the African Charter.

In particular, it should be viewed in conjunction with AC art. 2, stating the absolute principle of non-discrimination, and AC art. 18.3, according to which the State shall ensure that the national laws do not discriminate against women and children in accordance with international instruments. In many African states, including those dealt with in this study, women may be considered as minors, legally or in effect, in a number of areas such as tax law, family law, property law, inheritance law etc. In such instances one may consider applying AC art. 5 to ensure womens right to full enjoyment of their legal status equally with that of men.

AC art. 5 proceeds to declare a general prohibition against "All forms of exploitation and degradation of man", and gives two examples of specific cases hereof, one of which is the prohibition against slavery and slave trade, which is the subject of a separate section below.

The other, and potentially far more interesting and significant, example hereof is the prohibition against "all forms of torture, cruel, inhuman or degrading punishment or treatment" which is absolute and not subject to clawback clauses.

Looking to the regime of human rights regulation, we find that other international human rights instruments contain the same formulations of this concept, such as sec. 5 of UD as well as ICCPR sec. 7, which are identical to that of AC art. 5. On the regional level sec. 5.2 of the AMCHR applies the same formulation to prohibit torture as well as cruel, inhuman or degrading punishment or treatment. A similar provision is art. 3 of the ECHR, omitting the term "cruel", which still does not alter the scope of the provision since "inhuman" must be seen as encompassing cruelty also.

A specific international instrument in this area is the UN Convention against Torture and Other Cruel, Inhuman or Degrading Treatment or Punishment (UNCAT).[14] Here, art. 1.1 defines torture extensively as: "any act by which severe pain or suffering, whether physical or mental, is intentionally inflicted on a person" for a number of purposes including the obtainment of information or a confession, intimidation and coercion, and cases based on discrimination of any kind, where a person acting in an official capacity is somehow involved.

In order to delimit torture from the less severe concept of cruel or inhuman punishment and treatment, art. 1.1 proceeds to make clear that

---

14. Adopted by General Assembly Resolution 39/46 of 10 December 1984, which entered into force on 26 June 1987. As of 31 December 1995 the Convention had been ratified by 93 states.

torture "does not include pain or suffering arising only from, inherent in or incidental to lawful sanctions".

Given the uniformity of this principle, as well as the relatively large number of ratifications to the Convention,[15] it would seem that the prohibition of the use of torture at least on a legal level enjoys universal recognition, applicable to every cultural context.

The section on torture in AC art. 5 should therefore not present any formal legal problems or controversy in relation to the other international instruments, or in relation to the national law of its member states. Instead, the problem would lie with the member states' inability or unwillingness to prevent it on a practical level, falling within art. 1 and 26 of the Charter dealing with the national implementation and establishment of institutions guaranteeing African peoples' full enjoyment of the rights of the Charter.

This is particularly aggravating since we must regrettably acknowledge that violations of this right do occur on a frequent basis also in several States who are parties to the African Charter. Even more disturbing is the tendency, at least until recently, by the OAU and its institutions to refrain from taking action in such cases, claiming it to be an undue interference in the state's domestic affairs.[16]

We hereby see too clearly illustrated the schism between the legal and the factual world, where human rights recognition and formal compliance do not necessarily guarantee actual fulfilment hereof in every day life.

In contrast stands the other part of the provision, on punishment or treatment, which gives rise to an interesting and important discussion on the definition hereof, particularly in relation to the use of judicial flogging.

For a definition of the concept of cruel, inhuman or degrading punishment or treatment in any of the instruments, we look in vain, since none of these have clearly defined the ramifications of this concept. The closest we get, with respect to statutory provisions, is art. 16.1 of the UNCAT, which obligates each State Party to undertake to prevent within its jurisdiction "other acts of cruel, inhuman or degrading treatment or punishment which do not amount to torture as defined in art. 1, when such acts are committed by or at the instigation of or with the consent of or acquiescence of a public official or other person acting in an official capacity".

---

15. Ibid.
16. These include Mauretania, the Central African Empire, Sudan and Nigeria; Bello 1987, p. 153f. See also the Annual Reports as well as individual country studies published by Amnesty International on the subject.

On this basis we can therefore not determine whether the use of flogging, defined as a given number of strokes with a cane to be given either instead of or in conjunction with another form of sentence, constitutes a violation of this freedom.

The only clear interpretation hereof comes from the ECourtHR, where it was determined that the use hereof did constitute a violation of the provision in the European Convention.[17] The significance of this decision has been extended to representing the international view in the matter by the HRC under the ICCPR, which in addition has included under the prohibition excessive chastisement as an educational or disciplinary measure.[18] Also Amnesty International has stated without reservation that "Corporal punishment is a cruel, inhuman and degrading form of punishment and as such prohibited by international law".[19]

Looking now to the national Constitutions of Botswana, Malawi and Mozambique, the central question is whether this interpretation on the concept also applies to the member states to the Charter, or if the African Commission may adopt a different approach to the issue.

BC sec. 7, MAC sec. 19 and MOC art. 70

The first section of AC art. 5, on the recognition of every persons legal status, has no direct counterpart in the national Constitutions of Malawi, Mozambique or Botswana. The only approximation hereof is MAC art. 41 sec. 1, stating that "Every person shall have the right to recognition as a person before the law", which could be applied with the same meaning.

Still, this provision is followed by sec. 2 and 3 of the same article on the right to access to the courts and to an effective remedy for violations of human rights, suggesting that in this context the provision is directed more towards the area of fair trial instead of the very personal and basic meaning in AC art. 5.

Looking first to the constitutional provisions, BC sec. 7.1 in accordance with art. 5 of the African Charter and other instruments mentioned above simply states that "No person shall be subjected to torture or to inhuman or degrading punishment or treatment", without any further declar-

---

17. Judgment of the European Court of Human Rights, 25 April 1978 in Tyrer, Series A.26.
18. GenC7/16, § 2, GenC 20/44, § 5; Nowak, 1993, p. 134.
19. AI, September 1993.

ation of the right to personal integrity. An identical formulation was used in MIC, revealing their common origin, which in addition was heavily inspired by the formulation used in the European Convention a decade younger.

Looking at the Constitution of Malawi, we see the principle expanded, making MAC sec. 19 by far the most comprehensive of the provisions. It declares in sub-sec. 1 and 2 that "The dignity of all persons shall be inviolable", and that every State organ shall guarantee respect for human dignity in all criminal and other proceedings as well as during the enforcement of a penalty.

Then, in sub-sec. 3 we find the standard formulation repeated, that "No person shall be subject to torture of any kind or to cruel, inhuman or degrading treatment or punishment", which in this context seems to appropriately exemplify the general principle already stated in the first part of the provision.

A further addition, which is both unique and interesting in the way it reflects a modern-day interpretation of the fundamental principle, is sub-sec. 5 which declares that "No person shall be subjected to medical or scientific experimentation without his or her consent".

In contrast hereto MOC art. 70.1 simply declares that "All shall have the right to physical integrity, and may not be subjected to torture or to cruel or inhuman treatment", to be viewed as an extension of the right to life contained in the first half of the provision. In contrast to the other provisions MOC art. 70 does not include any prohibition against the use of inhuman or degrading punishment, which is unfortunate since this particular aspect has key significance as discussed below.

The part which gives rise to discussion, identical to the MIC sec. 5.2, is BC sec. 7.2, which states that "nothing contained in or done under the authority of any law shall be held to be inconsistent with or in contravention of this section to the extent that the law in question authorizes the infliction of any description of punishment that was lawful in the former Protectorate of Bechuanaland immediately before the coming into operation of this Constitution".

This means that if the use of flogging is recognized as a legitimate sentence since before the Constitution came into force, the various provisions throughout the Acts and regulations prescribing the use of and detailed procedures for the administration of flogging as a sentence and a disciplinary measure would not violate BC sec. 7.

However, this historically based correspondence between the legal position in Botswana and Malawi is fundamentally abridged through the introduction of the new constitution for the latter. Here MAC sec. 19.4 explicitly states that "No person shall be subject to corporal punishment in connexion with any judicial proceedings or in any other proceeding before any organ of the state". In light of the principle of *lex superior* as well as *lex posterior*, it is evident that this provision invalidates the various legislative provisions on judicial flogging as described below, which would then have to be amended or repealed by the legislative organs of Malawi in the near future.

Examples of such provisions are sec. 25 and 28 of the MPC, corresponding with minor variations to sec. 30 of the BPC and sec. 301 of the BCPEA, in which a number of specific criteria to be fulfilled in each case are established.[20]

According to these criteria a sentence of corporal punishment would mean to be caned specifying the number of strokes not to exceed 12, or, in case of a person under eighteen years, six strokes. Neither females nor males sentenced to death or considered by the Court to be more than forty years of age must be sentenced to caning (Sec. 30 of the BPC). The caning shall be carried out in a manner and with the use of such a cane as has been approved by the Minister, and only after certification by a medical officer that the person in question is fit to undergo this type of punishment. The medical officer or magistrate shall furthermore supervise the administering of the sentence. No sentence of caning shall be carried out by instalments, and it must be administered privately in a prison (Sec. 301 of the BCPEA).

According to the, now outdated, MPC sec. 28, the maximum number of strokes is 24, and there is no particular restriction for minors. Similarly, no women or persons convicted of a death sentence may be flogged, but the age limit here is 45. Otherwise the provision corresponds to that of Botswana.

In addition to the judicial area, we find also in Botswana education system, i.e. the various Regulations under the EA, that corporal punishment

---

20. Two separate Acts mention the legitimate use of flogging in connection with sentencing. The first of those is the BPC, Act 2 1964, which entered into force on 10 June 1964. The second is the BCPEA, No. 52 1938, which entered into force on 1 January 1939. In contrast hereto the present Constitution was adopted as L.N. 83, 1966, and entered into force on 30 September 1966.

may be applied as a disciplinary measure.[21]

Looking at the Botswana case law in this area, we find 3 examples where the Courts have decided on the use of corporal punishment.

On the firmer side is the case *State vs. Keakitse* from 1982, concerning the sentencing of a fourteen-year old boy who had been convicted at first instance of theft and sentenced to two strokes with a light cane. The appellate judge increased the number of strokes to six, finding that under the circumstances it was important to indicate to other young people the severity of the law.[22]

In contrast hereto the Court of Appeal ruled in the famous case *The State vs. Petrus and Another* from 1983 that corporal punishment by repeated and delayed instalments did amount to inhuman and degrading punishment.[23]

The final case is *R. Radithose vs. the State* from 1990, where the Court of Appeal ruled in favour of the appellant, who had been sentenced to a combination of 4 years of imprisonment and 6 strokes of whipping for shopbreaking and theft. Granting leave for that part of the sentence which related to corporal punishment, the Court declared the futility and inappropriateness of the combination hereof with a long prison sentence. This decision was strengthened by the fact that the appellant had already been sentenced to corporal punishment on a number of occasions.[24]

Any such case law from Malawi would be of historical relevance only, since not only the Legislature but also the Judiciary would be obliged to follow the Constitutional provision in sec. 19, prohibiting future use of corporal punishment.

Finally, Mozambique abolished the use of judicial punishments of flogging in September 1989, before the adoption of their new Constitution three months later. It should be noted here, however, that the former provisions allowed the use of flogging up to a total of 90 lashes to be given to persons serving a prison sentence![25]

Adding to the multi-faceted picture of Southern African approaches to

---

21. Sec. 29 of the Education Act, Law No. 40, 1966, S.I. 4, 1975; Education (Primary Schools Regulations), S.I. 127, 1980; Education (Government and aided Secondary Schools) Regulations, S.I. 145, 1978.
22. Rev. Case No. 4 of 1982; Neff, 1986, p. 18.
23. Court of Appeal 8/12/1983.
24. Court of Appeal, No. 14/1990.
25. Law no. 5/1983.

the tender issue of corporal punishment, one may note that in Zimbabwe, where the constitution contains a provision similar to that of the African Charter and the other national instruments mentioned above, corporal punishment is still available as an option in the Criminal procedure and Evidence Act and in the Magistrates Courts Act. However, in a case from 1988, the three defendants were sentenced separately of rape by a regional magistrate's court to varying periods of imprisonment in conjunction with whipping of six strokes. The Appellant judge ruled that the whipping constituted a case of both inhuman and degrading punishment, quoting the European Tyrer-case and the Botswana Petrus-case mentioned above.[26]

Drawing up a conclusion, we can clearly see that the case law and statutes leave no doubt that in Botswana the use of corporal punishment, under the conditions stated above, is widely if not unanimously recognized, and administered in a way which would not seem to constitute a violation of BC sec. 7. Whether or not this also means that Botswana does not violate AC art. 5 is a slightly different and more complicated matter.

It is revealing to see how the interpretations of a seemingly universal concept are not without variation, even within the national laws of neighbouring countries, representing as wide a scale of approaches to the subject as one might expect to find in the African continent as a whole - at least among those states which prescribe to some form of Rule of Law. There is no doubt whatsoever that the use of judicial flogging contravenes the European conception of freedom from cruel, inhuman or degrading treatment or punishment, which has so far impacted on the international interpretation hereof. Still, whether or not this interpretation also applies to the African Charter is not easily answered, and in the end the answer will have to depend on the position one takes in relation to maintaining a universal conception of human rights.[27]

We should keep in mind that Africa suffers a general state of underdevelopment particularly in the public sector,[28] and that such sentences as prison or the payment of fines may often have far more severe consequences for the person and potentially also for his close as well as

---

26. State vs. Ncube; State vs. Tshuma; State vs. Ndhlovu, Supreme Court of Zimbabwe (1988)(2) SA 702; Naldi, 1989.
27. An-Na'im arrives at the similar conclusion, arguing that the definition of this particular standard should be "the product of internal discoure and cross-cultural dialogue". ed. An-Na'im, 1992, p. 39.
28. Neff, 1986, p. 19.

extended family. At this point AC art. 7.2, according to which "punishment is personal and can be imposed only on the offender", should be kept in mind, since the use of corporal punishment is less likely to constitute a violation hereof.[29]

In the end it will be up to the African Commission to interpret AC art. 5, and decide accordingly which countries violate it or not. Here, one should take note of the precise formulation of AC art. 60 and 61, on applicable principles of interpretation, according to which such sources should be those international and UN bodies and instruments expressly acknowledged by the African states. Subsequently, the African Commission may apply the interpretation adopted by the HRC under the ICCPR, which has been ratified by a large number of the African states, but potentially only in relation to those states which are in fact also party to this instrument. And the direct application of a decision from any of the other regional bodies, such as the European or Inter-American Commission or Court clearly falls outside the mandate of the African Commission in favour of, for instance, "practices consistent with international norms on human and peoples rights" and "customs generally accepted as law".

As mentioned before, this is an area where no definite conclusion can be drawn separately from the acknowledgement of one's ideological view. If a universalistic approach should be applied,[30] the interpretation of AC art. 5 should follow that of the other international instruments, and in that case Botswana in particular would violate this provision in a number of cases.

If, on the other hand, one wants to adopt a more pluralistic conception of law, where basic provisions are subject to global consensus but where the actual elaboration and definitions hereof may vary from region to region, one might cautiously allow for an individual evaluation of the appropriateness. In case of Botswana, where the process is administered under tight judicial control and in accordance with very specific criteria, I would be inclined to accept the use of corporal punishment in its present form, at

---

29. This does not mean that I personally like or wish to see people being beaten physically, and that I don't find that it would be a degrading form of punishment in a European society where the stigmatisation following such an act would be severe. I merely contest that an European point of view should automatically apply in any given case, and that the question for me is how the Africans themselves regard this type of punishment.

30. See ch. 2 for a discussion hereof.

least for the time being.

Freedom from slavery

AC art. 5

The concept is found in AC art. 5, which states that "all forms of exploitation and degradation of man, particularly slavery, slave trade ... shall be prohibited". This article is very thorough in its formulation, and covers a wide array of different specified provisions, the majority of which have been discussed separately above as they relate to freedom from torture or cruel or inhuman punishment or treatment. The stressing of the prohibition against slavery and slave trade must be viewed on the history of the African continent, in light of the atrocities committed by the colonialists for centuries as well as the common practice among various African tribes of taking prisoners of war or conquest as slaves.

Unfortunately, the importance of protecting this freedom legally has not just a historic value, since it might still occur that African parents in desperate circumstances give away their children in return for money to pay for basic necessities. An aspect hereof is the marrying off of young girls, so that their families can use the dowry given by the husband for maintenance.[31] Again, this problem is related to the inequality of married women all over the Continent; women who cannot dispose of their own income, and who consequently may find themselves in such a state of total dependence on their husbands or other male relatives that it amounts to a situation of servitude.[32]

As stated above, particularly AC art. 18 and 2, on particular protection of the rights of women and children and non-discrimination, should be applied here as well. Since this provision again refers to relevant international instruments and includes the provisions contained herein,[33] to a limited extent they support AC art. 5 in cases relating to women and children. Examples of these instruments are the Declaration and Convention on the Elimination of (All Forms of) Discrimination against Women from

---

31. Bello, 1985, p. 154.
32. See below on the question of discrimination against women in Botswana.
33. See the section on freedom of movement and the right to asylum in AC art. 12.3, for a further discussion on the legal implications of such a reference to international instruments.

1967 and 1979, the Equal Enumeration Convention from 1951 and the Convention on the Political Rights of Women. With respect to children, such instruments as the Declaration and Convention on the Rights of the Child from 1959 and 1989, and The Convention and Recommendation on Consent to Marriage, Minimum Age for Marriage and Registration of Marriages from 1962 and 1965 apply.

The general concept of slavery is protected in several international instruments, such as the Universal Declaration art. 4, the ICCPR art. 8. These provisions are supplemented by a number of global and UN instruments such as the Slavery Convention with Protocol from 1926, the Supplementary Convention on the Abolition of Slavery, the Slave Trade and Institutions and Practices Similar to Slavery from 1956, and the Convention for the Suppression of the Traffic in Persons and of the Exploitation of the Prostitution of Others from 1949.

However, since AC art. 5 contains no reference of the kind found in art. 12.3 and 18.3, the provisions in the conventions and declarations mentioned above have no substantial or independent status in relation to AC, except to the extent following from the general reference in the Preamble of AC to the principles of other international instruments.[34] In addition AC art. 60 and 61 concerning applicable principles for the interpretative functions of the African Commission, as discussed above, should be noted, but at the same time it is dubious whether these instruments can be applied by the Commission in light of the fact that the various slavery conventions have been ratified by less than half the state parties to the AC.[35]

It is important to note that AC does not contain an express prohibition of forced labour, contrary to the other general conventions.[36] Neither, in fact, does the UD, but in light of the examples outlined above, there are still a number of unfortunate situations occurring in Africa, which at the same time do not amount to slavery. In these cases a provision protecting the freedom from forced labour, as a less severe variation of the same concept,

---

34. The second-last section of the Preamble reads "... Reaffirming their adherence to the principles of human and peoples' rights and freedoms contained in the declarations, conventions, and other instruments adopted by the Organization of African Unity, the Movement of Non-Aligned Countries, and the United Nations".

35. Human Rights International Instruments, Chart of Ratifications as of 31 December 1995, UN 1995.

36. ECHR art. 4, AMCHR art. 6, and ICCPR art. 8.

could be applied instead.

The lack of a provision on forced labour in AC is therefore an omission which should be regarded critically, even though these cases could be included under other parts of AC art. 5 such as the prohibition against "exploitation and degradation of man".

BC sec. 6, MAC sec. 27 and MOC art. 88

BC, MAC and MOC establish this principle in accordance with AC, and as will be seen below some of them even go beyond the scope laid out by the regional instrument. Similar to the graduation found in the relation to AC art. 5 on torture and cruel punishment or treatment, we here find that the concept of freedom from slavery is prohibited by all the various instruments without reservation. In relation to the concept of forced labour or servitude, seen as being of a less severe nature, there are some variations in the national instruments.

BC sec. 6 protects the individuals right to freedom from slavery corresponding to AC art. 5, declaring that "No person shall be held in slavery or servitude", and the same provision is found in MAC sec. 27.1. The provisions of the two instruments are not identical to AC art. 5, since they both add the concept of servitude. The main difference lies with the fact that while MAC sec. 27.2 continues to follow AC art. 5 by prohibiting slave trade, it is not included in BC sec. 6.

Whether this latter aspect should lead to a conclusion that BC hereby does not comply with AC is more doubtful, since the fairly unlikely occurrence of such a situation in Botswana would probably be encompassed by the other parts of the provision.

MOC has no provision prohibiting slavery, and from a formalistic point of view it could therefore be questioned whether Mozambique then violates the provisions of AC. Here, however, attention should be brought to the formulation of AC art. 1 on the duty of state parties to recognize the rights of the Charter and undertake to adopt legislative "or other measures" to give effect to them. As such it can therefore not be concluded that there is a violation in this case, since the provision doesn't necessitate legal, or even less constitutional, enactments. What is important, as stated above in relation to Botswana, is that some other form of protection is available, and in fact MOC not only stipulates in art. 88.3 that forced labour shall be forbidden, but proceeds in art. 89 through 91 to list a comprehensive catalogue of employees' rights.

The other two Constitutions also state the right to freedom from forced labour, BC in sec. 6.2 and MAC in sec. 27.3, and the latter goes even one step further by declaring in sec. 27.4 a prohibition against "tied labour that amounts to servitude". Here the people of Malawi consequently enjoy a wider protection of these rights than is afforded by the other national Constitutions as well as the AC.

An important question is whether freedom from forced labour is an absolute right, and an examination of the three Constitutions reveal that this is only the case in relation to MAC art. 27. In contrast hereto MOC art. 88.3 states the prohibition of forced labour "with the exception of work performed in the context of penal law".

BC sec. 6.3 lists a number of cases, which are to be excluded from the definition of forced labour and consequently do not constitute a violation of sec. 6.2. These cover areas relating to consequences of a sentence or court order, cases of persons who are either lawfully detained or members of a disciplined force, and instances of public emergencies, sub-sec. (a) through (d), all of which are identical with those of the 1962 Constitution of Uganda. In the light of this the BCC, along the same lines as the Kenya CC, added two sections to the Uganda-provision, the first of which deals with public emergencies in sub-sec. d and limiting the extent to that which is "reasonably justifiable in the circumstances of any situation". The second provision is sub-sec. e on "any labour required as part of reasonable and normal communal or other civic obligations", an example of which would be the obligation to serve as member of a jury when elected.

When dealing with these provisions of BC sec. 6, and in particular the last one mentioned directly above, one may keep in mind the provisions of AC Part I, Chapter II, on individual duties, and in particular art. 29, where subsections 1 through 8 establish the framework for a substantial amount of individual obligations. These provisions have to be upheld through national legislation in order to have any effect, since an international instrument such as AC only binds its member states and not their individual citizens.[37] As such BC art. 6 is one of the few areas in the Constitution where such obligations may be given effect in national law.

One example of this correlation between the two instruments is, for

---

37. See for instance AC art. 1, which only includes member states as subject of obligation in relation to AC., and the various provisions in art. 30 through 59 relating to the procedures of the African Commission, which can only deal with communications relating to transgressions by member states.

instance, BC sec. 6.1 (c) relating to members of a disciplined force and AC art. 29.5 on the duty to preserve, strengthen and protect national independence and the territorial integrity of one's state. Another example is BC sec. 6.1 (e) on communal and civic obligations in relation to AC art. 29, subsections 1., 2., and 6. on the duty to maintain one's parents in case of need, to place one's physical and intellectual abilities at the services of one's community, and to work and pay taxes in accordance with the law.

The corresponding provision in the MIC was identical to BC sec. 6.3, and the question is then whether we must see MAC sec. 27 as absolute, and the omission of such a catalogue of exceptions as was found in the first Constitution as deliberate and binding. If this is the case, there are several provisions in the statutes of Malawi which would then have to be repealed or revised, in particular sec. 27 of the MPC which authorizes that "All imprisonment shall be with or without hard labour in the discretion of the court".

We cannot rule out the possibility that it was indeed the intention of the drafters of the MAC that no forced labour should take place under any circumstances, not even those normally accepted by most societies in the world. The mere fact that statue rules concerning various forms of forced labour are still in force can really not be taken as an indication, since the process of legal reform in lieu of this very young instrument is still going on, also bearing in mind the example of provisions in the Penal Code concerning corporal punishment shown above. If the scope outlined in MAC sec. 27 is deliberate, this state awards a higher degree of protection of this right than most other national constitutions, not to mention the African Charter and other international instruments.

The right to a fair trial

AC art. 7

The right to a fair trial is stated in AC art. 7, which hereby contains some of those rights and freedoms of the individual which are the prerequisites for the Rule of Law in a given society. One should also keep in mind that the importance of this concept, and the rights encompassed by it, is especially significant in relation to human rights protection, since it refers to a situation where an individual is already at odds with society and the state and totally subjected to the powers hereof.

On this background it is not surprising that the right to a fair trial is therefore included in all the general global and regional human rights instruments as well as in most national law. The differences of scope and interpretation lie in the degree to which the instrument in question specifies and gives legal substance to the general concept through specific provisions.

Thus, while we can consider the principle of fair trial as being of universal character, we will see in the following that the details hereof and the degree to which its various elements are given priority or even included, might vary to some degree depending on the instrument in question.

Art. 7 sub-sec. 1 of the AC states the right for a person under a criminal trial[38] to have his or her cause heard in sub-sec. 1, to appeal to competent national organs in sub-sec. 1 (a), to be presumed innocent until proven guilty in sub-sec. 1 (b), to have defence of one's own choice in sub-sec. 1 (c), to be tried within reasonable time, and to have the court or tribunal be impartial in sub-sec. 1 (d). In addition hereto, art. 7 sub-sec. 2 deals with the problem related to *ex post facto* laws by banning the use of retroactive penal legislation. Finally, the article contains a provision on the personality of punishment.

Contrary to the other international instruments covering the principle of fair trial,[39] all of which follow a roughly similar outline with minor variations, AC does not cover a number of the rights specified herein. These include the lack of provisions securing the right to a public trial, to call witnesses, to have the accusations communicated in a language which the defendant can understand, or if not to have the aid of an interpreter, and the freedom of the defendant not to have to plead guilty or testify against himself.

Without these provisions, too much room is still left open for trials being unjust, random, and at the mercy of the individual court, and as such AC art. 7 does not give satisfactory guarantees for an individual facing charges. The effect of these omissions resulting in, for instance, the inability of the accused person to defend him- or herself, may even result in an actual miscarriage of justice arising from the infringement of the person's rights.[40]

But, realizing this, the ACom has taken an important initiative to remedy this situation by considering the area of fair trial under art. 7 of the Charter at its 11. Session in Tunis, March 1992. The result of their delibera-

---

38. D'sa, 1985, p. 107.
39. UD art. 10, ICCPR art. 14, ECHR art. 6, and AMCHR art. 8.
40. D'sa, 1987, p. 106.

tions was a Resolution on the Right to Recourse Procedure and Fair Trial,[41] which in section 1 enhances the significance of every individual's right to have his or her course heard. More important, sec. 2 contains a number of the specific provisions relating to fair trial, which have so far been missing in AC in relation to other instruments as shown above.

These include the right for persons arrested to be informed at the time of the arrest "in a language they understand" about the cause for their arrest, and to have the free assistance of an interpreter if they cannot speak the language of the court. Furthermore, the Resolution states the right for a person charged with an offence to "examine, or have examined, the witnesses against them and to obtain the attendance and examination of witnesses on their behalf under the same conditions as witnesses against them". Still, no reference is made of the right to a public trial, or the freedom not to have to plead guilty or testify against oneself.

The Resolution states a number of aspects of the right to fair trial, which are already to be found in AC art. 7, and this undeniably gives rise to some confusion. This is also the case when we ponder more closely on the nature and consequences of such a resolution, the key question being whether the Resolution can add a larger scope of rights than those already encompassed by AC's art. 7 and whether such additional provisions are equally binding on member states to the Charter.

Clearly, if the form used to broaden the scope of the Charter had been an additional protocol, the problem would have been solved, because the instrument would then be subject to additional ratification and binding on those member states only.

Here, on the other hand, we find an interpretative statement issued by the Commission subsequent to its self-pronounced mandate to consider substantive rights, "in accordance with its policy to deepen the understanding of substantive rights guaranteed by the Charter". It should be noted that this mandate is distinct from interpretations made under AC art. 45 sub-sec. 3, which requires a request to do so by a State party, an institution of the OAU or an African organization recognized by the OAU, and not *ex officio* as in this case. Generally, such institutional declarations have the status of

---

41. The African Commission, 5. Annual Report 1991-1992, Annex X.
   A similar resolution on the right to free association in AC art. 10 and 11 was also adopted at the same time.

soft law, and are not legally binding for the member states.[42] They do contribute guidelines on how to interpret a given provision, but the State parties are not necessarily bound by these interpretations, at least not unless they voluntarily choose to be so. One may also hold the view that in cases where the interpretative contents of the statement do not go beyond the generally accepted ramifications of the provision or concept in question, the State parties may not derogate from these merely with a reference to soft law being non-binding.

Looking at the present Resolution from the African Commission, we may therefore attempt to decide to which extent the different aspects hereof go beyond the concept of fair trial as generally recognized in international human rights law.

This is fairly easily done, since most parts of the resolution are merely repetitions of what is already included in AC art. 7. As for the remaining sections as outlined above, concerning language and witnesses, we can look to the corresponding provisions in other international instruments such as UD and ICCPR, both of which are encompassed by AC art. 60's reference to those instruments which the African Commission may draw from. Here, UD art. 10 is very brief and contains no reference to these particular aspects, but so does the very thoroughly formulated ICCPR art. 14, where sub-sec. 3.a, 3.e and 3.f contain the same provisions, even with an identical formulation which suggests that this particular provision did indeed serve as the source of inspiration for the ACom when drafting the Resolution.

Therefore one may be justified in claiming that the parties to AC in their implementation hereof shall have regard not only for art. 7, but also for the Resolution issued by the AComm, even though it may not possess as strong a character as the Charter itself.

BC sec. 5.2 and 10, MAC sec. 42, MOC sec. 98-102

In relation to Botswana, the rights encompassed by the concept of fair trial are contained in BC sec 10, under the heading "Provisions to secure protection of law", and a provision which is almost completely identical to sec. 8 of MIC.

---

42. Art. 38 (1) of the Statute of the International Court of Justice; Oscar Schachter 1991 in Steiner/Alston, 1996, p. 134.

Here we find the most extensive, but not the only,[43] example of the national law of the member states affording both a more specific and extensive protection of individual human rights and freedoms than AC. An obvious explanation is of course that the drafters of this provision, at least in relation to BC and MIC two decades before AC came into being, followed the layout established by the main international instruments in existence at the time of its genesis, namely the ECHR. With respect to MAC and MOC, also the ICCPR adopted by the UN in 1966 would have served as a source of inspiration; not that the provisions herein differ much from those found in the ECHR, but at least the controversy of legitimacy arising from the copying of one region's perception of human rights to another is avoided. In addition, both Malawi and Mozambique are parties to the ICCPR.

When looking at the national instruments, MOC is by far the most narrow, and it will have to be assessed whether it is comprehensive enough to reflect even the relatively limited provisions of AC. It is clear that the one offering by far the widest degree of protection is MAC, followed by BC.

Another noticeable difference is that BC limits the scope of sec. 10 and its protection to persons who have formally been charged with a criminal offence (sec. 10.1), and deals with the question of pre-trial detainees in sec. 5.2 on the right to personal liberty. Here MAC sec. 19 merely declares the principle of every person's entitlement to personal liberty, and affords the rights of sec. 42 to "every person who is detained, including every sentenced prisoner". This is a significant extension, since this article hereby protects groups of individuals both before and after the period outlined by BC, i.e. persons in both pre- and post-trial detention, all of which are probably more vulnerable to human rights violations, since they are not under the direct supervision of the judiciary.

Adding to the emphasis, MAC sec. 42 sub-sec. 1 continues to list a number of specific rights particularly directed towards the protection of persons in detention, which have no equivalent in either BC, MOC or AC. An example hereof is the basic right in sub-sec. 1 (a) to be detained "under conditions consistent with human dignity", which may be self-evidently included also in the other instruments, but with the crucial addition that this as a minimum shall include "the provision of reading and writing materials,

---

43. Other examples are the right to personal liberty and to secure protection by the law, in AC art. 6 and 3 and in BC sec. 5 and 10 respectively.

adequate nutrition and medical treatment at the expense of the State". Also sub-sec. 1 (d) addresses the practical needs of detainees acutely by stating that they shall "be given the means and opportunity to communicate with, and to be visited by, their spouse, partner, next-of-kin, relative, religion councillor and a medical practitioner of his or her choice". Finally sub-sec. 1 (e) and (f), following naturally from the right to personal liberty established in AC art 6 and from the essential non-judicial nature of pre-trial detention in particular, go beyond the explicit scope of BC by declaring the rights of persons in this situation to challenge the lawfulness of their detention either in person or through a legal practitioner before a court of law and to be released if such detention is unlawful.

In order to be able to maintain a clear overview of a number of provisions which are both extensive and complex, a distinction has been made in the following between, first, those provisions in BC, MAC and MOC which have no correspondence in AC, and, second, the different aspects of AC's provisions on fair trial compared to those of the national Constitutions.

i. Provisions of BC, MAC and MOC which are not included in AC

Examples of some of the provisions found in BC sec. 10 and MAC sec. 42 but lacking in MOC and in AC art. 7 are those mentioned above, such as BC sec. 10.1 (b), on the right *to be informed "as soon as reasonably practical" in a language understood and in detail of the nature of the offence* charged, and BC sec. 10.2 (f) on the right to free assistance by an *interpreter* if the language is not understood. It should be noted that while BC sec. 5.2 repeats the formulation and scope of sec. 10.1 (b) in sec 5.2 for pre-trial detainees, sec. 10.2 (f) has no correspondence in this provision.

The right to be informed of the charge is encompassed by MAC sec. 42, sub-sec. 1 (a), which replaces the term used by BC sec. 10.1.b with the slightly stronger "promptly", and the concept of understanding of language is protected by this provision also. The same concept repeated in relation to some of the other rights in MAC sec. 42.2 applying to persons who have been arrested or formally accused, such as sub-sec. (a) on the right to remain silent, as well as during the trial proceedings, where the general provision in sub-sec. (f)(ix) on the right to be tried in a language which one understands, applies. This is also the provision where we find the right to an interpreter, paid for by the State, and it might appropriately have been included under MAC sec. 42.1 (a) and sec. 42.2 (a) concerning persons in pre- or post-trial detention. Still, we may instead see it as a natural practical consequence of these provisions, since some form of translation is obviously necessary in the case where the person does not speak the language of, say, the members of the police force. Hereby sec. 42.2 (f) (ix) acquires a particular meaning by stressing that during the course of the trial qualified and professional interpretation should be available to the defendant, rather than simply translation by any person who might happen to speak the language in question to some degree, and as such the relevance of this provision in relation to the right to a fair trial is emphasized.

BC sec. 10.2 (d) states the right to be given facilities to examine the prosecution's *witnesses* in execution of one's right to defence, and to obtain the attendance and examine one's own witnesses on the same conditions as those applying to witnesses called by the prosecution. Here, MAC sec. 42.2 (f) (iv) merely declares the right for the accused "to adduce and challenge evidence", and links it to the right to remain silent and not testify during trial. A parallel to this provision is found in BC sec 10.7 stating an individual's right to refrain from giving evidence at his or her own trial.

Another provision which has been included in BC and not in AC, ensuring rights and freedoms of importance to a fair trial, is the right in BC sec. 10.2 to *be present at one's own trial*, unless one has either given consent to the opposite or in other ways behaved so as to "render the continuance of the proceedings in his presence impracticable" a formulation allowing for a fair measure of discretion with respect to possible derogation from the right itself. This right has not been included in MAC, which is remarkable in light of the fact that this was secured by MIC, and is contrasted by sec. 42.2 (f) (v) which specifically underlines that everybody has the right "to be represented by a legal practitioner". Under the present democratic spirit inspired by the Rule of Law in Malawi, one might argue that trials *in absentia* would be unthinkable, and that such a provision might be superfluous or at least could be covered by the general principles of fair trial in the rest of sec. 42. Still, times and governments change, and in an unfortunate situation the fact that MAC does not prevent this still stands uncontested.

MOC has also no provision covering this right, apart from a general clause in art. 98 stating that "no-one may be arrested and put on trial except within the terms of the law", hereby addressing the right to personal liberty rather than fair trial.

BC sec. 10.3. gives the right for the accused to receive a *copy of the judgment* within reasonable time, subject to payment of a reasonable fee, and similar to the example mentioned above neither MAC nor MOC contains any reference to such a right.

BC sec. 10.5. and 10.6 state the principle of *ne bis in idem*, that a person who has either been pardoned for an offence, or convicted or acquitted by a competent court, shall not be tried for that same offence again. The exception to this is appeal or review proceedings before a superior court relating to the conviction or acquittal. MAC sec. 42.2 (f) (vii) states the same right, but without the exception of appeal in BC sec. 10.5 and 10.6. Instead, MAC sec. 42.2 (f) (viii) gives the positive right to have "recourse by way of appeal or review" to a Court of higher instance than the court of first instance, a provision which has no explicit parallel in BC.

Finally there is the right in BC sec. 10.10 to have a trial of any form in *public*, unless all parties agree otherwise. This right is subject to the limitations in sec. 10.11, examples of which are interest of justice, public safety, order or morality, the welfare of persons under 18 years of age or privacy of persons concerned by the trial. This is a clawback clause[44] resembling those to be found at several places in the provisions of AC. It takes two different shapes, one in form of a general reference to national law, such as AC art. 6 on the right to liberty and personal security, art 9.2 on freedom of expression and art. 12.1 on freedom of movement, and with more specific considerations such as AC art. 11 on freedom of assembly and art. 12.2 on the freedom of movement across borders. On this point MAC is more simple, and just includes the term "public" in the introduction to the part concerning fair trial in sec. 42.2 (f) (i). At the same time it opens up for the setting aside of this principle in relation to children after sec. 42.2 (g), where sub-sec. (vi) gives children the right "to be dealt with in a form of legal proceedings that reflect the vulnerability of children while fully respecting human rights and legal safeguards". This aspect of fair trial will be dealt with separately in relation to AC art. 18 on the rights of children.

None of these provisions are included in AC art. 7, or in MOC.

ii. Provisions of AC art. 7 compared to BC, MAC and MOC

---

44. Defined by Higgins as a clause that "permits, in normal circumstance, breach of an obligation for a specified number of public reasons", differing from a derogation clause in that it applies to everyday circumstances while the latter allows suspension only in circumstances such as war or public emergency (D'sa, 1987, p. 109). An example of such a derogation clause in BC is sec. 16.

Shifting the focus and taking the opposite approach related to the question of transforming the African Charter to national law, we find that most of the provisions in AC art. 7 have corresponding provisions in BC and MAC, and to some extent also in MOC.

AC art. 7.1 deals with the basic right of *access to justice*, e.g. the right of an individual to have his or her case heard (sec. 1), and to *appeal to competent national organs* against the violations of his or her fundamental rights as established by conventions, laws, regulations and customs in force (sec. 1 (a)).

The corresponding provision in BC is sec. 18, which gives the High Court of Botswana original jurisdiction to hear and determine any question related to the situation where a person alleges that his or her individual civil and political rights according to sec. 3 to 16 have been, are being or are likely to be contravened.

In Botswana, the Ombudsman was established in 1995, and may investigate, *ex officio* or following a complaint from a member of the public, any actions taken by the public administration, except from those relating to matters in an extensive number of areas, according to sec. 3 and 4 of the Act.[45]

With respect to Malawi, sec. 15 declares the duty of the State of Malawi and all its organs to uphold and implement the provisions of the Bill of Rights, and sub-sec. 2 states the right for any person or groups hereof "with sufficient interest" herein shall be entitled to the assistance of the courts as well as other relevant institutions to ensure "the promotion, protection and redress of grievance" of these rights. In addition, MAC sec. 46 on enforcement of the rights and freedoms states, in sub-sec. 2, that any person claiming that one of his or her fundamental freedoms has been infringed, is entitled to apply to a competent court and to seek assistance from the Human Rights Commission in doing so, the latter in accordance with MAC sec. 129 through 131.[46]

Also the newly established Ombudsman may *ex officio* investigate such instances, and take appropriate action as established by MAC sec. 120 through 128, which regulate the appointment, functions and available

---

45. Quansah, 1995, p. 220 f.
46. The Constitution of Malawi, Chapter XI.

remedies of the Ombudsman.[47]

For Mozambique, MOC art. 100.1 merely states that "The State shall guarantee the access of citizens to the courts", and no constitutional provision has been made with regards to the establishment of an Ombudsman.

The term "competent national organs" must refer to institutional competence as a whole, encompassing the personal competence of the members as well as the issue of jurisdiction. The formulation does not, on the other hand, indicate that it applies only to the judiciary, but also to various administrative institutions.

Here it should be noted that MAC sec. 43 states the right for every person to "lawful and procedurally fair administrative action which is justifiable in relation to reasons given where his or her rights, freedoms, legitimate expectations or interests are affected or threatened", and to be given reasons in writing for such administrative action. This is a provision which has no correspondence in either of the other two Constitutions or in AC, and once more illustrates the thoroughness with which the drafters of MAC proceeded.

In relation to Botswana, Malawi and Mozambique as well as any other State parties to the African Charter, the term must also include *customary courts* to the extent which these have been recognized and accredited competence by the state's constitutional or legislative law, a point which is further enhanced by the inclusion of customary law in the formulation of AC art.7.1 (a).

The Customary Courts are recognized in Botswana through the Customary Courts Act. In Malawi, the traditional courts were in effect up to 1992, and were empowered to deal with death sentences and political crimes. Now, MAC sec. 110.3 still states that "Parliament may make provision for traditional local courts presided over by lay persons or chiefs" with the important restriction that their jurisdiction shall be limited exclusively to civil cases at areas of customary law and certain minor common law and statutory law. Accordingly, the situation now closely corresponds to that of Botswana.

This is different from Mozambique, where art. 167 sec. 1 outlining the various Courts does not include any reference to traditional or customary courts, and further stipulates in sec. 2 that "other than the courts specified

---

47. Constitution of Malawi, Chapter X.
    The Ministry of Justice have drafted two Ombudsman Bills, the latest in February 1996, which further outlines the principles governing the functions of this office.

in the Constitution, no other court may be established with jurisdiction over specific categories of crimes".

AC art. 26, second part, states that the states must allow "the establishment and improvement of appropriate national institutions entrusted with the promotion and protection of the rights and freedoms guaranteed by the present Charter".

The term "appeal" in AC art. 7.1 (a) can also be interpreted in the general sense as the right to appeal a decision of a lower court to higher judicial organs. In this sense it is not repeated in one general provision of BC, but left to be dealt with in the particular legislation regulating access to and procedures of the various instances such as the Customary Courts, the Magistrates and Children's Court, the High Court and the Court of Appeal.[48] As mentioned above, MAC has a specific provision, sec. 42.2 (f) (viii), which states the right for a person to appeal a decision from a lower Court to a higher instance.

The principle of *independence of the judiciary and the Rule of Law* as a prerequisite for the individual's right to a fair trial is specified in a number of the provisions of AC in conjunction. AC art. 7.1 (d) states the right for an individual to be tried within a reasonable time by an impartial court or tribunal, and AC art. 26, first part, according to which states have an obligation to ensure "the independence of the Courts".

This concept must be separated into two independent rights or concept, the first concerning the establishment and impartiality of the judiciary, the second into the right of *habeas corpus*. Only the first of these will be dealt with here, since the question relating to the right to be brought before a judge after arrest falls within the right to personal liberty and the protection hereof, and is subsequently analysed in that chapter

In relation to the first, BC in sec. 10.1 states that, with respect to any person charged with a criminal offence, the case shall be afforded a fair trial by an independent and impartial court, thus reflecting the provisions of AC. The important addition in BC is that this court must also be "established or recognized by law", a requirement of institutional legality corresponding to the demand in relation to criminal offences and punishments described above, where AC also lacks a general provision. With respect to civil cases, the same principle as in BC sec. 1 is expressed in BC sec. 10.9, which

---

48. See the Magistrate's Courts Act, S.I. 121, 1983; The High Court Act, S.I. 157, 1976; The Court of Appeal Act, S.I. 36, 1975; The Children's Act, S.I. 5, 1981, art. 31; and the Customary Courts Act, S.I. 12, 1977, art. 41.

states that any court or tribunal prescribed by law to deal with any civil rights and obligations shall be independent and impartial, and that persons appearing before such a court shall be given a fair hearing within a reasonable time.

MAC has an identical provision, sec. 42.2 (f) (i), according to which an accused person (hereby excluding civil cases) has the right to be tried before an independent and impartial court of law.

MOC has no reference to this.

The right to be *presumed innocent until proven guilty* is stated in AC art. 7.1 (b), and in BC sec. 10.2 (a), MAC sec. 42.2 (f) (iii) and MOC art. 98.2 respectively. With respect to Botswana, the provision also includes the freedom not to plead guilty, while MAC goes a step further and states the right to remain silent and not testify during trial. This principle is enhanced by sec. 42.2 (f) (iv), stating the right not to be a compellable witness against himself or herself as well as the general right to adduce and challenge evidence. Additionally, MAC sec. 42.2 characteristically extends this principle to the period of time preceding the actual trial, as shown in sec. 42.2 (c) according to which a person arrested or accused shall not be compelled to make a confession or admission which could be used in evidence against him or her. To emphasize this principle sec. 42.2 (a) additionally states that any person arrested or accused shall be informed "promptly" of the right to remain silent and of the consequences of making such statements.

In relation to Botswana the presumption of innocence may in effect be transgressed in cases such as those related to stock theft, where the legislation[49] places the burden of proof that the animal was not stolen upon the person charged with the offence.

But, as pointed out by *Neff*, as long as this demand does not go further than the obligation to establish certain facts on a balance of probabilities, it cannot be defined as a transgression of the right to be presumed innocent.[50] In any case of doubt, the principle of *lex superior* should prevail, to the effect that a principle relating to fundamental human rights and freedom established by the Constitution should take precedence over a provision in a legislative Act, since the latter derives its legitimacy from the former.

The right to *defence by legal counsel of one's own choice* is stated in

---

49. Botswana Stock Theft Proclamation of 1921; Neff, 1986, p. 27.
50. Neff, 1986, p. 27ff.

AC art. 7.1 (c) and has corresponding provisions in BC sec. 10.2 (c) and (d), in MAC sec. 42.2 (f) (v), and in MOC art. 100. BC here contains the important supplement to AC art. 7.1 that the defendant has the right to be given adequate time and facilities for the preparation of his or her defence, a provision which has no counterpart in MAC sec. 42. Instead, sec. 42.2 (c) grants detainees the right to "consult confidentially with a legal practitioner".

MOC art. 100 states the duty for the State to guarantee to persons charged with an offence the right to defence, and the right to legal assistance and aid.

BC stresses that counsel must be given by a legal representative, and looking at the recommendations from the Sub-committee under the Constitutional Conference for Botswana,[51] which took the Uganda Constitution at its basis, an addition was made to the provision of this instrument. It expressly stated that the term "legal representative" meant "a person entitled to practice in Uganda as an advocate",[52] and the Botswana recommendations added that reference should be made to an advocate *or attorney*. Instead of including the definitory provision in the article itself, as had been done in the Uganda case, the legislators of Botswana decided that it should be included in the general provisions on interpretation and savings regarding the entire Bill of Rights, BC sec. 19.1. This provision states that the term "legal representative" means "a person entitled to practise in Botswana as an advocate or attorney". The same conclusion was reached in relation to MIC, where sec. 8.13 has a similar clause of interpretation, but was not repeated in the new Constitution of Malawi in 1994, presumably because it no longer gives rise to serious concern.

Regarding the question of *free legal aid* services, this is a question which is being confronted in a number of African countries, including Botswana, Malawi and Mozambique. The text of AC itself is silent on this point and merely states the right to defence, without clarification as to whether this is an absolute right regardless of the client's ability to pay or the general availability of such services. However, this is one of the points specifically addressed in the African Commission's Resolution on Fair Trial mentioned above, in which the Commission in sec. E.5 "recommends to States party to the African Charter on Human and Peoples' Rights - to provide needy with legal aid". Notwithstanding the discussion on the extent

---

51. Report of the Botswana Constitutional Conference Committee.
52. The Constitution of Uganda art. 13.12, S.I.1962/405.

to which this Resolution is legally binding for the member states, this is clearly just a recommendation, something one should aim for or at least consider seriously, and AC therefore does not necessarily impart on its member states an obligation to establish legal aid institutions and programmes.

In accordance with the text of AC art. 7.1 (c), but out of harmony with the Resolution, BC clearly states in sec. 10.2 (d) that such legal representation must be paid for by the defendant himself, and in case he or she is not able to do so, the person must handle his or her own defence. In other words, the State must not deny an individual the right to legal representation, but on the other hand has also no obligation to ensure it.[53]

On this point the drafters of MAC took a different position, which removed them from the rather restrictive attitude found in both BC and AC, by confirming the principle of right to legal aid provided by the State. Here, however, they distinguished rather uncharacteristically between the situation of detention and that of the actual trial, in a way which reveals itself only through a closer analysis of the exact formulation of the two provisions: in relation to detainees MAC sec. 42.1 (c) states that, apart from the right to consult confidentially with their counsel and be informed promptly of this right, they have the right, where the interests of justice so requires, "to be provided with the services of a legal practitioner by the State".

In contrast hereto stands the provision covering the period of the actual trial, sec. 42.2 (f) (v), according to which one has the right to be represented by legal counsel of one's own choice or, where it is required in the interests of justice, "to be provided with legal representation at the expense of the state". In the first case there is a duty for the state of Malawi to provide practical access to legal practitioners, but the client may have to pay their fees themselves. In the second case, however, it is clear that the state has a duty to provide the same service if necessary, but free of charge.

The background for such a differentiation is of course that the potential consequences of not having legal assistance at the trial are far more serious than at the time of detention, provided that the other safeguards are upheld, and it is a positive step which the state of Malawi has taken by guaranteeing this right constitutionally.

MOC art. 100 does not specify whether the legal aid provided by the State shall also be free of charge, similar to the situation described in the discussion above. Given the formulation of the provision, stressing "legal

---

53. For a further discussion on this topic, see Nsereko, 1988, p. 211.

assistance and aid" as a separate right besides "defence", one might legitimately argue that the provision does grant the right to assistance free of charge, or at least only subject to a nominal fee. In fact, this is a prerequisite for the full enjoyment of this right by the majority of the population, since they will be without economic means to pay for such services. Another point of concern, which gives rise to serious practical problems, is the lack of trained lawyers to do the actual defence work, but here a demand on the State to provide legal aid funds as well as adequate education and training facilities for jurists could rest on MOC art. 100.2, according to which "The State shall make provision to ensure that justice is not denied for lack of resources".

Taking a more general view, we here have an example of the need to look at the different provisions of the African Charter within the context of realities in which it operates and on the basis of which it has been conceived. It is tempting to judge this obvious lacuna in the African Charter from a European background and criticize it as being an example of the failure of the Charter to impose substantial obligations on its member states.

However, looking at realities, we find that the actual administrative and financial situation of most African countries, and in particular countries like Malawi and Mozambique, renders the providing of free legal services to everybody charged with a criminal offence a desirable but presently hopeless goal to be strived towards.[54] In fact, Botswana might be one of the few states with the financial ability to provide these services, but still faces problems related to the lack of trained personnel to perform these services in the municipal areas as well as outside the cities, as well as the general infrastructure of the administrative and judicial system.

Ironically enough, we can see from the text above that Botswana goes further than the other instrument in emphasizing that legal services must be paid for by the person himself.

On this background the formulation of AC art. 7.1.c should be understood, if not completely excused, given that this is only one among many areas of the Charter where vision and reality are often far apart.

Similar to the example used above regarding stock theft and the possible transgression of a constitutional principle, BC sec. 10.12 (b)[55] authorizes the legislative setting aside of the right to legal counsel before subordinate courts, when the offence and the person in question operated

---

54. D'sa, 1985, p. 108.
55. This provision was introduced as an amendment to the Constitution, Act 30 1969.

under the jurisdiction of African customary law. An example hereof is found in the Customary Courts Act of 1961[56] sec. 31, which precludes the use of any type of legal counsel by the parties before the Customary Court. The background for this is, of course, the fact that the judges have no actual legal background but rely on knowledge of legal custom and tradition, with which the general legal practitioner is not familiar. In short, the official and the customary legal systems in Botswana operate as two separate entities, and in fact the use of legal council by one or even both parties may easily lead to a situation of miscarriage of justice. An even stronger and potentially far more problematic provision is BC sec. 10.12 (e), according to which the general rule that only offences criminalized by the statutes are punishable may be abridged in cases where the court in question is authorized to convict a person of a criminal offence under any African customary law as long as he or she is under the jurisdiction hereof.

A similar provision in relation to legal counsel could also be found in sec. 8.12 (b) of MIC, but the second example of possible offences under customary law was not introduced here.

In a European context the right to legal counsel established by ECHR 6.3 (c) is considered an absolute right which cannot be suspended. This, therefore, is an example of universal recognition of a concept such as the right to a fair trial on the one hand, but where the actual definition of the various elements hereof varies enough to reject the notion of universality in favour of regional or national diversity.

The principle of *nulla crimen sine lege, nulla poena sine lege*, in this case freedom from retroactive condemnation or punishment, is stated in AC art. 7.2. as well as in BC sec. 10.4. and 10.8, MAC sec. 42.2 (f) (vi) and MOC sec. 99.

These provisions all establish that no person may be condemned for an act or omission that did not constitute a legally punishable offence at the time it was committed. Also, BC sec. 10.8 demands that a person may only be convicted where both the criminal offence and the penalty therefore have been defined and prescribed by written law, a provision corresponding to the principle in AC art. 6 that "no one may deprived of his freedom except for reasons and conditions previously laid down by law".

In this case, MOC art. 99.2 does allow for a potential significant weakening of this otherwise universal principle, by stating that criminal laws may be applied retroactively, albeit only in favour of the accused. The

---

56.   S.I. 12, 1977.

problem here lies with how this decision is made, by whom and based on which criteria, since even good intentions can turn out bad in the end, and something which was intended to be in the favour of the accused may very well end up being the opposite. Therefore this section must be applied by the judiciary only in cases where there can be no doubt whatsoever about the appropriateness of applying retroactive criminal legislation. An attempt has been made at correction, however, through the insertion in the Concluding and Transitional Provisions art. 201, which states that in Mozambique "law may only be retroactive when this is to the benefit of citizens and other legal persons". This provision does emphasize that there must be a clear and evident benefit for the individual in being subjected to retroactive law, but the problems in defining the accuracy hereof may still give rise to concerns. Also, the placement of each of these provisions indicates that this was an area where the drafters of MOC had mixed feelings, and surely the structural clarity of the Constitution would have benefited from, at least, the joining of these two provision into one.

Regarding the question of punishment there is, however, a difference in formulation, which suggests that the interpretation may be different in AC on the one hand and the national Constitutions on the other hand. While AC art. 7.2 merely demands that a provision for a given offence is in force at the time of conviction, BC sec. 10.4 and MAC sec. 42.2 (f) (vi) both go one step further by not only demanding that the sentence is in accordance with legal provisions, but that it must also not be more severe than the maximum penalty prescribed for such an offence. Finally, MAC sec. 42.2 (f) again takes the lead with respect to protecting the rights of the individual, by stating that a person has a right to receive the sentence in whatever form "within a reasonable time after conviction".

Finally AC art. 7.2 contains a feature which is unique to the African Charter, probably because this principle is usually perceived as cemented beyond questioning in European legal and, not the least, moral thinking and tradition. Whether this is in fact always true may very well be questioned, but not in this particular study. It is the demand that "punishment is personal and can be imposed only on the offender", a provision which has its roots in the not infrequent occurrence where an African individual is punished for an offence, but where the punishment also directly or indirectly is imposed upon those who support him within his family or local community.[57]

---

57. Bello, 1985, p. 157.

Another possible interpretation, which transcends the gap between socio-economic and civil rights, is that the provision could be used to disempower imprisonment or substantial fining of a family's breadwinner. Hereby his or her family would suffer without cause, and such an interpretation might also entail that especially a woman with infants or small children should only be punished in a way that the child or children relying on her would not suffer from it.

A distinction can be made in relation to the personality of punishment with respect to general and specific deterrence. An example of the first type is the Botswana case *Jaba vs. State*[58] mentioned by Neff, where the defendant was sentenced harder for concealing a birth, the reason given by the lower court that this type of crime was becoming too prevalent. Since the defendant had no way of foreseeing or taking into account this argument at the time the crime was committed, the superior court justly reversed the sentence downwards, and hereby rejected the clear prioritizing of the interests of the individual under those of the community.

With respect to the second distinction, specific deterrence, Neff quotes the Botswana case of *State vs. G.Ikanyeng*,[59] where the defendant was charged with unlawful possession of diamonds, and where the sentence was made exemplary on the background of the seriousness of the crime in relation to the country's economy, a consideration which has been given legal formulation in sec. 9 of the Constitution of Botswana.

The difference between the two situations is that the defendant in the second case, but not in the first, has a way of foreseeing and taking into account the potential harshness of the sentence on that basis. At the same time I would tend to see the distinction as more of a technical than as a legally valid nature, since both cases represent the subsumption of the interests of the individual to those of the society as a whole. On this background I would rather label both cases under the heading of general deterrence, and reserve the distinction of special deterrence for those considerations related to the individual himself. Criteria to be applied here would be the number of previous sentences, the likelihood of recurrence of the crime, whether the person is a potential danger to himself or to society, and other special circumstances surrounding the person both in relation to the commitment of the crime and with respect to the appropriate sentencing, keeping in mind the point made above with respect to dependent relatives

---

58. Jaba vs. State; Criminal Appeal No. 47, 1982.
59. State vs. G.Ikanyeng, 1974 1 E.L.R. 98.

etc.

The right to personal liberty

AC art. 6

The concept of personal liberty has been considered one of the most important aspects of human rights in an African context, to the extent that it was included already in the law of Lagos from 1961, which ultimately led to the creation of the African Charter and other initiatives.[60] But, as pointed out by Bello, balancing liberty of individual with the national independence and security of young states has not been without problems, making this an area where theory and practice of African leaders have not always been mutually consistent.[61]

AC art. 6 states the right for every individual to "liberty and the security of his person", and underlines as a general rule that deprivation of freedom as well as arbitrary arrest or detention must not take place. The exception which, however, has major implications, is that conditions "previously laid down by law" can constitute the basis for such infringements and limitations on the rights and freedoms stipulated in the article.

Here we have another example of a "clawback" clause similar to those mentioned in connection with the right to fair trial, which seriously serves to limit the protective measures of the provision on personal liberty. The effect hereof is that national legislation created before the coming into force of this Charter, i.e. before 1981, can constitute the basis for deprivation of freedom in the form of arrest or detention, even though such acts go against the other provisions of the Charter.

As in relation to AC art. 4 on the right to life, the question arises whether art. 6 implies not only a passive but also a more active obligation for the state to guarantee the security of its citizens. In effect this could mean an obligation to refrain from acts of war against other states, which could lead to danger for its citizens, or even to actively protect them against violations committed by another state or its representative. At least total negligence by the state should not be tolerated, especially when it lies within the power of the state to take effective action to protect its citizens in such cases.

---

60. "Law of Lagos", January 1961.
61. Bello, 1985, p. 154-155.

As in relation to AC art. 4 on the right to life, the question arises whether art. 6 implies not only a passive but also a more active obligation for the state to guarantee the security of its citizens. In effect this could mean an obligation to refrain from acts of war against other states, which could lead to danger for its citizens, or even to actively protect them against violations committed by another state or its representative. At least total negligence by the state should not be tolerated, especially when it lies within the power of the state to take effective action to protect its citizens in such cases.

In relation to AC art. 6, the question could be raised whether constitutional or legislative provisions introduced by a member state between the time of its signature or ratification of AC and the time of its entering into force would be encompassed by the term "previously laid down by the law" in AC art. 6.

The Charter takes legal effect from the date of its coming into force, which in accordance with AC art. 63.3 happens three months after the reception by the OAU Secretary General of a simple majority of the instruments of ratification or adherence from member states. At the same time AC art. 65 further stipulates that the Charter takes effect three months after the date of adherence to or ratification of the Charter by the individual states.

Now, according to the principles of international law in relation to the two-stage procedure of signature and ratification, a state which has signed a convention is obliged to observe the provisions hereof in good faith already from this point.[62] This means, for instance, that the state must not enact new legislation, the contents of which would expressly contradict the provisions of the instrument in question. Such a situation could leave member states in a legislative vacuum in a situation where the international instruments in question take very long to come into force, or in a situation where the instrument does not come into force at all, as was indeed feared would be the case with the African Charter.[63]

My own bid in the matter would be, that in cases where a state ratifies the African Charter, it must also expect it to come into force at some point in time, and must therefore act upon it consequently. In this case, the term "previously" in AC would therefore not be fixed as one objective date, but would depend on the date of ratification by the member state during the

---

62. Vienna Convention on the Law of Treaties, art. 18
63. See ch. 5.

period from 27 June 1981, when the Charter was adopted by the OAU General Assembly, to 21 October 1986, when the Charter entered into force.

In relation to Botswana the date of ratification plus three months, in accordance with art. 65, gives the date 17 October 1986, leaving the period in question to be only four days. With respect to Malawi, the records (if correct) show a fairly unusual picture, since the date of ratification is 17 November 1989, while the date of signature as well as the deposit of instrument of ratification is 3 months later on 23 February 1990. Mozambique deposited its instrument of ratification on 7 March 1990, but without a preceding signature, similar to the approach chosen by Kenya, Madagascar, Namibia and several others. The problem described in relation to Botswana and other states therefore does not arise in relation to either of these two states.

For some states such as Congo, Liberia, Senegal and Togo, all of which ratified the Charter during 1982, the problem could be of a more significant nature, since such a situation in reality would have persisted for several years. I do not, however, know of any concrete examples where this has given rise to legislative difficulties such as those described above.

As an effect of the formulation of AC art. 6, no specific enforceable demand is made of national legislation already in existence, and as such the protection against violations of these rights and freedoms must be found in the other remaining articles of the African Charter, or in various other instruments or ratified by the parties.

BC sec. 5 and MAC sec. 18 and 19.6

With respect to Botswana, the right to personal liberty is established in BC sec. 5, which simply states that nobody may be deprived of his or her personal liberty. However, neither this nor any of the other provisions in BC include the other part of AC art. 6, the right to personal security.

We cannot excuse this lacuna exclusively with the fact that BC was modelled upon a European rather than an African conception of human rights, since art. 5 of the ECHR mentions every persons right to freedom as well as to personal security. So does art. 3 of the UD as well as art. 9 of the ICCPR, too. Seeing this formulation in relation to other provisions of AC, particularly art. 5 on the individual's right to "respect of the dignity inherent in a human being" as well as the enhancing of the inviolability of every human being in AC art. 4, the general picture indicates that these concerns have a higher priority in the context of the African Charter than in the national Constitution of Botswana.

Whether or not this also gives rise to concerns that the person residing in Botswana is more susceptible to violations of his or her personal integrity is another story. The substantial content of this particular principle of personal security is in any case of such an ambiguous nature that it needs to be filled out through other forms of regulation and in actual practice. Given that the political situation in Botswana does not indicate that this type of human rights violation is prevalent, in addition to the other points just made, we may be less alarmed of the lack of provisional protection of personal dignity here than in many other African states. We do find, however, that problems exist in Botswana, mainly with respect to interrogations by the police and the judiciary's use of involuntary confessions.[64]

One might therefore claim that the lack of a legal provision on the right to personal safety does represent an example of an area of human rights regulation, where Botswana cannot be said to fully comply, on a legal level, with the provisions of the African Charter.

The MIC sec. 3 was, not surprisingly, identical to BC sec. 5, and as such contained a similar extensive list of situations where the personal liberty could legitimately be set aside. The only exemption to this is BC's last sub-sec. (k), which refers to "the purpose of ensuring the safety of aircraft in flight". There is no obvious explanation why such an otherwise reasonable provision should not apply to Malawi, except for the assumption that Malawi's status with respect to technical and other forms of infrastructure at that time did not make it very appropriate !

In the MOC sec. 18 simply states that "Every person has the right to personal liberty", a provision which in its brevity comes closer to the form used by AC than any of the other sections. It is supplemented by sec. 19 declaring in sub-sec. 1 the inviolability of all persons' dignity, which again is followed by sub-sec. 6, according to which every person shall have the right to freedom and security of person. The article clearly complies with AC art. 6, but as in many other cases MAC goes further, in this case by adding a number of specific situations which are to be encompassed by this provision. The first hereof is sub-sec. 6 (a) stating freedom from detention without trial, a provision which does not go beyond what is already established by the main section of the provision as well as the comprehensive sec. 42 on fair trial and the rights of detainees.

Of far more significance is sub-sec. 6 (b), according to which no

---

64. Nsereko, 1995; Solo, 1995.

person may be detained "solely by reason of his or her political or other opinions". This is a provision which, in addition to those mentioned above, is closely related to AC art. 9, 10 and 13 on freedom of opinion, association and political participation, reflected in MAC sec. 32 through 37 and sec. 40.

Finally, MAC sec. 19.6 (c) declares that no one may be imprisoned for inability to fulfil contractual obligations. This is a provision which has no corelate in AC, BC or MOC, but is identical to ICCPR sec. 11 and hereby gives due recognition to Malawi's ratification hereof.

MOC has no explicit provision on personal liberty or security, and particularly the first of these may to some extent be grounded in the marxist tradition which influenced the Frelimo drafters of the 1990 Constitution. The protection hereof may therefore be found in the other provisions such as the freedom from arbitrary arrest and detention in art. 98, 101 and 102 and the right to physical integrity in art. 70, dealt with in the sections on right to life and freedom from torture, and in conjunction these provisions do in fact cover AC art. 6 fairly well.

The right to liberty and personal freedom is not everywhere viewed as an absolute right, insofar as AC contains the clawback clause of reference to national law shown above. A similar provision exists in BC sec. 5, which states that deprivation of personal liberty may "only" happen according to the law in quite a substantial number of cases listed below. MAC sec. 19 makes the right "subject to the Constitution", which is a far more restrictive allowance than BC and AC, first and foremost because it does not allow for the setting aside of this principle through statutes alone, but subjects them to constitutional control and hereby limits the exceptions to particular and appropriate cases. We here see an example of one of the most criticized aspects of AC, because virtually no actual qualifications on national law are imposed on member states in this case. This means that even the extensive exceptions listed in BC would be compatible with AC art. 6 regardless of their actual contents.

Looking at BC sec. 5.1, sub-sec. (a) through (k) may be divided into two main categories, where the first, (a) through (f), concern legal and judicial matters, where a court order is required for the imposing of restrictions on personal liberties. These provisions cover cases such as convictions of criminal offences, contempt of court, ensuring the fulfilment of legal obligations, excecution of court orders, suspicion of the person having committed or being about to commit a criminal offence, and the education and welfare of a minor. In the last area, where the personal liberty of a minor may be restricted by the Court, the Botswana Constitutional Conference (BCC) decided to expand on the Uganda provision, which has otherwise been applied directly and which did not contain any of the following restrictions. Instead the BCC included the qualification adopted from MIC,[65] that such deprivation of liberty must be restricted to cases where either the order of a Court or the consent of the parent or guardian of the person concerned has been obtained.

The other group of cases where personal liberty may be restricted, and for most parts even without a court order, covers areas of public interest and welfare, which will typically be handled by the police or other authorities on a day-to-day basis.

The provisions in BC sec. 5.1 (g) through (k) deal with cases of the spreading of disease, insanity, addiction to alcohol or drugs, vagrancy, and security in aircrafts during flight. In fact, these examples indicate that this latter category of exemptions to the absolute right to personal liberty is closely linked to the concept of personal security and safety according to AC art. 6, since they refer to situations which might entail potential dangers to the individual himself or to others.

Finally, BC sec. 5.1 deals with two areas of particular relevance to freedom of movement, the restriction of unlawful entry into Botswana and of movement within Botswana, both of which will be dealt with below in relation to the section on freedom of movement and residence.

All of the examples listed above refer to very particular situations, the occurrence of which are seen on a limited scale. The following section deals with the very basic and important aspect of personal liberty, namely freedom from arbitrary and illegal arrest or detention and the right to *habeas corpus*, expressed by the last sentence of AC art. 6, which states that besides the requirements already listed, in particular, "no one may be arbitrarily arrested or detained". Here we find a strong overlap between the provisions regulating the right to a fair trial, and we also see that the national Constitutions structure these rights differently. An example hereof is that while MAC sec. 42 contains an extensive catalogue on the rights of detainees in addition to those under trial, BC sec. 5 sub-sec. 2 through 4 on personal liberty deal particularly with the period of time preceding an actual trial in addition to the rights relating to fair trial under sec. 10.

BC sec. 5.3. complies with AC art. 6 by stating that any person who is arrested or detained in accordance with sec. 5.1. (d) and (e), e.g. in execution of a court order or when reasonably suspected of having com-

---

65. The Nyasaland (Constitution) Order in Council, 1963, S.I. 1963, no. 883.

mitted or being about to commit a criminal offence, shall be brought before a court "as soon as is reasonably practicable". Here the BCC decided to abandon the formulation of the corresponding sec. 8.3 in the Constitution of Uganda, which used the term "without undue delay" in favour of that adopted by the later Kenya-provision. They hereby indicated that they agreed with the recommendations of the KCC of 1962 that "the phrase "without undue delay" - does not provide sufficient protection for an arrested person".[66] On this point, BC sec. 10.1 and 10.9 merely state that the trial must take place "within a reasonable time", and the corresponding provision in MAC is sec. 42.2 (f) (i), which applies the same formulation (see below).

BC sec. 5.3 proceeds to state that in cases where a person cannot be found to have been tried "within reasonable time" from the time of arrest or detention, the person in question shall be released without prejudice to any further proceedings against him, either unconditionally or subject to reasonable conditions ensuring his appearance at later trial-related proceedings. A corresponding provision in the Criminal Procedure and Evidence Act sec. 36 and 43[67] states that a person who has been arrested shall be brought before a Court as soon as possible, where he shall either be released unconditionally or on bail, or any further detention be authorized. Here it is interesting to note that the BCC apparently did not, contrary to the case of the first formulation as listed above, go along with the improved provision of the Kenya-recommendation. This provision declared that in case the person had not been brought before a court within 24 hours, the person in whose custody he or she had remained, had to lift the burden of proof that compliance with the provision listed above existed. In fact, the BCC sub-Committee recommended that the provision in the Constitution applied the same phrasing as the Kenya-provision, with the exception that the 24-hour time limit was extended to 48 hours. Still, not even this softening was approved by the final decision-makers of the BCC, and so the formulation of the latter provision remained the same as the Uganda-formulation, "within reasonable time".[68]

---

66. Report of the Kenya Constitutional Conference, Committee on a Bill of Rights, London 1962.
67. Criminal Procedure and Evidence Act No. 52, 1938, Laws of Botswana, Cap. 0802.
68. For an illustration on how this can be applied in practice, see Modukwe-case, where the defendant was held in custody for more than 48 hours; Review Case 117/1980, 14 Comparative and International Law of Southern Africa 1981, 347; Maope, 1986, p. 52-54.

But the same emphasis in MAC on the particular vulnerability of people in pre-trial detention described above, which is unique in relation to AC as well as BC, also asserts itself here. MAC sec. 42.2 (b) declares the right for every person "arrested for or accused of the alleged commisison of an offence" to be brought before an independent and impartial court of law "as soon as it is reasonably possible, but no later that 48 hours after the arrest". Here, the person shall either be charged or informed of the reasons for his or her further detention, and if neither of these happen the person shall be released. If the person awaiting trial is kept in custody, MAC sec. 42.2 (d) states that "save in exceptional circumstances" he or she has the right to be segregated from convicted persons and to appropriate treatment in accordance with his or her status as an unconvicted person. Also at this point MAC sec. 42.2 (f) (ii) should be noted, since it stresses the right for an accused to be informed "with sufficient particularity" of the charges made against him or her.

To emphasize this principle, MAC Sec. 42.2 (e) states that the person has a right "to be released from detention, with or without bail, unless the interest of justice require otherwise". This provision is highly important, because it establishes the norm that unnecessary and unvalidated pre-trial detention must be avoided, and that a person awaiting trial remains free unless it can be reasonably justified by the authorities that he or she should be held in custody. Also, it goes far beyond the rather vague scope of BC and of MIC, as well as that of AC. Still, by not defining the acceptable criteria for pre-trial detention more closely, for instance by limiting it to certain types of serious crime, the door is opened for an abridgement of the principle, and it will therefore be the responsibility of the judiciary to apply a strict and consistent practice on this point.

This is an area where MOC is surprisingly strong, laying down the fundamental principle in art. 101 that "Preventive imprisonment shall only be permitted in cases provided for by law, which shall limit the duration of such imprisonment". Sub-sec. 2 furthermore states that the person in question shall be brought before judiciary within the period fixed by the law, which alone shall have the power to decide the validity and continuation hereof based on a writ of habeas corpus which the detainee shall have the right to submit according to art. 102. By operating with a time limit on the period allowed for pre-trial detention, MOC goes further in individual protection than both AC and BC, since the formulation hereof may be perceived as stronger than the term "reasonable time" herein, and is surpassed only by the strict maximum rule of 48 hours in MAC.

In addition BC sec. 5.4 states the right to compensation for any inlawful arrest or detention, referring to sub-sec. 3, a provision which has no correspondence in neither MAC or MOC, nor in AC. We must assume that it was deliberately omitted from AC by its drafters, not because they did not recognize its importance, but because it might give rise to too much controversy among potential State parties with a sensitivity towards any financial obligations combined with the not infrequent occurence of such cases all over the African continent. With respect to MAC and MOC, there would also have to have been some deliberate intention among their drafters to leave it out, probably because such a right would give rise to an overwhelming number of cases, particularly if applied retroactively.

With respect to Botswana, the derogation clauses in BC sec. 16 and 17 which cover situations of war or public emergencies should be noted, since pre-trial detention in such situations may be applied within far wider limits than what is normally permitted. There are still some safeguards in effect, stated in BC sec. 16.2 according to which the person in question must be informed of the grounds for his detention, a public notice hereof shall be published, his case must be reviewed at intervals, and he must have access to legal counsel. The significant difference is that while pre-trial detention under normal circumstances should not last for more than 48 hours without authorization by the Court, the time-limits for detention under BC sec. 16.2 are 5 days for the giving of reasons for the detention, 14 days for the public notice hereof, and one to six months in relation to the review procedure.

The right to property

AC art. 14

AC art. 14 states the right to property, but not as an absolute right since it may (only) be encroached upon in the interest of public need or in the general interest of the community, and in accordance with the provisions of appropriate laws.

As such this provision is yet another example of the use of a "clawback" clause similar to those seen in relation to most of the other provisions of AC, as dealt with above. It is, however, of a less extensive character than several of the other clauses, since the conditions are two-fold and encompass the requirement of legality as well as the need for justification of a situation of public need, both of which must be fulfilled.

In any case the State party would have the onus of proving the existence of such circumstances as to necessitate the interests of the community taking precedence over the individuals right to property. The most obvious example of such a legal annulment of the right to property is community expropriation, for instance with the purpose of expanding the infrastructure in a given area, and in most of these cases the conditions for public interest are satisfied. Still, given the open nature of the terms "public need" or "interests of the community", the practice by the states would need to be accordingly strict and limited to cases where it's beyond reasonable doubt that such infringements of the right to property are critical to the wellbeing of society.

Looking to the other international human rights instruments, we see that the concept of right to property has developed differently in the various instruments. The UD art. 17 states the right for everyone to *own* property, alone or collectively, and explicitly declares that no one shall be arbitrarily deprived hereof. This authoritative approach to a sensitive subject was not followed in the ICCPR, which contains no article on the right to property at all, and neither was such a provision included in the ECHR. On the other hand both the AMCHR art. 21 and art. 1 of the OP1 to the ECHR state the right for everyone to the *use and enjoyment* of one's property, subject to restrictions and modifications on conditions similar to those stated in the AC.

Analysing AC art. 14, it is interesting to note that the formulation hereof just refers to "property", without any indication of whether it should be understood as the right to own property, or just to have access to it. This is significant in relation to the question of ownership and access to land, if we interpret AC art. 14 as conferring on the individual the right to acquire individual ownership of, for instance, areas suitable for farming, grazing etc. This could cause extensive controversy in several African states, where there is a popular demand for land reforms and privatization, and where the African Charter art. 14 could be an important tool.

A less dynamic interpretation of art. 14 would be to see the provision as merely stating the right for an individual to have access to land and other forms of property sufficient to his needs, regardless of ownership as long as this does not affect the actual use. Furthermore, in cases where a person already has ownership of property, this can only be set aside when the criteria listed in art. 14 are fulfilled.

In any case, art. 14 match relates to AC's provisions on collective rights, particularly art. 21 on all peoples' right to wealth and natural resources, which must also be exercised "in the exclusive interest" of the people, and must under no circumstances be deprived them (sec. 1). Furthermore, every person's sufficient access to land can be seen as a prerequisite for self-sufficiency in food production, which again is closely related to the collective right to development as stated in AC art. 22.

The AC does not include in its provisions the right to compensation for property which has been confiscated or expropriated. Still, this also goes for any of the other instruments, except for the AMCHR, which in art. 21 gives the right to "payment of just compensation" for deprivation of property. It should be noted that in relation to the collective right to property as mentioned above, AC art. 21.2 states that "In case of spoliation the dispossessed people shall have the right to the lawful recovery of its property as well as to an adequate compensation".[69]

One of the reasons for this article must be found in Africa's cultural background, where association with the same land as one's ancestors traditionally is considered of great spiritual and cultural value. The concept of individual right to property would seem to break with the tradition in most African countries which have tended to, and in fact still do, operate with tribal ownership of land. Furthermore, recent history in several socialist African states has shown a pattern of similar communalization of land and property. On this background, and seen in relation to the other international instruments outlined above, AC art. 14 on the right to property has a remarkable status.[70]

BC sec. 8, MAC sec. 28 and MOC sec. 86 and 46

With respect to Botswana, BC sec. 8. on the right to property is more elaborate and detailed in its formulation than the corresponding provisions of AC, but the scope of rights does not differ significantly in the various instruments.

BC sec. 8.1 states the right to property and freedom from repossession or any other infringement hereof, a formulation which is similar to AC art. 14.

Again, we see that MAC is both more precise and explicit, stating in sec. 28 the right for every person to acquire, including but not limited to the right to own or possess, property alone or in association with others.

The communal aspect in the last section has no explicit counterpart in

---

69. D'sa, 86, p. 113.
70. Neff, 1983, p. 48.

either AC or BC. One must, however, take into account the general extent of the collective perspective in AC, as well as the formulation of BC sec. 8 which deliberately seems to avoid the formulation of an individual right and merely protects from arbitrary interference with interests in property.

On this background, it seems that the interpretation of the various instruments' provision on the right to property has roughly the same subjects, namely the individual as well as other legal persons. MAC sec. 28 becomes particularly relevant in relation to social and religious organizations and institutions, corresponding to MOC art. 78, and to some extent implied in BC sec. 11 as well.

The right to property is not an absolute right in either AC, BC or MAC. However, there are differences in the formulation of the criteria for which it may be set aside, where MAC is the briefest and merely states in sec. 28.2 that deprivation of property must not be "arbitrary" without further specification.

Following the line of AC sec. 14 more closely, BC sec. 8.1 states that it must not be set aside, except when it is necessary or expedient on the grounds specified in the three sub-sections of sec. 8.1 (a).

Sub-sec. (i) mentions interests related to "defence, public safety, public order, public morality, public health, town and country planning". This general provision is supplemented by sub-sec. (ii), which includes actions taken "in order to secure the development or utilization of that, or other, property for a purpose beneficial to the community", which also has a general application. Finally, sub-sec. (iii) is of a more specific nature, insofar as it authorizes the acquisition of property "in order to secure the development or utilization of the mineral resources of Botswana." While (i), upon closer analysis, corresponds reasonably well to AC's concept of "general interest of the society", (ii) and (iii) may or may not always fall under the category "public need" in AC art. 14, depending on the actual circumstances.

It is necessary here to weigh carefully the pressing and obvious needs of the society against the welfare and interest of the individual. This should be done by ensuring that the relative balance between the two is maintained, and keeping in mind that the individual's loss of property must be in relative proportion to the needs of society when infringing upon it.

In none of the instruments does this dichotomy reveal itself more clearly than in the Constitution of Mozambique, where MOC art. 86 states the fundamental human rights principle that ownership of property shall be guaranteed by the State. In addition, sec. 2 emphasizes that expropriation hereof may only take place "on grounds of public need, usefulness or interest as defined by law", as well as the requirement that just compensation for this shall be awarded. We hereby see that the individual's right to property, seems to be guaranteed on the same level as in the other instruments.

Still, one must look also to the other articles in MOC, and this gives a somewhat clearer picture of art. 86, making it very clear that this article should be understood as excluding land and other natural resources.

MOC art. 46 undisputedly states in sec. 1 that "All property in land shall vest in the State", and in sec. 2 that land may not be sold, mortgaged, encumbered or otherwise alienated.

Furthermore, MOC art. 35 specifies that "Natural resources...shall be property vested in the state" (sec. 1) and that the public domain of the state in addition to a number of different types of resources shall include "other goods and assets classified as such by law". There is therefore no doubt that the interpretation of the right to property in MOC art. 86 is meant so as to exclude all forms of ownership in immovable objects related to land or natural resources.

The opportunity for a wider interpretation of the exemption clause in AC becomes even more clear in BC sec. 8 (5), which specifies a number of areas of legislation exempt from inconsistency with the right to property. Examples hereof are satisfaction of tax or dues, as a penalty for breach of law under civil or criminal law and in the execution of court orders or judgements, or as an incident of lease, mortgage, pledge or contract. Here the argument, that such infringements on the individual's right to property can not be fully contained under the formulations of public need or general communal interest in AC, may be even more appropriate, even though the provisions do not conflict directly.

In order to give the individual even greater security against such violations, BC in fact takes an important step further than AC by stating in art. 8.1 (b) sub-sec. (i) that in the case of deprivation of property, the law must make provisions guaranteeing to the individual prompt payment of "adequate compensation". This is noteworthy, since the only precedence in other international human rights instruments is the AMCHR, as stated above. As mentioned above, this is also stated in MOC art. 86.2, but MAC has no such requirement, which sets this provision somewhat behind the general standard in this area.

Finally, BC sec. 8.1 (b) sub-sec. (ii) states the right to have all matters regarding limitations on the right to property tried by the High Court of

Botswana, in order to establish both the legality and the amount of compensation for such deprivation. This serves as another example of how various articles in AC and BC relate to one another, since this provision in effect serves as a direct correlate to AC art. 7.1.a. on the right to appeal to national organs against violations of one's human rights and freedoms. It is also in direct accordance with BC sec. 18, which establishes the first-instance jurisdiction of the High Court in matters relating to alleged violations of individual rights and freedoms in Botswana.

On the question of access to the High Court, the Bechuanaland Constitutional Conference decided to adopt the Kenya-recommendation on such a provision, rather than the Uganda version which served, otherwise, as the general model for most other provisions in BC. This provision in the Constitution of Uganda only secures "a right to access to a court or other authority", and Botswana thus decided to go along with this improvement in the legal guarantees already established by Kenya. This is all the more interesting to note, since on the first of the provisions regarding compensation, BCC chose the contrary approach and stayed on the Uganda-formulation on the right to "adequate compensation". They hereby abandoned the formulation "full compensation", which was used already in the first Kenya Constitution and adopted again by the KCC.

Corresponding to this, MAC sec. 15 gives a general right to seek the assistance of the courts as well as other organs of government such as the Ombudsman and the Human Rights Commission, for ensuring the promotion, protection and redress of grievance of the rights contained in MAC Chapter IV. MOC art. 81 and 82 state the right for individuals to contest acts that violate their rights, and have the right of recourse to the courts in these matters, and gives the various other state institutions similar jurisdiction according to their individual mandate in the Constitution.

The right to participate in democracy

AC art. 13

This provision can be divided into two parts, the first of which is the right for every citizen to freely participate in the government of one's country in art. 13.1.

The second part of art. 13 is the right for every citizen to equal access to the public service of his country, art. 13.2, and the right for everybody to enjoy public property and services, art. 13.3. Since the latter part is dealt

Individual Civil and Political Rights and Freedoms 145

with in sec. 12 of this chapter on freedom from discrimination, only the first part on the right to participation in democracy will be looked at here.

AC art. 13.1 corresponds to similar provisions in the UD (art. 21), ICCPR (art. 25), and AMCHR (art. 23). The important difference between these three provisions and AC art. 13.1 is that all of them establish more definite criteria for the fulfilment of this right.

Here, the UD art. 21 as well as the ICCPR art. 25 and the AMCHR art. 23 state the right to vote in periodic and genuine elections by universal and equal suffrage and held by secret ballot or other similar procedures, and the AMCHR even adds the right to be elected in addition hereto. Also art. 3 of the First Protocol to the ECHR ensures these principles, expressed as the duty for the State parties to the Convention "to hold free elections at reasonable intervals by secret ballot under conditions which will ensure the free expression of the people in the choice of the legislature".

Seen in the light of these other provisions, AC art. 13.1 stands out as meagre and without substantial legal content, particular in light of the clawback reference that this right shall be exercised " in accordance with the provisions of national law". The requirement that it shall be exercised "freely" hardly remedies the situation.[71]

An important question to be raised is whether AC art. 13.1 is compatible with the existence of a one-party state, of which there are several among the member states of the African Charter. If the formulation of AC art. 13.1 had been similar to that of the other instruments, it is clear that this would not have been the case. However, in its present formulation we cannot establish clearly that the one-party state under some conditions, when for instance this form of government is made lawful under domestic law, would be in violation of AC art. 13.1.[72] This, in fact, proves that the guarantees of AC art.1 are virtually empty simply because of the clawback clause referring to national law.

This is one of the provisions of AC where the historical and political realities are clearly reflected, illustrating the distinction between the traditional tribal community and the nation state on the other; on the one hand the right to participate in the benefits and decision-making powers of the community is a traditional concept in African customary law.[73] On the other hand the post-colonial era has seen a large number of dictatorships on

---

71. Kotey, 1982-85, p. 137f.
72. D'sa, 1987, p. 112.
73. Ibid.

the continent, and in light hereof a more substantial provision would have been very hard to accept for a majority of the potential member states of the Charter. The alleged reasons for that would be that in many of the young African states political stability is still very fragile, due to ethnic, social and economic factors in conjunction, and that the price of democracy might therefore be too high to risk.[74]

In light hereof, AC art. 13.3 therefore seems to appear as expressing a fairly remarkable commitment towards democratic government.[75] This would indicate that liberal democracy on the level of the national state is perceived as being somewhat alien to Africa, and allegedly unsuitable to tackle its needs.[76] In relation to a number of countries, including those three used in this study, we find that democracy is either a permanent tradition, as in Botswana, or is progressing rapidly, albeit not without understandable difficulties following long periods of foreign domination, dictatorships or civil wars, as is the case with both Malawi and Mozambique. The new Constitutions found in both of these states not only provide for an extensive catalogue of human rights, which are the object of this study, but also provide for a democratic system of government, and multi-party elections have taken or will be taking place shortly after the entering into force of these new Constitutions.[77]

Another aspect of AC art. 13.1 reveals itself once we move beyond the legal right and into the question of actual opportunity to participate in the process of democracy. Here the full enjoyment of AC art. 13.1 becomes inseparable from the fulfilment of a number of the other rights and freedoms of the individual, particular freedom of information and expression, and freedom of association, assembly and discrimination in general. Also some of the economic and social rights are significant, since education, including the ability read and write, as well as basic health and social security will often determine the degree to which a person is able to participate effectively in the political life around her.

These will be dealt separately below under their individual headings, since they present themselves as distinct concepts in both the international and national instruments as shown below.

---

74. See ch. 2 for a discussion of these points.
75. Ibid.
76. Naldi, 1989, p. 121.
77. Mozambique held their first elections in 1994, and Malawi is scheduled to have local elections in the very near future.

MAC sec. 40, MOC art. 73 and 30-34

Interestingly enough, this is one of the few provisions on civil and political rights in the AC which has no direct counterpart in BC.

One of the explanations, however, is found when keeping in mind the history of the Constitution and the background on which it was drafted, as outlined in chapter 7 of this study. One of the primary sources of inspiration was the ECHR, not only for BC but for the similar Bills of Rights in the other former British colonies who gained their independence in the beginning of the 1960s and earlier.[78] As seen above, a provision corresponding to the right to participate in democracy did not form part of the original ECHR, but was added to it by the First Additional Protocol already in 1952.[79] Still, the new African states did not take it into consideration when elaborating their own constitutions.

This, therefore, explains why this particular provision was not included in the Constitution of Botswana, and more importantly it can therefore also be made clear that the omission did not signify any indication that Botswana did not wish to present itself as a democratic society.

Looking beyond the Bill of Rights, we do in fact see a clear reflection of a democratic society in the entire framework of the BC. Chapter IV, on the Executive (with provisions concerning the President and the Vice-President, the Cabinet and other Executive Functions in sec. 30 through 56) and Chapter V (on the Parliament, the National Assembly, and the House of Chiefs in sec. 57 through 94) in detail regulate the basic procedures relating to a democratic society. Since Botswana is a multi-party state with universal suffrage,[80] where free and fair elections are held in accordance with the provisions outlined above, we cannot criticize Botswana for non-compliance with AC art. 13.1 in the legal sense.

---

78. These include such states as Nigeria, Kenya, Uganda, and the former Nyasaland (Malawi).
79. First Additional Protocol to the European Convention on Human Rights, on Enforcement of Certain Rights and Freedoms not included in Section I of the Convention. Signed in Paris 20 March 1952.
80. Sec. 67 states that the requirements for being qualified to vote is (a) citizenship of Botswana, (b) age 21 or above, and (c) residence in Botswana for a continuous period of at least 12 months immediately preceding the date of application for registration as a voter, or permanent domicile following one's birth in Botswana.

Furthermore, these provisions are supplemented by the Electoral Act,[81] which in detail prescribes the procedures to be followed with respect to the registration of voters, elections, polling and election petitions. Here sec. 30 specifically states that a person must be registered as a voter in a given constituency and that he shall produce his voter's registration card in order to be allowed to do so.

In relation to Malawi, MIC was based on the same model as BC, and almost identical to it, which has been demonstrated continuously throughout this study. But in the years following independence the political development of Malawi followed a completely different route, and already a few years after independence Malawi was a one-party state with Dr. Banda as the autocratic Head of State. Even worse, he banned any political opposition, and instituted a regime which both from a legal and a practical perspective was responsible for numerous and comprehensive human rights violations, which lasted until the beginning of the 1990s.[82]

Whether or not an inclusion of the right to democracy or other similar safeguards in the first Constitution of the state would have made much difference in preventing the unfortunate human rights abuses in Malawi is perhaps doubtful - ill will always finds a way, and if the intention is strong enough, even legal safeguards are easily set aside. On the other hand it would have served as a message to the people of Malawi as well as to those aspiring to rule the country that the guiding principles should be those of democracy and the Rule of Law, and might have made the task easier for those working towards such goals.

In MAC, sec. 40 contains a number of provisions which show different aspects of the right to participate in the political process. It should be noted that the rights given herein are under the restriction clause "subject to this Constitution" (sec. 1) and "save as otherwise provided in this Constitution" (sec. 3), which works two ways at the same time. First, it means that limitations on this right can only be made through other constitutional provisions and not through the ordinary statutes, in contrast to MAC sec. 37 on freedom of information which subjects that right to "any Act of Parliament". Second, it does allow for limitations on the political rights, and as such this provision is less absolute than most of the other sections in MAC's Bill of Rights. Such a reference would, however, be appropriate since other sections of the Constitution restrict these right to nationals of Malawi only.

---

81. Electoral Act, Laws of Botswana, Act 38, 1968 (latest amendment Act 16, 1984).
82. Kaunda, 1994, p. 18ff.

The first two parts of MAC sec. 40 are closely related to the positive freedom of association in sec. 32, and sub-sec. (a) states that every person shall have the right "to form, to join, to participate in the activities of, and to recruit members for, a political party", while sub-sec. (b) states the right to "campaign for a political party or cause".

Sub-sec. 2 of sec. 40.1 is very important in relation to these two provisions, since it obliges the State to provide the funds, when necessary,[83] to ensure that any political party which has secured more than one-tenth of the national vote of a Parliamentary election will continue to be able to represent its constituency during the life of that Parliament. This is a provision which goes far beyond the duties explicitly or even tacitly implied in AC, but it is highly relevant since it seeks to remedy the inequality of financial affluence, which is one of the obstacles opposition parties in particular will encounter.

Sub-sec. 1 (c) proceeds to state the right for every person to participate "in peaceful political activity intended to influence the composition and policies of the Government". This is a provision which seems to address particularly the last section of AC art. 13.1 on every citizen's right to participate in the government of his or her country "through freely chosen representatives". Finally MAC sec. 41.1 (d) declares a person's general right "freely to make political choices", a provision which should be read in conjunction with MAC sec. 34 stating the freedom to hold opinions without interference.

The very last part of MAC sec. 40 is sub-sec. 3, according to which every person shall have the right to vote, in secret, and to stand for public office. Particularly this latter aspect is subject to the restriction clause mentioned earlier in this section, but also MAC sec. 24 on the equal rights of women should be kept in mind in conjunction with this right. However, it should give rise to some concern that MAC sec. 24 does give a general right for women to protection against discrimination, but in sub-sec. (a) and (b) only covers civil and family law, and has no reference to public life. The omission seems even more obvious when one looks at sec. 24.2, which invalidates all laws which are discriminatory and requires that positive legislation is introduced to eliminate "customs and practices that discriminate against women", including discrimination "in work, business and public

---

83. This provision, as the only one in this Chapter of the Constitution so far, was amended in 1995. Here, the phrase "when necessary" was deleted in order to make the provision unconditional. Constitution (Amendment) Act no. 6, 17 May 1995.

affairs", sub-sec. 2 (b). We may therefore assume that the intentions of the otherwise liberal drafters of the Constitution of Malawi did not exactly want to directly encourage women to take part in the political life, even though none of the provisions mentioned above are in any conflict with AC art. 13 or 18.

With respect to Mozambique, the right to participation in democracy is remarkably well reflected in the Constitution. Art. 73 sets the format by declaring that "All citizens shall have the right and the duty to participate in the process of extending and consolidating democracy at all levels of State and society", with sec. 3 adding that this right is "personal". For once, this is an area of human rights where the restrictive term "citizen" would have been used correctly, and we should read it as such, differently from other provision where the term, but not its implications, would be extended to include other nations' citizens residing in Mozambique as well. The provision's inclusion of the duty to participate in democracy, underlined by sec. 3 stating that the right to vote is a "civic duty" is interesting, in the way it reflects the general reference to individual duties of AC art. 27 through 29. It is, however, hard to imagine how non-compliance with MOC art. 73 could be established or legitimately sanctioned in actual practice.

While MAC sec. 40.3 made no reference to the minimum age in relation to the right to vote and to be elected, MAC art. 73 gives these rights to every citizen 18 years of age and over, "with the exception of those legally deprived of this right". Different from the similar exception clause in MAC sec. 40, there is no requirement that such limitations are constitutional, examples of which would be the restriction that only citizens of Mozambique may be elected for President (art. 118) and restrictions on naturalized citizen's exercise of public functions (art. 29).

The principles governing the electoral process are found in art. 30, according to which the people of Mozambique shall exercise their political power through elections of their representatives "by universal, direct, secret and periodic suffrage". Other mediums are public referenda, which should be held on major national issues, as well as citizens' "permanent democratic participation" in the affairs of the nation. A similar system should guide the election of public officers, according to art. 107.

MOC has an extensive number of other provisions concerning the establishment of political parties, an example of which is the basic freedom to form or to participate in political parties established in MOC art. 77 sec. 1. In addition, sec. 2 states that "party membership shall be voluntary", deriving from the freedom of citizens to associate on the basis of the same political ideals. We here see the negative freedom from party membership as well as the positive right to freedom of political opinion expressed similarly to MAC art. 40.1, and also here the connection to the general freedom of association in MOC art. 76 is strong.

MOC art. 108 states that legally constituted political parties may compete in elections and shall hold public office in accordance with the results of these. Again, this provision seems to state the obvious, looking from a tradition of parliamentary democracy, but addresses some of the obstacles which may unfortunately be very real in this context.

Finally, sec. 31 through 33 establish the general legal framework governing the life of political parties, among other things stating in art. 31 that they are "expressions of political pluralism" and must operate and be structured on a democratic basis. Art. 32.2 sub-sec. (a), (b) and (d) lay down a number of conditions to which political parties are subject, so that apart from adhering to the Constitution in general they shall also be national in scope, defend national interest, and strengthen the patriotic spirit of citizens and the consolidation of the Mozambican nation. In addition sub-sec. 2 (c) and 3 obliges the political parties to contribute to the formation of public opinion and towards peace and stability in the country through political and civic education of citizens. Particularly the first groups of these provisions, with its strong emphasis on patriotism, reflects the catalogue of individual duties in AC art. 27 through 29, particularly art. 29.4 on the duty to preserve and strengthen national solidarity. As such, it should give rise to some concern, since these extensive requirements may in fact be applied so rigidly that only a dominant party in power may be seen as fulfilling the criteria, legitimizing the banning of all other political coalitions on this ground. This is a situation which must be avoided at all costs, and the authorities as well as the judiciary will therefore have to interpret MOC art. 32 in a way that the normal democratic pluralism of the country does not suffer unnecessarily.

Still, no question remains that with respect to safeguarding the citizens' right to political participation, MOC surpasses MAC extensively, not to mention BC and AC, and this marks a shift from the tendency seen in many other sections of this study.

Freedom of conscience

AC art. 8

AC art. 8 states the individual's freedom of conscience and the freedom of religion, which may be seen as one duality covering, respectively, the inner conviction and its expression in outward practice. The provision must be interpreted both in the positive and in the negative sense, i.e. both the right to belong to a given religion or faith and the freedom from being forced to adopt certain religious beliefs or to follow the state religion. Contrary to the corresponding provisions in UD, ICCPR and ECHR, the African Charter only states the right to the "profession" of one's religion. As such, AC art. 8 does not explicitly state the right for a person to change one's religion or to manifest his or her religion in worship, observance, practice and teaching, whether individually or in community with others.

To some extent the formulation of AC art. 8 can be seen as responding to a situation where tribalism and religious fanaticism has resulted in violations of the freedom of religion in several African states. Examples hereof can be found among different faiths, such as the muslim extremism found in Nigeria at some point, resulting in massacres of several thousand individuals resisting conversion, and the persecution of christian and particularly catholic priests and bishops in other African states.[84]

In contrast, the catholic church was always revered in Malawi, at least until the Pastoral Letter was issued in 1992. See chapter 4.

BC sec. 11, MAC sec. 33, and MOC art. 9 and 78

Looking at the national Constitutions, we see that those of Botswana and Malawi both reflect the same scope of protection of this right as does AC, while the situation is somewhat different with respect to Mozambique.

BC sec. 11 states the principle of freedom of conscience and of religion, defining the former as including freedom of thought and the freedom to change one's religion or belief. Included also in the concept is the freedom to manifest and propagate one's religion or belief in worship, teaching, practice and observance, both in public and in private, and either alone or in community with others.

The only provision of this article which differs from that of the Uganda

---

84. Bello, 1985, p. 158.

Constitution is BC sec. 11.2, stating the right of every religious community to establish and maintain places of education and, within this context, to provide religious instruction. Here, the BCCC adopted the recommendations of the KCC, and in further accordance herewith specified in sec. 11.2 that such activities would be funded by the religious communities themselves.[85] In contrast, the drafters of MIC applied the original formulation and included no parallel to the first part of BC sec. 11.2, but otherwise the formulation of the article remained the same.

An important addition, serving as a balance to the previous sub-section, is BC sec. 11.3 declaring that no person attending a place of education shall be required to participate in any religious ceremony or education in a faith or belief other than his own.

Finally, BC sec. 11.4 elaborates further on the principle of freedom of conscience by stating that no person shall be compelled to take any oath contrary to, or in a manner contrary to, his or her religion or belief.

MAC sec. 33 is short and general on this point, stating simply that "Every person has the right to freedom of conscience, religion, belief or thought, and to academic freedom". The latter is an addition which we do not find in any of the other instruments, reflecting the growing recognition of as well as the need to afford particular protection of this right.[86] We must assume that the brevity of this provision is deliberate in the sense that it should encompass all the different aspects of an individual freedom of religion. It is not clear, however, whether we can also interpret this provision as comprehending the collective aspect, such as the right of religious denominations to establish themselves, collect property etc., and thus MAC may seem relatively weaker than the other instruments on this point.[87]

MOC art. 78 states that all citizens "shall have the freedom to practise or not to practise a religion", corresponding to the provisions on freedom of conscience in the other instruments. It continues, in sec. 2, to give religious denominations the right to pursue their religious aims freely, and

---

85. The recommendation from KCC read that "- the Committee considers that the Constitution should not give a communal school the right to receive State aid or State recognition, though such aid and recognition should not be denied on discriminatory grounds".

86. Academic freedom was violated systematically during Banda's rule, and large numbers of academics and writers were detained without trial during those decades. Human Rights Watch, 1991, p. 35ff.

87. In 1969, Jehovah's Witnesses was declared to be "dangerous to the good government of Malawi" and banned under the Unlawful Societies Order no. 127/1969.

to own and acquire assets for realising those aims. This latter part is interesting, first because the subject is not the individual believer but rather the congregation as a legal person, and second because it follows closely the framework established by BC sec. 11.2 and leaves MAC art. 33 a good deal behind in the protection of the rights of institutionalized legal entities. Still, MOC art. 78 must necessarily be viewed in conjunction with the other provisions in the Constitution, since a number of these may cast a different light on the context in which MOC art. 78 shall be enjoyed. One should look to the basic principles in Part I where art. 9.1 declares that "The Republic of Mozambique shall be a lay state", proceeding in sub-sec. 2 to state that the activity of religious institutions shall be subject to law.

To some extent these categorical and potentially very restrictive provisions are balanced by sub-sec. 3 which emphasizes that "The State shall respect the activities of religious denominations" in order to promote a climate of social understanding and tolerance as well as strenghten national unity. These are worthy objectives, but nevertheless it is clear that the intention of the drafters of the Constitution of Mozambique was to discourage religious practices and institutions in favour of secular social justice and democracy.

In order to fulfil the promise of MOC art. 78 as well as living up to the provisions on freedom of religion in both AC and ICCPR, a forthcoming and tolerant attitude towards religious communities would therefore have to be displayed by the Government of Mozambique.[88]

AC art. 8.2 establishes that "no one, subject to law and order, be submitted to measures restricting the exercise of these freedoms", an interesting formulation which at the same time modifies and maintains the clawback clause in a way that leaves open the possibility of extensive limitations on freedom of conscience and religion by the individual state.

In correspondence with AC art. 8.2, BC sec. 11.5 (a) and (b) list a number of such applicable opportunities for derogation. While sub-section (a) covers reasons like defence and public safety, order, morality, sub-section (b) refers to the rights and freedoms of others, and in particular the

---

88. A concrete example of which I have, albeit only anecdotal, knowledge is the surprisingly positive reception which the Indian yogi and world renowned spiritual teacher Guru Maharaji has received in Mozambique, particularly among the political elite. However, the Parliament's denial of his request for a very large piece of land on which to build "Heaven on Earth" would hardly have been deemed a violation of freedom of conscience, even if such a right had been included in the Constitution !

right to observe and practice one's religion without unsolicited intervention from others. This provision contains the possibility of conflict with the extensive right in BC art. 12.1 to propagate one's religion, and looking from a more general perspective we see that the legal ramifications for the enjoyment of freedom of religion are quite similar to those found in relation to Mozambique, with an equal basis for concern.

A score of different rights and freedoms, which in many ways are similar, are freedom of conscience and religion, freedom of expression and freedom of association and assembly. What these provisions mainly have in common is their relative short and precise formulation in the various instruments.[89] The most problematic aspect in relation to these freedoms is a formulation found in all of the relevant articles in BC, but not in MAC, stating that the rights and freedoms contained in the articles cannot take place "except with the consent of the person".

Even though AC is full of various clawback clauses mainly referring to national law,[90] such a clause of consent on behalf of the person vested with rights and freedoms cannot be found in the Charter.

BC contains no qualifications as to the nature of or requirements for such consent, and does not specify whether it must be written, tacit or given in any other form. Furthermore, a person subject to various forms of duress ranging from informal group pressure to more direct forms of coercion may involuntarily consent to the setting aside of some of his most personal rights and freedoms associated with religion.

The question which must therefore be raised, is whether the clauses of consent in BC sec. 11, 12 and 13 conflict with the provisions of AC obliging states to ensure that the rights and freedoms guaranteed in the Charter can be enjoyed by everybody. It would seem appropriate that at least some restrictions on the ability to renounce protection of one's rights and freedoms, following the requirement of legal age of majority, mental and emotional capability as well as some demands of the form and circumstances of the consent, would have to be included in BC in order to comply

---

89. A clear illustration of their limited controversy is the fact that few or none of them apparently gave rise to serious discussions during their drafting by the Botswana Constitutional Conference.

90. This is a feature which has been one of the most criticized aspects of the Charter because it hollows out the protection of rights and freedoms and hereby entails a strong likelihood that the protective measures will be weakened in individual states' practice. See previous sections of this chapter on the right to fair trial and personal liberty for a further discussion of this point.

with AC art. 1.

Freedom of information and expression

AC art. 9

AC art. 9 declares the right for every individual to freely receive information in sec. 1, and sec. 2 states the corresponding right to impart information formulated as the right to express and disseminate one's opinions.

Regarding sec. 9.1, it should be noted that AC only mentions the right of an individual to receive information, and hereby follows the example of the ECHR art. 10.

This is a more narrow formulation than in UD art. 19 and ICCPR art. 19.2. Both of these provisions state not only the right to receive and impart information, but also to seek (and consequently also to question) information given by the government or other sources from inside as well as outside the country.

On this last point it should further be noted, that while the two global instruments and the ECHR stress that freedom of information is unlimited by geographical borders, a similar provision is not included in AC art. 9.1. If we apply a narrow and literal interpretation of AC art. 9.1 to this effect, the difference would be that while an individual has the right to enjoy information made generally available to the public, he or she may not necessarily have the more extensive right of the global instruments in this area.

In other words it is up to an African (or European) government to select out the information it considers to be "suitable" for general dissemination, without any criteria of objectivity attached, and with the power to restrict access to all other sources of information, alternative as well as official.

The difference between the two provisions in AC art. 9 is, that while the freedom to receive information in AC art. 9.1 is absolute, art. 9.2 subjects the individuals' right to express and disseminate his or her opinions to limitations "within the law". As such we have another example of the "clawback" clause already found in connection with several other provisions of AC. The real weakness of the Charter is that this formulation does not in any way establish any criteria for the qualifications and limitations in national legislation, which leaves it entirely up to the individual state party to decide how real the freedom of expression may actually be.

This in effect would mean that AC on this point would be considered useless from a protection perspective, since such rights would be entirely subjected to the ramifications of national law. A constructive suggestion is therefore to interpret AC art. 9.2 as referring to the manner in which the freedom of expression is exercised.[91] Hereby the reference would not be to the national law in general, but to provisions in, for instance, the Penal Code or other provisions regarding public meetings, court proceedings etc.

The concept of freedom of expression is an area where the individual's exercise hereof is likely to have a comparatively more significant effect on other members of society or the community as a whole. It is therefore appropriate that it be limited by a legal prohibition against slander and defamation, incitement to violence and racism and other concerns related to *ordre public*.

On the other hand the formulation of the article also leaves room for excessive restrictions such as censorship and infringements on the freedom of the press. This is a practice which unfortunately is common in many nations in Africa, particularly in several dictatorships and one-party states.[92] This right is important also in relation to the promotion and accomplishment of democracy and governance, especially when reflected as the opportunities for the media to be a constructive agent in this process by providing links between various groups in society.[93]

BC sec. 12, MAC sec. 21 and 33 through 37, and MOC sec. 74 and 104

Following the concept of freedom of conscience as looked at above, the same pattern of similarities and differences between the provisions of AC and the national Constitutions can be found regarding freedom of expression.

Here, AC art. 9 states the right to "express and disseminate" one's views, and within this concept BC sec. 12 specifically defines it as the freedom to hold opinions, freedom to communicate ideas and information, and the right to privacy of one's correspondence, all of which must be

---

91. Neff, 1986, p. 38.
92. Okere, 1984, p. 146f.
93. Summary of workshop, Panel on Issues in Democratization, ed. Kpundeh, 1992.

enjoyed without interference.[94] The provision on freedom in relation to correspondence is also closely linked with the freedom to receive ideas and information without interference, which is a fulfilment of the principle of AC art. 9.1 on the right to receive information.

In this area MAC covers the same scope of rights, but divides them out into several different provisions. Beginning at the most personal level, MAC sec. 33 declares that, apart from freedom of conscience and religion, every person has the right to freedom of belief and thought, and MAC sec. 34 states the right to hold opinions without interference.

Moving to the more public aspect, MAC sec. 35 declares that every person has the right to freedom of expression, followed by the right in sec. 33 to academic freedom and the right to impart and receive opinions in sec. 34. Finally, MAC sec. 37 states the right of "access to all information held by the State or any of its organs at any level of Government", and in relation to this provision there is no ambiguity. In contrast to the provisions of AC and the other instruments, this must imply the right to information in its broadest scope.[95]

However, this right is restricted by two limitations, the first of which is that it is generally "subject to any Act of Parliament", examples of which could be laws relating to state security issues, pornography, privacy of individuals etc. The second limitation is specific and personal, and potentially gives rise to far more concern, since this freedom can only be exercised "insofar as such information is required" for the persons' exercise of his or her rights. If this provision was to be interpreted in the strictest sense, it would in many cases be difficult for persons with a legitimate interest to prove that it was also necessary for their exercise of any particular right, and the interpretation in practice should therefore follow a relatively liberal course on this point.[96]

---

94. Even though this right is not directly stated in AC, one may argue that it is of such an intrinsic character that, as long as the other provisions are fulfilled, it will naturally be included in the general concept of freedom of information and expression.

95. It was submitted to the Constitution Commitee in Feb. 1995 that this provision should be deleted, because it would entail the danger of allowing for "all sorts of frivolous litigation in the courts", e.g. cases against branches of government by private organisations, labour unions etc. contesting Parliament's right to limit access to such information in accordance with the first half of the section; Kalaile, 1995.

96. During the years of Banda's rule, particularly in 1973 and 1974, a number of additions to the Penal Code, concerning "Prohibited Publications", were enacted to the effect that more than 2000 books, pieces of music, videos and films were banned in Malawi.

The principle of privacy of correspondence is found in MAC sec. 21.c, according to which every person shall have the right to personal privacy, expressed among other examples as freedom from "interference with private communications, including mail and all forms of telecommunications". We must assume that the terms "correspondence" and "telecommunications" in BC sec. 12 and MAC sec. 21 (c) should be understood so as to cover the same, extensive, scope of situations, and that the difference of formulations merely is yet another example of how the drafters of MAC took into account the technological progress of the last three decades since the drafting of BC.

MOC has no direct provision on freedom of opinion, which could be seen as a structural weakness, but which has less significance in light of MOC art. 74, where sec. 1 declares the right for every citizen to freedom of expression as well as the right to information. The provision does not give any details as to whether the latter should include not only the right to receive but also to seek information, as discussed in relation to AC above. Sec. 2 continues to define freedom of expression as "the ability to make known one's opinions by all legal means", and declares that neither of the rights mentioned in sec. 1 shall be subject to censorship.

It is interesting to note that while neither AC nor BC pay any particular interest to the freedom of the press, this is an area which has high priority in the other two Constitutions. MAC sec. 36 states that "The press shall have the right to report and publish freely, within Malawi and abroad, and to be accorded the fullest possible facilities for access to public information. Again, MOC art. 74.3 is the most extensive, defining freedom of the press as including in particular (but not exclusively) "the freedom of journalistic expression and creativity, access to sources of information, protection of professional independence and confidentiality, and the right to establish newspapers and other publications".

AC gives the right to express and disseminate one's opinions "within the law", and the Constitution of Botswana has the most extensive catalogue of opportunities for setting aside freedom of information and expression. As such, BC sec. 12.2 (a) through (c) contain a number of conditions for

---

Those include a large number of pornographic and violent production of a general dubious quality, but also books by Mario Puzo, James Michener and Doris Lessing, as well as the movies "Flashdance" and "Bonnie and Clyde". Finally, on the more curious end, are books on astrology such as "The Gemini" and "Leo on the Ascendent", on the basis of which we may get an idea of the more precise birth data of Dr. Banda.

dispensation, providing that these measures must not exceed what is "reasonably justifiable in a democratic society (BC sec. 12.2).

Such criteria cover the following three areas, the first of which is sub-section (a) including interests of defence as well as public safety, order, morality or health.

Sub-section (b) is of a rather miscellaneous nature, encompassing such different interests as the protection of rights and freedom of others, and in particular the privacy of persons concerned in legal proceedings, information given in confidence, maintenance of the authority and independence of the courts as well as the technical operation of mass-media, and the regulation of educational institutions for the benefit of its students and pupils.

Finally, sub-section (c) allows for restrictions on freedom of expression to be imposed upon public officers and employees of local government bodies and teachers. The latter part of sec. (c), regarding the areas of teaching and related institutions, was not included in similar Uganda-provision, which has otherwise provided the format of BC sec. 12, but was inserted into BC in 1969. As a consequence this reference can also not be found in the otherwise identical sec. 10 of MIC. It is, however, in accordance with the related provision, dealt with above, regarding the right of religious and other communities to establish schools and other educational institutions. These provisions in sec. 12 must therefore be viewed in this context.

With the exception of the general reference to Acts of Parliament in sec. 37, all of MAC's provisions in this area are of an absolute nature and have no other references to possible grounds for exemption from these rights. In contrast hereto, MIC was formulated identically to BC sec. 12, with the exception of the reference to employees of local government bodies or teachers mentioned above.

MOC art. 74.4 follows a course relatively similar to BC, but is more simple and states that the exercise of the freedoms found in art. 74 shall be regulated by law based on necessary respect for the Constitution, human dignity and mandates of foreign policy and national defence.

The BPC contains a number of provisions, which all serve as examples of restriction on freedom of expression based on the general regard for *ordre public* under sub-sec. (a) of BC sec. 11.2. These provisions include sec. 90 on the general breach of peace, sec. 91 and 93 on abuse of contempt of national symbols as well as the President and other public officers, and sec. 92 on expressions of contempt based on another person's race, origin etc. Sec. 197 through 204 deal specifically with cases of defamation, and finally sec. 184 restrict the use of "insulting language" in general.

The tendency of the Courts in applying these provisions has indicated that as a general rule the concept of freedom of expression must prevail. The key factor in determining to which extent it should be restricted seems to be whether the incident has led to a breach of general peace, or is likely to do so.[97]

A slightly more restrictive interpretation of the freedom of expression is applied in cases concerning contempt of court, where similar concerns for public order might be raised in cases of extreme or on founded allegations of incompetence or lack of impartiality of the judiciary. Still, in those cases the Court of Botswana has allowed for a reasonable measure of criticism.[98]

Going back to the fundamental character of freedom of information and expression it is important to take note of the fact that this is an area where the relationship between various individuals' exercise of this freedom and other individuals' right to protection of their privacy is most sensitive and likely to result in conflict. On this background it is remarkable that AC does not, like the other international and regional instruments,[99] protect this right. There is also among the various instruments a difference in scope, which does not follow the distinction between the international and the national levels, in relation to the protection of name, honour and reputation. While UD art. 12, ICCPR art. 17 and AMCHR art. 11, as well as MOC art. 71, all include this immaterial aspect of privacy, this is not the case in ECHR art. 8, MAC sec. 21 or BC sec. 9. It is hard to imagine the background for such an omission in the latter three instruments, other than the fact that it would almost always have to be subordinate to freedom of expression, which has then been given very high significance in these three cultures.

Freedom of association and assembly

AC art. 10+11

These two provisions cover aspects of the democratic rights and freedoms which are closely connected, in the sense that the fulfilment of one without

---

97. Neff, 1986, p. 39ff., who quotes a number of specific cases.
98. Neff, 1986, p. 43.
99. UD art. 12, ICCPR art. 17, ECHR art. 8 and AMCHR art. 11.

the other seems unlikely to result in any substantial guarantees of political and democratic freedom. As such, they should also be viewed in close connection with AC art. 13 on the right to participate freely in the government of one's country.

The interesting aspect of these provisions in AC art. 10 and 11 is the formulation of the "clawback" clauses, where both provisions of AC contains examples hereof similar to those found in relation to some of the articles of AC discussed elsewhere.

They vary in formulation, to the extent that art. 10.1 states that "Every individual shall have the right to free association provided that he abides by the law", while AC art. 11 states that "The exercise of (the right to free assembly with others) shall be subject only to necessary restrictions provided for by law". The difference in formulation of the clawback-clauses in AC art. 10.1 and AC art. 11 thus implies that the freedom of assembly is of a more absolute nature, subjecting infringements hereof to harder conditions of legality than those applying to freedom of association. Whether there is any substantial difference in the opportunities for setting aside the provisions is more doubtful, since AC art. 11 gives as examples "interests of national security, the safety, health, ethics, and rights and freedoms of others", without excluding other reasons.

Discussing each article separately, AC art. 10 covers the right to freedom of association, stated in art. 10.1. as the positive right for an individual to belong to an association, and in art. 10.2. as the negative freedom of association. Given that art. 10.1. does not impose any restrictions on national legislation, as shown above, any association as such could be declared as being contrary to the interest of the State or other entities, and subsequently membership hereof would be considered illegal. Therefore art. 10.1. does not in itself provide actual guarantees for the individual, except for those following the demand for the legal and administrational practice to be consistent with national law and Constitution once it has been established.

Associations in general are covered, without specification, contrary to the ECHR art. 15 and UD art. 23.4., both of which explicitly mention trade unions. Furthermore, there is no specific provision on the right to form or to join an association, including trade unions, but only the more passive right of belonging to an association.[100]

The negative freedom of association in art. 10.2 can also be found in

---

100. Neff, 1986, p. 43

UD art. 20.2, but neither in ICCPR nor in the AMCHR or ECHR. This should be noted, since, around the time when the AC was conceived, the ECourtHR ruled in a case regarding negative freedom of association, the so-called British Rail-case.[100] Here the ECourtHR stated that although it was not specified separately in the ECHR art. 11, no one may be compelled to join any association. Therefore the AC on this point is one step ahead of the other conventions, directly continuing the line of thought from UD.

The reference made to the obligation of solidarity in art. 29, which is an obligation on the individual to "preserve and strengthen national solidarity".[101] It makes the actual scope of the guarantees in art. 10.2. very weak, given that almost any kind of organization may be labelled as a threat to social and national solidarity. More particularly, this formulation refers to the situation of the one-party state, where membership of the political party and freedom of association may seem in effect to be incompatible. Also, in this relation, AC art. 10.2 should be viewed in connection with AC art. 9.2 on freedom of expression.[102]

This is one of the most explicit examples of AC "softening" the rights and freedoms of the individual by imposing counterbalancing duties. This is an approach which leaves a great deal of space for such limitations to be carried out at the discretion of the individual state and its representatives. The state therefore has to lift the burden of proof in the individual case, and validate that the conditions have been of such a nature that the precedence of the interests of the state, over the free will and interests of the individual, were critical to the welfare of the community in the given situation.

AC art. 11 covers the freedom of assembly, which also appears in the other regional and international instruments in a similar form. The limitations to the exercise of this right cover a wide spectrum of interests, from national security, safety, health and ethics, to the rights and freedoms of others. This is not exhaustive, according to the term "in particular", but the list of criteria of possible grounds for derogation in this article is still more extensive than in any of the other articles of the Charter. At the same time it is also more specific, and therefore affords a higher degree of protection

---

100. ECourtHR, No. 44, 13 August 1981, James, Young and Webster.
101. Attention should be paid to the fact that in the first (Dakar) draft of the Charter, this right was unconditional, since the reference to national solidarity was not included until the final edition by the Council of Ministers. See chapter 5, p. 6.
102. For a more expansive discussion of the ramifications of the one-party state in relation to human rights, see Bello, 1985, p. 163ff, as well as the chapter on AC art. 13 below.

than the corresponding provisions in the two other regional human rights conventions, which allow for unqualified limitations as long as they are in accordance with the law and considered necessary in a democratic society.[103] Those limitations can only be imposed by law, i.e. not in administrative practice or in more specific cases only, but does not exclude laws imposed under state of emergency etc.

In a case against Greece,[104] The ECommHR has stated the right of freedom of assembly to be of fundamental and key importance for the social and political life of a country, especially when the freedom of assembly is interpreted to cover political parties also. Also in a case from 1979,[105] the ECommHR concluded that the freedom of assembly relates to private as well as public meetings, but that in case of the latter the local authorities can demand a permission to hold the meeting, thus enabling them to ensure the peaceful character and progress hereof.

In an attempt to remedy some of the weaknesses inherent in AC art. 10, the AComm adopted a "Resolution on the Right to Freedom of Association" in 1992, during the same session as the Resolution on fair trial was adopted[106]. In contrast hereto the Resolution on freedom of association does not add to the material scope of the provision, but merely seeks to make clear the importance of the right to freedom of association.

The Resolution's sec. 1 and 2 emphasize that the state Parties' competent authorities "should not override constitutional provisions or undermine fundamental rights guaranteed by the Constitution and international human rights standards", or enact provisions which would limit the exercise of this freedom. Particularly the latter aspect seems to be an attempt to limit or even nullify the exemption clause in AC art. 10, which is of the most general nature, and as such the resolution has both formal and material value.

Finally, sec. 3 of the Resolution states that the regulation of the exercise of freedom of association "should be consistent with States' obligations under the African Charter of Human and Peoples Rights". This provision would for instance refer to the explicit duties for state Parties under AC art. 23.2 to ensure that individuals enjoying asylum in one of the member states

---

103. ECHR art. 11.2, and AMCHR art. 15. D'sa, 1986, p. 111.
104. The Greek Case in Yearbook 12, ECommHR.
105. ECommHR. No. 8191/78, DR. 17 p 93.
106. 11. session, Tunis, March 1992; Fifth Annual Activity Report, Annex VIII.

shall not engage in subversive activities or that their territories shall not be used for subversive or terrorist activities against other states. By applying this interpretation of the reference in sec. 3, apart from the general positive obligation to ensure rights and freedoms through national law in AC art. 1, some of the more restrictive aspects on freedom of association are brought back into focus.

The Resolution is also interesting because it emphasizes the AC's adherence to other international human rights instruments such as UD and the two UN Covenants ICCPRR as well as ICESCR. No reference is made to the ECHR or other regional non-African arrangements, which is in accordance with the Commission's mandate in AC art. 60 and 61. Instead, credit is given to the UN Sub-Commission on the Prevention of Discrimination and its Resolution no. 13 of 11 September 1980 adopting freedom of association.

Whether this means that state Parties to AC, who have not ratified the two Covenants, may still be bound by the provisions herein through the reference of the Resolution, is a discussion which has been carried out in relation to the Resolution on Fair Trial as well as the rights of women and children in AC art. 18, and shall not be dealt with further here.

BC sec. 13, MAC sec. 32 and 38, and MOC art. 75, 76 and 34

The concepts of freedom of association and assembly, which have been dealt with separately in AC art. 10 and 11, are contained within one provision in BC, which states in sec. 13 that "no person shall be hindered in the enjoyment of his freedom of assembly and association".

In line with the European conception at the time of the drafting of BC as well as the ECHR, the principle of negative freedom of association was not specifically included in BC sec. 13. An interesting approach, which might seem appropriate in this case, would be to adopt a dynamic interpretation of BC sec. 13 in light of AC art. 10.2, to the effect that also the negative freedom of association should be protected under BC sec. 13. This notion is supported by the fact that in the European context negative freedom of association is now included in the concept in accordance with the British Rail-case mentioned above. Such an interpretation would add to that which is already contained in the second half of BC sec. 13.1, which, contrary to AC art. 10, specifies that freedom of assembly in particular should be understood as including the right to form or to belong to trade unions as well as other interest associations.

Looking to Malawi, we find once again that the drafters of MAC used formulations of rights and freedoms which are less ambiguous than those in the other instruments. As such, MAC clearly states in sec. 32.1 that "Every person shall have the right to freedom of association" with no references to legal or other exceptions similar to the clauses found in AC and BC as described below. In addition, the provision states that freedom of association shall also include the right to form associations, which is one of features missing in AC as stated above.

The same picture is seen with respect to freedom of assembly, where MAC sec. 38 states that "Every person shall have the right to assemble and demonstrate with each other peacefully and unarmed". Here, the inclusion of the concept of demonstration is unique to this instrument, as well as the fact that no restrictions, such as the obligation to register meetings with the authorities or the obligation to preserve public order, are included through a general reference similar to those found in AC and BC. The only criteria in sec. 38 are that such a demonstration or gathering is unarmed and peaceful, and even though this gives some room for the authorities to claim lack of fulfilment of one or the other as an excuse for banning such activities, the provision is still far more protective here than in the other instruments.

The MOC protects both freedom of assembly and of association, stating in art. 75 that all citizens shall have the right to freedom of assembly "within the terms of the law". This latter reference to law and statutes resembles those of BC, but is less qualified than the one found in AC art. 11. In order to fulfil the obligation of AC art. 1, the judiciary and authorities of Mozambique will therefore have to accept only such restrictions which are necessary and can be referred to "interests of national security, the safety, health, ethics and rights and freedoms of others".[107]

With respect to freedom of association, MOC has quite an extensive catalogue of provisions, as shown in the chapter on democracy, where the question of the right to participate in and to form political parties was discussed. The fundamental right is established in MOC art. 76, where sec. 1 simply states that "All citizens shall enjoy freedom of association", without a restriction clause referring to national law like in art. 75. Additionally, MOC art. 90 states the right for all employees to organize professional associations and trade unions, and even though sec. 2 of the provision subjects trade union activities to legal regulation with no limitations, this is a provision which brings MOC ahead of AC and MAC and up

---

107. AC art. 11.

on line with BC as well as ICCPR and ECHR.

MOC art. 76.2 further states a set of rights not for individuals but for those legal entities falling within the definition "social organisations and associations", defined in MOC art. 34 as "associations of citizens having joint interests and affinities. As long as they act in accordance with the (unspecified) terms of the law, they shall have the right in accordance with MOC art. 76.2 to pursue their aims, to create institutions designed to achieve their specific objectives, and to own assets to carry out their activities. These are rights similar to those given to religious denominations in MOC art. 78, and it is evident that the Constitution of Mozambique here goes a long way further in protecting these rights than any of the other national or even international instruments, all of which have the individual's perspective only. Similar to the principles governing political parties in art. 31 through 33, MOC art. 34 emphasizes the important role these organizations play in promoting democracy and citizens' participation in political life. The provision also declares, rather than demands, that "social organisations contribute to achieving the rights and freedoms of citizens, as well as towards raising individual and collective consciousness in the fulfilment of civic duties".

Going back to BC sec. 13, the main difference between the provisions of AC and BC lies within the various derogation clauses, listed in BC sec. 13.2. sub-sec. (a) through (d). These limitations do not contravene the rights of assembly and association stated in section 1 of the article, although they are modified by the general requirement that such measures of restriction must be shown to be "reasonably justifiable in a democratic society" (BC sec. 13.2 *in fine*). The requirements to be complied with are found in AC art. 11.2, since this is the only part of AC art. 10 and 11 which contains more than a general unqualified reference to national law.

BC sec. 13.2 sub-sec. (a) and (b) combined correlate to AC art. 11, listing such interests as defence, public order, morality and health, and the rights and freedoms of others, and therefore they do not give rise to any immediate controversy with relation to the implementation of AC in the national law of Botswana. In contrast hereto, the last two sections (c) and (d) will have to undergo closer examination in order to determine their compliance with AC. Both of these cover various forms of political activities of trade unions and other related organizations, adding in sub-section (c) to the provision regarding restrictions upon public officers, the possibility of imposing similar restrictions upon employees of local government bodies or teachers. This final addition, as well as sec. 13.2 (d) in its entirety, was not included in the corresponding provision in the Constitution of Uganda, which otherwise provided the framework for the formulation of BC sec. 13. Therefore they were also not included in MIC sec. 11, which is otherwise identical to BC sec. 13. Sub-sec. (d) lays down rules according to which legal provisions for the regulation and registration of trade unions and associations are allowed, including the right to refuse registration of a trade union or association on the grounds that such an organization is already in existence and is considered "sufficiently representative" of the interests of the potential members.

Here, one senses clearly the intention of the Botswana government to regulate the activities of trade unions as well as important groups such as teachers and local officials in a more restrictive way than other political activities. It should be kept in mind that neither of the provisions formed part of the original Constitution, but were added along with other constitutional amendments in 1969[108] in order to facilitate closer government control in areas important to the political stability and economic development of the country.

This argument would in most cases seem to be acceptable, considering the importance of political stability in what was then a recently formed independent state. On the other hand the virtually unlimited scope of restrictions upon public officers' and teachers' exercise of their freedom of assembly and association may not be in accordance with neither art 10.1 nor art. 11 of the AC. When looking for an answer to this question, it should be taken into account that the provisions in question authorize the legislators to restrict, for instance, the participation in public and legal demonstrations, meetings, and all forms of trade union activities of those groups. This is particularly serious, because the union members, teachers and people in the administration often have a higher level of education and articulation than the average Botswana, and the effect hereof is that the Government hereby is less susceptible to criticism and opposition.

In order to ensure a more satisfactory compliance with the provisions of AC, a solution would therefore be to specify the conditions under which such restrictions on freedom of assembly and association may be imposed, as well as inserting a clause in BC sec. 13.2 (c) specifying the specific interests to be served and the criteria for the determination of such interests.

---

108. Some of these provisions were articles 5, 8, 13 and 15 in the Bill of Rights, dealing with areas of government control in the areas of air transport safety, mineral exploitation, trade union organizations as well as the application of customary law.

With regard to freedom of assembly and, in particular, association, the Constitution of Botswana sec. 13 is supplemented by a number of important legislative Acts.

The right to free assembly is regulated by the Public Order Act of 1967,[109] which distinguishes between gatherings taking place in the so-called "uncontrolled" and in "controlled" areas, which may be defined and declared by the Minister. All meetings in the latter type of locations, which have usually been of an urban character,[110] must be authorized by the Police, and are otherwise considered illegal and subject to termination.

This general rule is modified by a number of restrictions, listing instances where freedom of assembly can be enjoyed without particular qualifications. It should be noted, however, that these exceptions do not extend to processions, and that for instance trade unions are not subject to any particular exemptions either.[111]

Apart from those exemptions covering a wide range of social, religious, educational or charitable purposes, as well as events related to sports, trade or entertainment, the interesting exemptions are those impacting various political activities. According to the Act, such important meetings as those of the kgotla or by a town council or district, as well as those hosted by or on behalf of a member of the government or a candidate for election at the level of Parliament, council or town, are all exempt from public authorization.

Freedom of assembly in these cases is particularly important to ensure the process of democracy in Botswana, particularly in light of AC art. 13 on the individual's right to participate freely in the government of one's country.

With regards to freedom of association, the Trade Unions Act[112] and the Trade Disputes Act,[113] both 1969, supplemented BC sec. 13 for several years. But in 1983 new legislation entitled the Trade Union and Employers' Organisation Act[114] was introduced, which already at its concep-

---

109. Public Order Act, 1967, Laws of Botswana.
110. Maope, p. 104f.
111. Ibid.
112. Trade Unions Act, 1969, LoB.
113. Trade Disputes Act, 1969, LoB.
114. Trade Union and Employers' Organisation Act, 1983, LoB.
     On this Act, see Vaenerberg, 1990.

tion was strongly criticized for contravening the basic principles of the International Labour Organisation, of which Botswana is a member since 1978.[115] However, this argument is weakened, from a legal point of view, by the fact that Botswana has not ratified any of the substantial ILO-conventions such as Convention No. 87 from 1948 on the establishment of trade unions or Convention No. 98 on the right of organization and collective bargaining.

An important consequence of the Act is that a person cannot join a trade union unless he or she is also employed in an industry with which the union in question is directly concerned, while on the other hand a person employed by the trade union cannot at the same time become or remain a member of the union in question (sec. 21). Furthermore, sec. 22 states that a similar restriction is imposed upon the leader of a trade union, and according to sec. 24 a trade union cannot enter into a contract on full-time employment without approval by the Registrar of Trade Unions and Employers' Organisations appointed by the Minister. All of these provisions hereby severely restrict the individual's freedom of association.

On a collective level, the Minister has extensive powers of discretion, for instance regarding the formation or joining of trade unions, and his decision is final and cannot be appealed to a Court of law or any other instance (sec. 47). Finally, no trade union in Botswana can join organizations outside Botswana or receive foreign support or financial contribution without the Minister's permission (sec. 63 and 64).

Freedom of movement and residence

AC art. 12

This article compiles a number of different aspects of the right to move freely across and within the borders of a country. A distinction is made between regular movement and travel by people whose status is not questioned in the two first sub-sections, and the more extreme cases related to asylum and expulsion, cases where the status of the individual is challenged in some way, in sub-sec. 3 through 5.

Art. 12.1. states the individual's right to "freedom of movement and

---

115. Botswana has ratified only two ILO-Conventions, No. 14 on holiday in the industry from 1921 and No. 19 on equality with respect to compensation for working accidents.

residence within the borders of a state", provided that he abides by the law.

As in the clawback-clauses discussed in relation to several of the earlier articles, there are no criteria for the provisions in national law, and the formulation therefore leaves room for virtually unlimited restrictions on the freedom of movement. A minimal requirement would be that the legislation in question is, at least, consistent with the aims and contents of the African Charter in general, particularly in relation to the prohibition against discrimination of any kind, and naturally also with the national constitutional or legislative provisions on freedom of movement, if these exist. It should be noted that, given the formulation of the article, the right is not exclusive to the citizens of the state, since the freedom of movement applies to every person residing within the borders of a state, including also non-nationals and lawfully admitted refugees.[116]

Another consequence of AC art. 12.1 is that the unqualified reference to national law does not preclude any consequences rising from an individual's non-compliance with national law, to the extent that a person may be expelled from the state of which one is a national if he or she violates provisions in, for instance, the Constitution or even the Criminal Code or a National Security Act.

Art. 12.2. covers the right for every individual to freely leave any country, foreign as well as one's own, and to return to his or her country. The section contains no key to a definition of the term "his country", and it is therefore left to the State party in question to determine this, based on such factors as ancestry, birth, residence etc., in accordance with the criteria for nationality or citizenship applied in its national law. This could give rise to complicated situations, particularly in regions where geographical and ethnic borders do not coincide, and where problems related to discrimination on this basis might therefore occur.

This provision is also subject to a clawback reference to national law, and even though it is formulated more narrowly than in sub-sec. 1, the actual effects hereof are limited or non-existent, since virtually any reason for restrictions can be encompassed within the scope of the concepts of national security, law and order, public health or morality.

Therefore the unfortunate conclusion is that, according to AC art. 12 sec. 1 and 2, a national of a given state has no absolute right to either move within the borders hereof or depart from it, and no absolute right to return to his or her home State. This leaves the individual in a potentially delicate

---

116. Zetterqvist, 1990, p. 56.

position, where in effect it is only the provisions of national law and not those of the African Charter which protect the exercise of these rights. Finally, this form of banishment from one's community because of some form of socially unacceptable behaviour may have been applied in the history of several African countries, but should be considered unacceptable in modern societies.[117]

Comparing AC art. 12.1 and 12.2 to other general human rights instruments, UD art. 13 and ICCPR art. 12 both state that everyone has freedom of movement and residence within the borders of the state, and that no one may be deprived of his or her right to leave a country, including their own, and to return to their own country. To this extent all of the three instruments correspond, but the difference lies in the clawback-clauses, found in ICCPR and AC which have roughly the same formulation,[118] while UD art. 13 is absolute and contains no reference to national law.

It is interesting to note that in contrast both art. 3 of the P4 to the ECHR and art. 22.5 of the AMCHR both state, without reservation, that no person shall be expelled from or denied the right to return to the territory of the state of which he or she is a national.[119]

On the right to return to one's own country, ICCPR art. 12 states that deprivation of this right must not be "arbitrary". It must be interpreted as a requirement that legal provisions are in force regulating such measures, and that an individual decision is taken by a competent judicial or administrative authority in accordance with these provisions.[120]

The difference between AC art. 12.2 and ICCPR art. 12 hereby lies in the fact that ICCPR aims at the individual's guarantees for legality. In contrast the focus in AC is on the general consideration for Rule of Law, and the provision only requires some form of authorization by law and does not necessitate an individual decision similar to that of ICCPR art. 12. This again depends on what the State party in question defines as constituting a

---

117. Kotey, 1989, p. 136.
118. The formulation of ICCPR art. 12.3 states that the freedom of residence and movement as well as the departure from a country including one's own (sec. 1 and 2) shall not be subject to any restrictions except those which are provided by law, necessary to protect national security, public order, public health or morals or the rights and freedoms of others. Such restrictions must also be consistent with the other rights recognized by the Covenant.
119. Kotey, 1989, p. 136f.
120. Nowak, 1993, p. 208f.

valid source of law, and might give rise to some concern in cases where, for instance, legal precedents or customary law play a significant or even deciding role in the legal process.

A provision which partly serves to remedy this unfortunate situation at least in some cases, is AC art. 14.4, which states that a non-national who has been legally admitted in a State party's territory may only be expelled from it by virtue of a decision taken in accordance with the law, thus ensuring the principle of *non refoulement* of refugees.

But in relation to AC art. 12.2, the provision has two serious limitations. The first one is cases where the person has already left the territory of their own free will. The second limitation is far more significant, and lies in the simple fact that the provision refers expressly to non-nationals only.

The grotesque consequence of AC art. 12 might therefore be that a State party may decree that nationals presently residing abroad, who for instance have been found guilty (possibly *in absentia*) of "subversive activities" or any other crime in accordance with national law for that matter, may be denied the right to return to their country without any individual consideration of cases, or without the possibility of an appeal to legal or administrative instances.

In contrast, a non-national under the same circumstances has the right to an individual decision by a competent authority in the matter, a position which is far more favourable in terms of ensuring freedom of movement.

One senses that the drafters of the African Charter were conscious of the problems in relation to these restrictions on freedom of movement for nationals of AC art. 12.2, and stressed it by applying the qualified clawback-clause instead of just a general reference to national law as in section 1.

But, the fact still remains that AC on this point leaves too wide a room for State parties' violation of the rights and freedoms of their people, particularly since this has potentially far-reaching consequences for the individual thus affected. Finally, the seriousness hereof is stressed by the fact that AC contains no provision on the individual's right to a nationality, but only guarantees the right for every person to recognition of his or her legal status in art. 5.

Moving on to the provisions governing cases related to various distinctions of expatriates, AC art. 12.3 states the right for an individual to seek and obtain asylum in other countries, again with the modifying reference to the national law of the State parties. This right applies only in cases of persecution, understood as a reference to political refugees whose status is defined in accordance with international conventions.[121]

Section 3 is interesting, since this right to seek and enjoy asylum is not included in ICCPR or in the text of the ECHR itself. Still, the concept is included in the UD art. 14, and the ACHR art. 22.7. Furthermore, the Declaration on Territorial Asylum and the UN Convention on Refugees, with additional Protocol, deal extensively with the above issues.

The formulation "seek and obtain" must be interpreted according to the UD's "seek and enjoy", in the sense that it does not impose a corresponding absolute obligation for the individual state to grant asylum. This interpretation is supported by the explicit reference to national law, and it will therefore have to be established in the national legislation whether a person seeking asylum in accordance with AC art. 12.3 also has an absolute right to be given it. It should be noted that, although the individual state can establish its own policy in relation to the granting of asylum, the principle of non-discrimination must prevail, insofar as it is established in AC art.2 and to the degree that it is also included in the domestic law of the state.[122]

The superior criteria are implied in the words "when persecuted", indicating that some degree hereof must be taking place, without giving further account on what those qualifications are.[123] The guidelines for the interpretation hereof must be found in the UN instruments mentioned above, which specify in details the conditions and prerequisites for obtaining of asylum,[124] in accordance with the reference to international conventions in AC art. 12.3.

At this point attention should be paid to the fact that OAU already at an early stage established its own regional instrument to deal with the question of refugees in the continent.

The Convention Governing the Specific Aspects of Refugee Problems (OAUCR) was adopted on 10 September 1969 at the 6th Ordinary Session

---

121. D'sa, 1986, p. 111.
122. See also art. 3 of the Convention Relating to the Status of Refugees, which states that "The Contracting States shall apply the provisions of the Convention to refugees without discrimination as to race, religion or country of origin".
123. As a minimum, it must refer to political refugees as defined by international Conventions. D'sa, 1986, p. 111.
124. The Convention relating to the Status of Refugees art. 1 sec. A through F give an extensive definition of the term "refugee" by outlining the circumstances under which this status is either obtained or denied.

of the Assembly of Heads of State and Government, and entered into force on 20 June 1974. It has presently been ratified by 41 African states,[125] including Malawi and Mozambique but excluding Botswana. According to the Preamble (sec. 1 through 5) it has as its background the significant problems relating to the question of refugees in Africa. Also the frictions between member states with regards to the "subversive activities" of refugees directed towards their country of origin have played an important role. The Preamble in sec. 6 through 11 affirms its adherence to international instruments such as the Charter of the UN, the UD, the UN Declaration on Territorial Asylum and, most important, the UN Convention on Refugees of 1951 (UNCR) and its additional Protocol of 1967 (UNCRP). Still, the Preamble of OAUCR sec. 8 justifies the formation of a particular African instrument on the basis that, in spite of the existence of substantial international legal provisions on this subject, "all the problems of our continent must be solved in the spirit of the Charter of the Organization of African Unity and in the African context" (sec. 8 of the Preamble).

The OAU Convention should be seen as a supplement to the existing international instruments and not as a replacement hereof, which is clearly shown by its close adherence to the provisions of the UNCR. As such, its art. 1 adopts the same formulation as the corresponding provisions herein, with the important addition of a paragraph on the definition of a refugee, extending the term to cover also "every person who, owing to external aggression, occupation, foreign domination or events seriously disturbing public order - is compelled to leave his place of habitual residence" (art. I). Another provision which is unique to the OAUCR in relation to UNCR is the inclusion of art. III on a prohibition of subversive activities, and art. IV on non-discrimination where the OAUCR goes further than the International Convention by including the terms "membership of a particular social group" and "political opinions".

Finally, a provision which clearly outlines the circumstances to which the OAU was particularly adapted is art. II sec. 4, stating that if difficulties arise in relation to the accommodation of asylum to refugees, the State must then appeal to other Member States, and they shall then "in the spirit of African solidarity and international co-operation take appropriate measures to lighten the burden" of the Member State.

The above mentioned reference in art. 12.3 is fairly unique in the context of the African Charter, since the only other provision on individual

---

125. International Journal of Refugee Law, Jan. 1995.

rights and freedoms containing a similar phrase is AC art. 18.3 on protection of the rights of the woman and the child.

In this relation the question arises, how such a reference should be understood, in light of the principles governing international law on instrument's binding effect in relation to those states who are parties to the instrument in question as well as those who are not.[126]

Generally, a convention only imposes legally enforceable obligations on those states who have ratified it, and as such the reference in AC art. 12.3 would in its most narrow interpretation include only the provisions of those international conventions ratified by the state in question. If that particular state party had not ratified, for instance, the refugee conventions mentioned above, the provisions hereof should not be taken into account when analysing and applying the provisions of AC art. 12.3.

This would, however, not take into account the fact that some instruments and the principles embodied in them have over time achieved such a general global consensus and recognition of their importance, that they can be seen as forming part of international customary law.[127] The result would be that they achieve a superior and fundamental status, giving them at least some degree of legal significance beyond the limitations of the ratification procedure as outlined above.

If we acknowledge that in a particular relation to the question of refugees, some of the basic instruments, such as the above mentioned UNCR, have achieved this status, the reference in AC art. 12.3 would extend also to those state parties who have not ratified the instrument(s) in question. Still, there are also problems arising from the consequences of this wide interpretation, if one goes to the extreme and interprets AC art. 12.3 as conferring obligations on member states which are clearly beyond those following from the ratification of particular instruments. Those problems would result in a general insecurity as to the scope of rights and freedoms to be claimed by the individual in a given case, particularly since the reference term in AC art. 12.3 does not clarify whether these instruments must be global or if they can be of a regional character such as the OAUCR.

Balancing these two extremes, the way to an understanding of the reference to "international conventions" in AC art. 12.3, as well as in art. 18.3 on the rights of women and children, would be to clarify that the

---

126. See ch. 5 on the African Charter and international law.
127. Steiner/Alston, 1996, p. 27ff.

contribution of these instruments would merely regard the interpretation and definition of the provisions established by AC art. 12.3. As such, one might for instance look to them for a closer definition of the term "refugee", but not include them to expand the scope of rights and freedoms beyond that which is already outlined by the AC-provision in its brief form. Even though it will often be difficult to distinguish between the two situations, since the act of interpreting a concept always adds some depth or scope which was not already there, this solution seems to be the most appropriate.

Art. 12.4. deals with the right for non-nationals legally admitted in the territory of a state party to stay in the country and only to be expelled from it by virtue of a decision taken in accordance with the laws of the country. A similar provision can be found in the ICCPR art. 13, which also states the right to have the decision of expulsion tried by a competent national authority. The difference between these two provisions is that while ICCPR art. 13 establishes a two-instance system, which can still be of an administrative and not necessarily a judicial nature, AC art. 12.4 does not prescribe that the decision should be tried before the Courts or any other authority other than that which has already made the decision.

AC art. 12.4 must therefore be viewed in light of AC art. 7 on the right to appeal of a decision violating his or her fundamental rights as well as AC art. 2 on freedom from discrimination, the provisions of which must be included when implementing AC art. 12.4 in national law.

Finally, art. 12.5 contains a prohibition against mass expulsion of non-nationals, precising mass expulsion as being directed against national, racial, ethnic or religious groups.

In contrast to most of the other provisions of AC discussed above, this section does not contain any derogation or clawback clauses, and the immunity from such a violation of one's freedom of movement and residence therefore has an absolute character. Still, this is only the case within the framework of the formulation itself, to the extent that mass-expulsion of nationally, ethnically, racially or religiously heterogenous groups on the common ground that they are illegal immigrants would not constitute a violation of AC art. 12.5.[128] An example of how the application of AC art. 12.5 might be difficult in the actual situation, is the case of the Nigerian Government's expulsion of no less than 3 million non-nationals from its territory.[129] Despite the alarming number and the consequences for each

---

128. Kotey, 1989, p. 137.
129. Bello, 1985, p. 168.

individual affected by it, it was still claimed as being beyond the ramifications of AC art. 12.5, on the grounds that the common denominator for those expelled was their lack of valid entry and residence permits and not their nationality, ethnic origin, religion or race.

Unfortunately the occurrence of this type of large-scale expulsions has not been infrequent in Africa over the last decades, carried out by such states as Nigeria, Cameroons, Ivory Coast, Rwanda, Burundi, Ghana, Zaire, Uganda, Equatorial Guinea, Gabon and Congo.[130]

We should therefore view AC art. 12.5 as an example of the African Charter's close adaptation and adherence to the circumstances in which it must operate, strengthened by the fact that other instruments such as the UD, the ICCPR, or the ECHR do not contain a similar provision.

BC sec. 14, MAC sec. 39 and MOC art. 83

Freedom of movement as established in AC art. 12 has its correspondence in BC sec. 14., MAC sec. 39 and MOC art. 83, but the differences between the formulation, and therefore also the scope of protection, of provisions in each instrument give rise to various comments.

As stated above, AC art. 12.1 lays down the general principle of freedom of movement and residence within the borders of a state, as long as the person abides by the law, and BC sec. 14.1 accordingly here specifies freedom of movement as the right to move freely throughout and to reside in any part of Botswana.

Also MAC sec. 39.1 states that every person shall have the right of freedom of movement and residence within Malawi, a provision which is as brief and absolute as we generally find them in this instrument.

Finally, MOC art. 83 deals with the two aspects of this right separately, stating in sec. 1 the right for all citizens to take up residence in any part of the national territory, and in sec. 2 the right to travel inside the national territory. Again, we have to confront the formulations chosen by the drafters of MOC, since the use of the term "citizen" taken in its literal sense would rule out aliens legitimately residing in Mozambique and, as a consequence hereof, any protection of their right to freedom of movement and residence. If, on the other hand, we read it as corresponding to the term "person" or "individual" used in the other instruments, the extent of protection in MOC is at the same level as that which is offered by AC, MAC and MOC. Such

---

130. Okere, 1984, p. 147; Bello, 1985, p. 168.

an interpretation is facilitated by the addition in sec. 2, but not in sec. 1, that freedom of movement belongs to everybody "except those legally deprived of this right by the courts". It would accordingly be possible to restrict, for instance, the movement of aliens in particular cases, all of which would have to be decided within the framework of the Rule of Law.

On the question of cross-boundary movement, it should be noted that the concept established in AC art. 12.2 on freedom to leave any country including one's own has not been included in the Constitution of Botswana, affecting nationals as well as non-nationals of Botswana. Even though it could be justifiably maintained that this does not give rise to serious concern under the present state of affairs, where travel is unrestricted and passports and visas are easily obtained by citizens of Botswana, it still constitutes a lacuna of BC in relation to AC.[131]

The most extensive protection of this right is, characteristically, found in MAC sec. 39.2, stating that "Every person shall have the right to leave the Republic and return to it". In effect, this would mean that the introduction of any restrictions such as general visa requirements and limits on the duration of a visitor's stay could be a violation of sec. 39.

Also MOC guarantees travel across national boarders by adding "abroad" to the general right in art. 83.2, and again the problems in relation to distinctions between citizens and aliens may arise as outlined above. In relation to this particular aspect, the effects are potentially more significant, since restrictions for other nationalities would most often be imposed already upon their entering into Mozambique.

In relation to AC sec. 3, on the right to seek and to obtain asylum, we here find that none of the national Constitutions included in this study provide any guarantees, and it is one of the few areas where this is the case.

This should be viewed on the background of the geo-political situation in Southern Africa over the last couple of decades, where large groups of refugees have migrated across borders. Botswana in particular has experienced large influx of refugees, in particular from Zimbabwe, Namibia, and South Africa, and has continued to receive these in spite of pressure from

---

131. This provision gave rise to concern with the Drafting Committee for the Kenya Constitution, which subsequently recommended that the right to leave one's country was included along with the right of movement within Kenya in the first part of the article.

South Africa to cease doing so.[132] In contrast, large groups of Mozambicans have fled to the neighbouring countries because of the long-standing civil war. With respect to Malawi, many individuals have fled the country during the politically oppressive regime of Dr. Banda, but at the same time the country received many of the refugees from Mozambique, the number peaking at over one million in 1993.[133]

On this background it is perhaps no wonder that the states have been hesitant in establishing the right to asylum at the constitutional level, preferring instead to deal with these issues at the level of statute law, which can be more easily adapted to changes in the political situation. Again it should be pointed out that AC art. 1 does not require that the member states implement its provisions constitutionally or even through legislation at all, as long at it is ensured that the final result, the actual practices, reflects their obligations according to AC.

In relation to AC art. 13.3's reference to international conventions, it should be noted that this is one of the very few areas where Botswana has acceded to any of the international human rights instruments, and has ratified the UNCR from 1951 as well as the additional protocol from 1967. Both Malawi and Mozambique have ratified these instruments, as well as the OAUCR to which Botswana is not a party. Furthermore, Botswana has also ratified the UN Convention relating to the Status of Stateless Persons, but this is not the case with either Malawi or Mozambique.

As in relation to other aspects of AC, for instance the area of fair trial, we find that the national Constitutions offer more extensive protection. An example is BC sec. 14.1 and MAC sec. 39, stating the freedom to enter Botswana and Malawi for every person regardless of nationality, where AC art. 14.2 only gives a person this right in relation to his or her own country.

Similarly, BC sec. 14 also guarantees every person immunity from expulsion from Botswana regardless of their nationality, a provision which has no explicit parallel in MAC or MOC. It must be assumed that AC art. 12.5 is also covered by BC sec. 14, even though this article only speaks in terms of persons, in singulars, when allowing for the differences in emphasis of collectivity and individuality of the respective instruments. To be taken into account is also the fact that AC art. 12.5 is mainly directed against multi-ethnic states suffering from serious and widespread conflicts

---

132. See Granberg/Parkinson, 1988, p. 37f. An in-depth description and analysis of Botswana's practice in relation to refugees is given by Zetterqvist, 1990.
133. UNHCR Branch Office Malawi, Update no. 3, 15 June 1994.

and power struggles between various groups, a problem which does not dominate life in Botswana. In any case, this right is particularly significant in relation to refugees, who in accordance with the principle of *non-refoulement* must be ensured against an involuntary expulsion to their former home state.

While MAC sec. 39 is of an absolute character and MOC art. 83 only allows for limitations on an individual basis and controlled by the judiciary, BC contains an extensive catalogue of clauses authorizing restrictions on freedom of movement. They are stated in sec. 14.2 and 14.3 sub-sec. (a) through (e), and refer to areas of legislation and particular circumstances similar to those already discussed earlier in connection with other provisions of BC.

It should be noted that in spite of their extensive and far-reaching character, BC sec. 14.2 and 14.3 do not contravene AC art. 12 sec. 1 through 4, since all these articles of AC refer to the provisions of national law as the ultimate determinant of the scope of rights and freedoms for each individual. It is therefore an example of how extensively the protective and promotional measures of AC can be hollowed out and rendered ineffective as a result of the references to national law.

Sub-sec. (a) is a general clause allowing for restrictions which are reasonably required, and covers areas such as defence, public safety, public order, public morality or public health, similar to those listed in AC art. 12.2, and on the acquisition or use of land or other property in Botswana.

This entire section was, contrary to the rest of the article, not adopted from the Uganda Constitution, where the corresponding sec. 17.3 (a) and (b) include court orders, but excludes the provision on land or property. Instead, the BCC decided to apply directly the provision in MIC which contained the provision on land and property. It is likely that this was done in an effort to prevent foreigners, from the neighbouring countries as well as other expatriates from Europe and elsewhere, from gaining too strong a position in a country with a limited supply of, for instance, good farm land and other similarly attractive resources.

Very significant, particularly in relation to the provisions of AC, is BC sec. 14.3 (b), which states that any law is not inconsistent with or in contravention of the freedom of movement as defined above, when it imposes restrictions of this freedom on non-citizens of Botswana.[134]

These two provisions in conjunction unfortunately allow for virtually

---

134. This provision is similar to art. 17.3 of the Constitution of Uganda.

unlimited restrictions on all aspects of freedom of movement and residence, for Botswana nationals as well as foreigners, and the rights and freedoms stated in AC are therefore in reality without legal importance as a result hereof.

A provision with a particular reference to Botswana in formulation as well as substance, in fact one of the few, is sub-sec. (c), which enables restrictions on the entry into or residence within defined areas of Botswana for the protection or well-being of the Bushmen people. It should be noted that MIC has no provision of this kind.

We here see one of the few examples in BC of a provision aimed towards the protection and promotion of the human rights of a group rather than a single individual, and it will therefore be dealt with further below in relation to the question of how to implement the so-called Peoples' Rights of AC.

In contrast hereto stands BC sec. 14.3 (d), which allows for the imposition of restrictions upon the movement or residence within Botswana of public officers. This provision is particularly serious viewed in connection with a similar provision in BC sec. 12 and 13 which allows for limitations on the freedom of expression as well as the freedom of assembly and association for public officers. These provisions in conjunction enable the total scope of individual rights and freedoms to be severely limited for these groups, individually and collectively. It is difficult to find other motives for such a provision than the wish of the government to limit criticism and possible threat to the political stability and positions of power. It is even more interesting that the BCC sub-committee actually recommended that the provision, which forms a part of the Uganda Constitution, was left out of the Constitution of Botswana, but that the Conference apparently decided, as one of very few occasions, to ignore the recommendation and included it nevertheless.

BC sec. 14 contains two provisions which are relatively simple and do not give rise to larger problems, insofar as they may be considered to be natural modifications on the freedom of movement and residence. These are section 2, which exempts cases where a person is held in lawful detention, and section 3 (e) regarding removal of a person outside Botswana either to be tried for a criminal offence or to undergo sentence in accordance with a criminal conviction. Here we see an illustration of the close relation between the right to personal liberty and freedom of movement, where the latter is in reality an extension of the former, and as a consequence hereof any questions arising from these sections will be dealt with in the chapter on personal liberty.

It is important to take note of the fact that these conditions must rule out the possibility of expulsion to a possible death sentence, something which would bring Botswana under the eyes of organizations like Amnesty International, and severely damage the country's human rights record.[135]

The final sub-sec. 4. and 5., of BC sec. 14 concern cases where, when a person's freedom of movement has been restricted, he or she has the opportunity of access to bring the decision before a Court of Law, which may make recommendations to the relevant authorities concerning the necessity or expediency of continuing the restriction. The authorities in question are, however, not bound to follow the recommendations, according to sec. 5, and therefore the practical significance of this opportunity is diminished.

There are other factors which serve to diminish the guarantees of BC sec. 14.4, the first hereof being the particular reference to sub-sec. (a) of the article only, and the consequence hereof is that decisions regarding non-citizens, public officers and cases of bushman protection are excluded from the process of appeal. Secondly, the note in brackets in sec. 14.4 furthermore excludes restrictions "applicable to persons generally or to general classes of persons" from this procedure as well. In conjunction, these two exceptions cover a large amount of potential cases concerning violations of freedom and movement by the State of Botswana, making the actual applicability of this access to judicial appeal and review quite limited. According to the report of the BCCom., sec. 14.4 and 5, which are nonetheless an improvement of sec. 17 of the Uganda Constitution which contains no such provision, were included as an adaptation of the recommendations of the KCCC. The KCCC is, however, silent on this particular point, even though it comments on the majority of the provisions of this article in the Uganda Constitution.

With relation to refugees' freedom of movement and residence within Botswana, the Refugee Act[136] mentions no restrictions of these rights for a recognized refugee once he or she has been granted asylum. Before this

---

135. During the 1980s there were, in fact, investigations carried out by Amnesty International regarding the expulsion of Zimbabwean refugees convicted of murder, who were returned to a possible death sentence; Granberg/Parkinson, 1988.
136. The Refugees (Recognition and Control) Act, Act 8, 1967.
Latest amendment Act 11, 1982.

status is achieved, the provisions of the Immigration Act[137] applies, and in accordance with sec. 8.3 herein, the President of Botswana may impose restrictions on freedom of residence for aliens of a specified class. The Government has availed itself of the opportunities inherent herein, and has since 1980 adopted the policy of accommodating all refugees in a settlement in Dukwe, and only permitting them to live elsewhere if they are self-supporting.

Freedom of movement is also restricted for these residents of the settlement, since they need a leave permit to move freely throughout and across the borders of Botswana. In return, they are exempt from the requirement of obtaining a residence permit, which is mandatory for all other aliens in order to reside legally in Botswana.[138]

Freedom from discrimination

A. Discrimination in general

The African Charter on Human and Peoples Rights art. 2 and 3

These two provisions in conjunction cover the basic principle that all human beings should be regarded as equal and entitled to the same measure of respect, dignity and protection of their rights, and accordingly the law in its formulation as well as its application must therefore respect and ensure this.

Art. 2 contains a general clause against discrimination, establishing the equal right to the enjoyment of the rights and freedoms in the Charter for everybody "without distinction of any kind, such as race, ethnic group, colour, sex, language, religion, political or any other opinion, national and social origin, fortune, birth or other status". It should be noted that the provision refers only to rights and freedoms, not to duties.[139]

This article corresponds to the similar articles on discrimination in UD and the other instruments, and its broad nature serves as a corner stone for the protection and promotion of human rights in both the regional and national contexts.[140]

---

137. The Immigration Act; Laws of Botswana chap. 25:04.
138. Zetterqvist, 1990, p. 58f.
139. Neff, 1983, p. 12.
140. UD art. 1 and 2; ICCPR art. 2.1 and art. 3; ICESCR art. 2.2 and 3; ECHR art. 14; AMCHR art. 1.

Due to its general nature AC art. 2 could be seen as having the character of a governing principle rather than affording directly specific and enforceable rights and freedom. It therefore takes a dedicated national legislator to transform its intentions into specific enforceable rights, and as such the independent value of AC art. 2 is of a limited nature. On the other hand it is a strong statement from the drafters of AC on a subject where the realities of many African societies indicate the need to establish and manifest the principle of non-discrimination. This relates, in particular, to conflicts of power between various ethnic groups in a community, and the question of equality between men and women, which will be looked at further in relation to Botswana in particular.

Looking at the individual aspects of AC art. 2, the expression "ethnic groups" is not to be found in any of the other human rights instruments. It must be viewed within the context of dissimilar political and ethnic frontiers in Africa as mentioned above, following the "geometrical division" of the continent by the colonialist states, which created groups of ethnic and cultural minorities in almost every African country. The only other human rights instrument which contains a similar provision is ECHR art. 14 which speaks about "association with a national minority", also on a cultural and historical background.

The expression "fortune" is also unique to the African Charter, but has its parallel in the AMCHR art. 1 which uses the words "economic status". The other international conventions and UD use the expression "property" in the similar context, and as such there's no major difference in the substance of these concepts.

AC art. 3 is divided into two sections, where sec. 1 states the right for every individual to "be equal before the law", while sec. 2 states the right for every individual to be entitled to "equal protection of the law". Two problems arise from this provision, namely the question of its relation to art. 2 and its unique status in relation to other international instruments, and the determination of the legal content of the two sections of AC art. 3.

Regarding the first issue, there can be no question that art. 2 and 3 shall be viewed in conjunction, and that they are merely elaborations on the same concept, emphasizing particular aspects hereof. Looking at the other international instruments referred to above, we therefore find no single provision in any of these instruments corresponding directly to AC art. 3.

One might see art. 2 as included within art. 3, which would mean that art. 2 in itself would seem to be superfluous.[141] I would, however, apply the opposite interpretation and see art. 2 as the primary provision and art. 3 as merely an elaboration in formulation if not in scope hereof.

This brings us into the second question, since art. 3 in contrast to art. 2 emphasizes the legal aspects of the principle of equality and non-discrimination. The term "the law" can be seen in a material and in an institutional sense, encompassing both the legislative provisions and their administration by the judiciary. Therefore art. 3 implies that not only must the written law refrain from making distinctions between certain individuals or groups hereof regardless of reason. It must also be applied accordingly in judicial and administrative practice, for instance in relation to individuals' equal access to the Courts and the question of legal aid, areas where extensive inequality exists throughout the African continent.[142]

Also, it could be questioned whether the customary courts, found all over Africa and even officially established in Botswana but not in Mozambique or Malawi,[143] are in conformity with these provisions, since they apply the traditional law to members of their community only and not to Europeans or to members of other tribes. Still, this is not discriminatory, but merely a question of outlining the jurisdiction of the traditional law to a particular ethnic group or tribe. When, on the other hand, the Customary Court apply the general statutory law of the state in question, they will also have to adhere to the provisions of AC art. 2 and 3, and apply this law equally and without discrimination to all individuals concerned.[144]

BC sec. 3 and 15, MAC sec. 20, MOC sec. 69 and 66

As outlined above, AC in art. 2 states that "Every individual shall be entitled to the enjoyment of the rights and freedoms recognized and guaranteed in the present Charter without distinction of any kind such as race, ethnic group, colour, sex, language, religion, political or any other opinion, national and social origin, fortune, birth or other status".

A similar general article can be found in BC sec. 3, stating that "every person in Botswana is entitled to the fundamental rights and freedoms of the

---

141. Neff, 1986, p. 12.
142. Bello, 1985, p. 151. This question has been dealt with more extensively in the chapter on the right to a fair trial.
143. See ch. 6 on fair trial.
144. Neff, 1986, p. 12; Maope, p. 116ff.

individual - whatever his race, place of origin, political opinions, colour, creed or sex."

There is a basic correspondence between these provisions, except for the omission in BC of the concepts of religion, language, tribe, birth and fortune and other status. Some of these could still be included under the concepts already mentioned such as race, creed and place of origin. It is, nonetheless, an indication of the complex constellation of the Botswana society, characterized by diversions between various ethnic tribes and peoples and with a fixed hierarchy of status both between the various groups and within the individual group or tribe as well.[145]

In relation to Malawi we see the influence of AC, since the list of concepts in MAC sec. 20 is modelled almost entirely upon that of AC art. 2. The only exceptions to this is MAC's use of the term "ethnic or social origin" instead of a reference to ethnic group or national origin, indicating a softer and less conflict-oriented approach as well as the more internal nature than the formulation in AC provides for. Also the term "disability" is included, hereby taking into account AC art. 18.3. Another important difference is that while AC art. 2 directs protection against discrimination towards the other provisions of this particular instrument only, MAC sec. 20 refers to discrimination "in any form" in addition to stating that this protection against discrimination is extended to all persons "under any law". This implies that all forms of statute and customary law are subject to the prohibition against discrimination, even though this would already be the case based on the principle of *lex superior*.

That discrimination will often reveal itself in various areas of statute law, and therefore needs to be dealt with at this level, is emphasized by MAC sec. 20.2, according to which legislation may be passed addressing inequalities in society and prohibiting discriminatory practices and the propagation hereof, as well as rendering such practices punishable to the courts. In particular, this article can be seen as addressing the area of customary law and practices where discrimination against women may be extensive, and as such it marks a change in attitude from MIC. An example

---

145. For instance the bushpeople or San, often called Basarva, "The Untouchables", of the Kalahari have a markedly and overall low status in Botswana, even though it may not be expressed on a legal level but through general belief and attitude. This status and subsequent treatment is accredited to them mainly by their close neighbours, the Bakgalagadi, for whom they work as shepherds etc., a group which again is regarded as lower in status than the various Motswana, but higher than the San. Steen Preis, 1996, p. 299ff.

is sec. 13 herein, which exempted sex as a basis for discrimination in sec. 13.3, and furthermore in sec. 13.4 (c) excluded important legal areas typically dominated by customary law, such as adoption, marriage, divorce, burial, inheritance or other matters of personal law wholly from protection against discrimination.

With respect to Mozambique, MOC has no less than two provisions stating the basic principle of non-discrimination, namely art. 66 and art. 69.

They complement each other in the sense that while MOC art. 66 declares that all citizens are equal before the law and shall enjoy the same rights and be subject to the same duties, art. 69 criminalizes "all acts intended to undermine national unity, to disturb social harmony or to create divisions of privilege or discrimination".

Both provisions then list a number of criteria for discrimination, which are almost identical in art. 66 and 69, but vary somewhat from those found in AC and in the other Constitutions. In relation to AC the terms colour, race, sex and religion are the same; AC speaks of national or social origin and ethnic group, while MOC uses the phrases ethnic origin and place of birth. With the addition of the criteria of social position, profession, educational level and legal status of one's parent, which are unique to this instrument, MOC fulfils or even goes beyond this part of AC sec. 2.

Art. 69, but not art. 66, furthermore adds the term physical or mental ability, corresponding to the principle in AC art. 18.4 on the rights of the elderly or the handicapped. On the other hand MOC art. 66 and 69 omit some very important aspects of discrimination, such as language or political or other opinion, both of which reflect situations where discrimination is highly likely to occur. Examples hereof would be denial of the right for children belonging to linguistic or ethnic minorities to receive primary education in their own language, and the affording of preferential treatment and various perks to members of a political organization, and it is therefore unfortunate that MOC does not provide explicit guarantees against this. Accordingly, it will therefore be the obligation of the legislative, the executive and the judiciary branches of Mozambican society to pay particular attention to such situations arising, in order to prevent a violation of AC art. 2.

The general provisions in both MAC and MOC protecting against discrimination are formulated as being absolute, in the sense that they must be respected at all times, in all situations and in all areas of legislation. In contrast hereto is BC sec. 3.2, which must be viewed in conjunction with BC sec. 15. The latter regulates in greater detail the question of discrimination, and states that the provisions of the chapter of the Constitution shall have effect for the purpose of affording protection to the rights and freedoms "subject to such limitations of that protection as are contained in those provisions, being limitations designed to ensure that the enjoyment of the said rights and freedoms by any individual does not prejudice the rights and freedoms of others or *the public interest*".[146]

Such limitations can be found elsewhere in sec. 15, where sub-sec. 2 states that "no person shall be treated in a discriminatory manner by any person acting by virtue of any written law or in the performance of the functions of any public office or any public authority". Thus the protection of sec. 15 is limited to relations between individuals and representatives of the state, while relations between private individuals fall outside the sphere of regulation in the Constitution, and are regulated by the various provisions of other laws.[147]

The further and more significant limitations, however, are inherent in the formulation of sub-sec. 3, defining the term "discriminatory" as "affording different treatment to different persons, attributable wholly or mainly to their respective descriptions by race, tribe, place of origin, political opinions, colour or creed". This formulation is hereby leaving out prohibition of discrimination on the basis of language, fortune and, most important, sex. On this basis it might be argued that it is legitimate, according to art. 15 if not art. 3 of the Botswana Constitution, to discriminate against women in such important areas as citizenship, public housing, employment in government, social benefits and education.[148] A more in-depth examination of these questions is found in the last section of this chapter.

---

146. This accentuation is my own.
147. This is in conformity with one of the fundamental characteristics of human rights regulation in general, and does not give rise to any concern. However, a question which would be of interest, but one which will not be dealt with further at this point, is whether it would be possible to apply art. 3 to cases between individuals, based on the principle of Drittwirkung, or if the Bill of Rights in the Constitution can only apply, by virtue of the very nature of constitutional provisions, to the relations between state and individual.
148. Unity Dow vs. Attorney General, High Court of Botswana, Misca. 124/90.

B. Women's equality and human rights

AC art. 18.3

One provision which should be viewed in conjunction with AC art. 2 and 3, is art. 18 sec. 2, according to which "The State shall ensure the elimination of every discrimination against women". This can be seen as an elaboration of the prohibition against discrimination on the basis of sex stated in AC art. 2, enforced by the emphasis on the legal aspects hereof in AC art. 3. This provision should be interpreted as encompassing both the passive obligation for the State to refrain from any such act, as well as its duty to actively take necessary steps to eliminate discrimination against women.

This article is interesting in an African context, since discrimination against women is a traditional practice still prevalent in many African societies, in spite of modern legal provisions to the contrary.[149] Also it is particularly relevant to this particular study, since this is one of the areas where Botswana in particular has been criticized for not complying fully with the provisions of the African Charter, as will be looked at in details below.

This is the other of two examples, the first being AC sec. 12.3 on the right to seek asylum, where AC has a general reference to other international declarations and conventions. The discussion to which extent states party to the African Charter will be legally bound by an international instrument, such as the UN Convention on the Eradication of All Forms of Discrimination against Women, which they have not ratified, can be found in that chapter. It is particularly relevant in relation to Mozambique and Botswana neither of whom have ratified CEDAW, in contrast to Malawi which is a party to this instrument.

BC sec. 15, MAC sec. 24, MOC art. 57 and 67

While BC's introductory sec. 3 has a reference to discrimination on the basis of sex, BC sec. 15 on discrimination in general does not mention sex among its criteria, and this question was dealt with in the recent Unity Dow case[150] regarding discrimination against women in the area of citizenship, referred in detail below. Here Counsel for the defendant argued that since

---

149. D'sa, 1986, p. 115.
150. The Attorney General vs. Unity Dow, Court of Appeal, Civil Appeal no. 4/91.

Individual Civil and Political Rights and Freedoms 191

BC art. 15 did not include sex, discrimination on this basis did not constitute a breach of the Constitution. The judge, however, in the first instance chose to see BC art. 15 as an interpretation clause which gave examples rather than limit the scope of protection. He pointed out that the provision would have to be interpreted in accordance with the spirit of art. 3, and therefore declared that discrimination on the basis of sex did constitute a violation of the provisions of the Constitution of Botswana. This position was also taken by the majority of the judges in the appeal case.[151]

The formulation of BC sec. 15 indicates a failure by Botswana to comply with the above mentioned art. 19 sub-sec. 3 of the African Charter, which declares that "The State shall ensure the elimination of every discrimination against women and also ensure the protection of the rights of the woman - as stipulated in international conventions". According to this provision it would be the duty of the State of Botswana, in accordance with

---

151. This is a situation strongly influenced by the traditional notion of women as having a status of dependence on men, with the married woman legally a minor under her husband's dominance and without the ability to act without his consent in questions regarding finances and law. I have been told, but not able to verify, that it may have some significance that in Setswana, the national language understood by the general majority of the nation, there is no grammatical distinction between the two sexes. Subsequently distinct terms for "he" and "she", or "his" or "her", would not exist, and the language to a large degree relies on the traditional diversion of female and male occupations and tasks, which were fairly consistent in earlier times, as a way of distinguishing between sexes. This changing of such fixed roles and concepts now subject to the changing of time may, at best, cause curious results and misunderstandings in various fields of life based on the traditional concept of language. An illustrating anecdote, which was referred to me in 1990, concerned a recent case in a Magistrates Court regarding the question of child support in a case where the parents were unmarried. While the woman had very little income and needed financial assistance from the man in order to support the child, the man had a quite large flow of income from a small-scale beer-brewing industry, an occupation which used to be the privilege of women only. The Court confused the situation of the man and woman, on the basis of the traditional roles and occupation and the lack of distinction in terms between female and male, and ruled that there would be no financial assistance to the woman since she allegedly had a substantial income from the brewery, while the man was without any significant income ! This consistency, however, is breaking up as a result of the development of Botswana into a modern industrialized and urbane society, where men and women with few exceptions are eligible to equal jobs and positions. It is further enforced by the widespread existence of female-headed households, caused by a substantial frequency of the men working as migrant workers in South Africa and remote parts of the country for most of the year.

AC art. 18 subsection 3, to change the constitutional provisions in a way that discrimination on the grounds of sex is no longer allowed or condoned by the constitution, and in order to eliminate the discrepancies between the formulation of BC sec. 15 and 3, so that both of them include the concept of sex.

Another problematic aspect is the above mentioned sec. 15 sub-sec. 4, which exempts a number of legal areas from the prohibition against discrimination on any basis. The most significant of these are sub-sec. (c) and (d), where the former exempts the areas regarding adoption, marriage, divorce, burial, devolution of property on death or other matters in general. Sub-sec. (d) states that the entire area regulated by customary law applicable to a particular race, community or tribe is exempted from the prohibition against discrimination of any kind, whether provisions already existing in common law have to be set aside, or if the issue is left to be dealt with exclusively under customary law. These represent some of the areas which are of a high significance in everyday life, where women may already experience disadvantages.

This position, based on the legal and practical implications of the formulation and layout of sec. 15, makes only one conclusion possible, namely that BC sec. 15 is in conflict both with the above mentioned principle against discrimination on any basis, including sex, as stated in BC art. 3, and with art. 2 of AC on freedom from discrimination. In the section below some particular areas of Botswana's legislation will be examined, with a view to determining the extent of which the provisions herein reflect a tendency towards affording a different legal position to women because of their sex.

None of the 1960s Constitutions of other Commonwealth African states such as Uganda, Kenya or Nigeria included the concept of sex in the specific anti-discrimination clauses, nor did MIC sec. 13 which is identical to that of BC. Therefore it should be viewed not so much as an intended omission on behalf of the drafters of BC in particular, but rather as a reflection of the general attitudes relating to the question of women's equality in law and reality which prevailed in an African context at the time. Accordingly, a comparison with MAC and MOC reveals that this is perhaps one of the areas where the scope of constitutional protection differs most strongly, since both of the younger instruments, in line with AC, have particular articles protecting the rights of women.

With respect to Malawi, we see that the changes in international prioritization of women's rights since the 1960s are reflected in the higher degree of protection in the new Constitution.[152] MAC sec. 24.1 initially declares that "Women have the right to full and equal protection by the law, and have the right not to be discriminated against on the basis of their gender or marital status". The formulation of this provision indicates that not only shall the State refrain from acting in a discriminatory manner, but it shall also actively protect women's equality through legislative as well as practical measures. An important and appropriate addition is marital status as an independent basis for discrimination, since an unmarried woman of mature age may enjoy fair equality of status with men, but may lose a large scope hereof the moment she enters into marriage, as shown in relation to Botswana below.

The protectional measures of MAC sec. 24 shall include, but may presumably not be limited to, womens' equal rights in a number of areas of the law. Sec. 24.1 (a) deals with civil law issues including women's legal capacity to enter into contracts, and to acquire and maintain property rights independently and in association with others regardless of their marital status. Also a woman's equal capacity in relation to custody, guardianship, care and decision making over her children, as well as the right to acquire and retain citizenship and nationality, are included. Finally, sub-sec. (b) states that in case of dissolution of marriage, women shall have equal right to a fair disposition of property held jointly with the husband and to fair maintenance considering all of the circumstances and, in particular, the means of their former husbands as well as the needs of any children. What is missing from this provision is, as stated above in relation to the section on participation in democracy, an inclusion of the whole area of public life, where women may need material as well as legislative support in the form of affirmative action etc. in order to participate fully in the democratic process on an equal basis with men.[153] Even though such initiatives to some extent may be seen to be comprised by sec. 24 in general, the specific

---

152. Attempts were made to emulate the Convention on the Elimination of All Forms of Discrimination Against Women from 1967, to which Malawi is a party. These attempts were, however, only partly successful; Kamchedzera, 1995.

153. This is important in light of the fact that women in Malawi are in fact in a highly inadvantageous position, reflected in the fact that their illiteracy rate is 67 of the 85 per cent of illiterate people in Malawi, and increasing in spite of the opposite decreasing trend seen in other parts of the world. Less than 1 per cent of the women in Malawi actively participate in decision making organs such as Parliament, government, the diplomatic service and other local representations; Women's World Banking Malawi Affiliate, 1995.

and articulated inclusion hereof would have been a powerful statement as well as a legal ice breaker in this area.

MAC sec. 24.2, corresponding to the general non-discrimination clause in sec. 20.2, embodies the principle of *lex superior* by stating that any law that discriminates against women on the basis of their gender or marital status shall be invalid. Furthermore, legislation shall be passed "to eliminate customs and practices" that discriminate against women, referring in particular to sexual abuse, harassment and violence, discrimination in work, business and public affairs, and deprivation of property including that which is obtained by inheritance. The provision seems to be particularly suited to deal with customary law, and may be seen as an *en bloc* invalidation of large areas hereof. The good news is that the area of public life is included as requested above, and that the provision meets the state's obligation in AC sec. 1; the bad news is that sec. 24.2, in contrast to MAC sec. 20.2, does not intend to declare such practices criminal or make them illegal beyond the context of sec. 24 in general. Therefore the latter part of this section shall be seen as a declaration of intent with a noble aim, but without a significant independent impact on women's legal rights and status.

In MOC, particular protection of the rights of women is primarily found in art. 67, which states that "men and women shall be equal before the law in all spheres of political, economic, social and cultural life". As such, this provision has the advantage of being comprehensive enough to avoid the interpretative difficulties arising from the corresponding provisions of BC and MAC, but therefore also the disadvantage of not clarifying more precisely the conditions and situations where it may be applied.

While this article deals with the protective aspect, sec. 57 concerns itself with a more general approach, stating in sec. 1 that "The State shall promote and support the emancipation of women and shall act to increase the role of women in society", and hereby realizing the importance of the governments' active participation in assuring women status and opportunities equal to that of men.

Sec. 2 and the first part of sec. 3 reflect a political statement unique to this instrument, by recognizing the participation of women in the military field, both in relation to the national liberation process over the last decades and in the ongoing defence of the nation.

A significant addition to sec. 1, however, is the last part of sec. 3, according to which the state shall "encourage and hold in high esteem the participation of women - in all spheres of the country's political, economic, social and cultural activity". Even though the same argument as above may be presented here, that limited significance on the protection of women's legal status and rights is added, the provision nonetheless serves as an indication of the positive intentions which the drafters of MOC had in this area, and as a strengthening of MOC's other provisions addressing discrimination against women.

Discrimination on the basis of sex in the legislation of Botswana

In the following a number of areas of legislation will be examined, all of which are important to the status of women. This is done in relation to Botswana only, since BC does not sufficiently prevent discrimination on the basis of sex as stated above.

Citizenship This is an area which has undergone a series of important changes since the early 1980s, particularly with respect to the rights of women to pass on their citizenship to their children.

Before 1982, provisions regarding citizenship were included in BC, forming a separate chapter of 10 articles succeeding the Bill of Rights. At that time, the provisions recognized the right of every child born in the country to Botswana citizenship, regardless of the nationality of the mother and her residence at the time of birth. The child had the same opportunity to become a Botswana citizen as long as the father was a citizen, even though it was born outside the country. BC thus gave different treatment to men and women, in the sense that a Motswana woman married to a foreigner did not automatically pass on her citizenship to her child, while this was the case of the Botswana citizen father. Still, the problem was not as serious as it would later become, because as long as the birth took place within the territory of Botswana, women married to foreigners could still pass their citizenship to their children.

At the end of the 1970s the Law Reform Committee (LRF)[154] was given the task of looking into different areas of legislation, including the various provisions of the Citizenship regulations, and in 1980 the Committee submitted its report based on a survey carried out in a number of localities. One of the issues dealt with here was the status of children born

---

154. The Law Reform Committee is one of nine Select Committees of the National Assembly, and its task is to review legislations, implement the public's views on existing or proposed laws, and to submit its observations and recommendations to the National Assembly. It is appointed every 5 years, and consists of the Attorney General and seven members of Parliament.

abroad whose parents were both Botswana citizens, and those whose mothers were unmarried. According to the existing provisions, such children could only acquire citizenship by naturalization, but in accordance with the views expressed by the population, the Commission recommended that citizenship by birth should be replaced by a general concept of citizenship by descent.[155] This was done with a particular view to reducing cases of dual citizenship, because, it was feared, such persons might be less loyal to Botswana.

These changes had the effect that the provisions of the 1982 Citizenship law became more liberal towards children born outside Botswana, since they would now acquire their father's or unmarried mother's citizenship regardless of place of birth. On the other hand they also became more restrictive in the contrary case where a person born in Botswana of a non-citizen father would no longer acquire Botswana citizenship if he or she also acquired that of the father. This last provision meant that a child born of a mother who was citizen of Botswana, and a father who was not, could still chose to claim Botswana citizenship if he or she did not at the same time take that of his or her father. Thus, according to the 1982 Citizenship Act, a principal difference between the position of women and men in relation to their marriage to aliens and their children's citizenship was established: the children of citizen mothers had to chose citizenship at birth, while those of citizen fathers were allowed to uphold dual citizenship right up to the age of 21.

However, the situation deteriorated in 1984, when the Citizenship law was amended again, and sec. 4 then read as follows:

"A person born in Botswana shall be a citizen of Botswana by birth and descent if, at the time of his birth -
    (a)   his father was a citizen of Botswana;
    (b)   in the case of a person born out of wedlock, his mother was a citizen of Botswana."

The concept of citizenship by birth alone was hereby abolished, since similar provisions, in sec. 5, applied to persons born outside Botswana.

The gravest effect was that the option of dual citizenship, which had previously been allowed for those children of citizen mothers and alien

---

155. Report of the Law Reform Committee, 1980.

fathers who had renounced their father's citizenship, was no longer available. This, in turn, meant that there was no way these women could pass on their citizenship to their children, leading to a state of clear discrimination between the status of men and women.[156]

This provision was absolute, allowing for no exception of any kind, and the significant implication hereof is that a person had no way of acquiring status as a citizen of Botswana, if at the time of his birth his mother was a citizen of Botswana but his father was a foreigner. This was the case regardless of the place of birth or of the domicile of one or both parents, and whether or not the father has any citizenship to pass on to his children, either because his country only recognized citizenship by birth, or because he was stateless or a refugee whose citizenship may be lost. In any of these cases, the child may thus formally or in effect become stateless.

It is clear that such a lack of citizenship status has profound effects and implications not only on the child itself, but also on the mother, furthermore, it would be justified to claim that this provision endangers the full enjoyment of a number of other human rights and freedoms otherwise established in BC.[157] One of the most significant hereof is freedom of movement, since the mother is unable to travel in or out of the country alone with her children, because they cannot be registered in her passport. Another example is freedom from degrading treatment, since the children are, in fact, given a status of "second-class residents" in a place which they in every other respect regards as their only home. In order to stay in Botswana they have to obtain residence permits subject to renewal every 90 days and given at the will of the authorities, they are also not allowed to receive bursaries to the University, or to be enrolled in or attend a college or stay in a hostel, unless they are citizens of Botswana.[158]

Not only would these conditions seem to contravene human rights

---

156. Botswana did not ratify the African Charter until 17 July 1986, little more than 3 months prior to the coming into force of the Charter, and without a preceding signature, so for this reason it was not bound by the provisions herein before that time. If such a signature had taken place before the amendments of the Citizenship law in 1984, one might have argued that art. 18 of the Vienna Convention on the Law of Treaties would apply, according to which the states in an interim period such as this one, have the duty to refrain from taking legislative action in violation of the letter or spirit of the instrument.

157. This was also upheld and established in the Dow-case.

158. Teacher Training College Regulations, under section 29 of the Education Act, S.I. 98 1978, section 7.2.

provisions of the Constitution such as freedom of movement, as mentioned above, but also a number of the provisions on economic and social rights in the African Charter, particularly art. 17.1, on the right to education, and art. 13 sec. 1 and 2 on the right to equal access to public property and service. The ambiguity of AC art. 13, however, makes it difficult to determine whether such a conclusion is correct, insofar as it distinguishes between, on the one hand, the rights of *citizens* to equal access to *public service* (art. 13.2), and on the other hand the right for *individuals* to equal access to public property *and services* "in strict equality of all *persons* before the law" (art. 13.3).

It is clear that art. 13.2, with the use of the term citizen, aims at a situation exemplified in the provisions of Botswana's legislation, where the aim has been to give citizens first priority over others with regard to access to various public resources, particular when these may be limited, and consequently there is no conflict between the two instruments at this particular point. The problem arises from the interpretation of art. 13.3, which uses the terms of individual and persons, e.g. a much wider interpretation than in art. 13.2, and one which would not necessarily rule out non-citizen children with lawful residence permits. It would even give them the right to enjoy public services in an equal basis with children who are citizens of Botswana, in which case the provisions of the Teacher Training College Act, sec. 7.2, would be in contravention of AC art. 13.

There are, however, arguments against such an interpretation of art. 13.2. The first hereof is the clear indication in art. 13 by its use of different terms of personality that the drafters of the African Charter intended to allow for a distinction between those rights which were the prerogative of citizens, and the narrower scope of those to be accorded to everybody regardless of such status.

In this case, art. 13.3 would have to be interpreted in the light of art. 13.2, so that the emphasis in art. 13.3 would be on access to property and to various types of services generally available to the public, such as public transportation, rest rooms etc. This interpretation might even include institutions of education and health facilities subject to financial payment or compensation. Art. 13.2 on the other hand reserves the right for citizens only to certain state benefits such as free health care, pensions, and access to institutions of higher education. In both cases there would have to be equal access for all persons within those distinct groups defined by the provisions, such that art. 13.2 would preclude any discrimination between different types of citizens based on, for instance, their ethnic, social or religious affiliations. Art. 13.3 would aim at specific situations such as those known formerly in South Africa, where access to public facilities was restricted to "Whites Only", and not to all members of the public regardless of race.

In 1986, the Law Reform Committee again reviewed the Citizenship Act, with a view to looking into the arguments upheld by various women's groups that the law was discriminatory. After visiting 25 localities all over Botswana, soliciting the views of people in various communities on the matter, the Committee made the following conclusive statement: "The Committee read the 1982 Citizenship Act, clause by clause, to all the areas covered by the fact-finding mission. Each meeting saw unanimous support as it stands". It added, in a reference to the claims of the women's groups, that "while the Committee is not unmindful of these arguments and views, and while the Committee appreciates that these views may well represent a new trend in public opinion, the Committee believes that - these are a clear and unequivocal expression of the will of the people".[159]

Indeed, the views expressed by the majority of the people quoted in the survey state that the "natural order" of things is for children to adopt the nationality of the fathers and for women to follow their husbands. Even though one has to keep in mind the nature of such a survey, and the significant impact the mode of presentation of such issues would have on the answers and views expressed, the report still indicates that the Citizenship Act of 1982 follows the concepts of traditional beliefs. This does not, however, diminish the fact that it was at variance with AC art. 18.3, and with BC art. 3 on freedom from discrimination on the basis of sex.

This conclusion follows the verdict of the Unity Dow-case,[160] as mentioned above, where the first instance judge in 1990 solved the potential conflict between art. 3 and art. 15.3 of the Constitution, declaring that according to his opinion:

> "The effect of Section 15.3 is not restrictive to the definition but it extends the meaning of or is explanatory of the word "discriminatory", in that gives examples of different kinds of discrimination -
> Interpreting the subsection as limiting section (1) to the definition would nullify the spirit of the Constitution, because not to be discriminated against because of one's sex is in accordance with the guarantee of the fundamental liberties mentioned in the

---

159. "Report of the Law Reform Committee on Marriage Act, Law of Inheritance, Electoral Law and Citizenship Law; June to December, 1986", p. 13.f.
160. Unity Dow vs. Attorney General, High Court of Lobatse, misca. 124/90.

Constitution.
- It would be offensive to modern thinking and the spirit of the Constitution to find that the Constitution was framed deliberately to permit discrimination on the grounds of sex."

The case was brought to the Court of Appeal by the Attorney General, where three of 5 judges (presiding judge Amissah, Aguda and Bizos) concurred in the decision of the High Court. They found that a liberal interpretation of Constitutional provisions on individual human rights should be applied. Hereby BC sec. 15 should be seen as encompassing a prohibition against discrimination on the basis of sex also, in spite of its formulation. In addition hereto BC art. 3 serves as a substantial provision conferring rights and freedoms in its own respect. The State's appeal was therefore rejected, and sec. 4 of the Citizenship Act was declared *ultra vires*. Two of the judges, Schreiner and Puckrin, issued a minority judgment, rejecting the notion that BC sec. 15 should be read to include the term "sex", and stating that the status of BC sec. 3 was merely preambular. On this basis they would allow the appeal.[161]

As a direct consequence hereof[162], the Parliament (several years later) amended the Citizenship Act, so that sec. 4 and 5 read that "A person - shall be a citizen of Botswana - if, at the time of his birth, his father or mother was a citizen of Botswana". The Bill also amended sec. 6, 8 and 13 of the Act accordingly, and the amendment was declared to retrospective effect dating back to 30 November, the day before the commencement of the Act itself.

In the following other Botswana statutes will be looked at, providing examples of situations where women are treated in a different manner than men because of their gender.

Family law Within the spheres of family law, some of the provisions definitely prescribe different rules for men and women, indicating that the domination of the father and husband as head of the family is still prevalent.[163]

---

161. The Attorney General vs. Unity Dow, Court of Appeal Civil Appeal no. 4/91.
162. Memorandum on Citizenship (Amendment) Bill, no. 9 1995, which quotes the case Attorney-General vs. Unity Dow.
163. A general overview of problems for women in family law, including customary law, of Botswana and other Southern African countries is given by Armstrong et alia, WLSA Working Paper no. 7. See also Jensen/Poulsen 1993, with a particular inclusion of customary law and cultural relativism.

According to the Marriage Act[164] sec. 16, boys may marry from the age of 16, and girls already from the age of 14, but according to sec. 17 no person below 21 years may marry without the consent in writing of their parents or guardian, unless the person in question is already a widow or widower. In cases where the parents disagree, the consent of the father alone shall be sufficient, according to sec. 17 (i), which means that the mother has no ability to prevent her sons' or daughters' marriage against the will of her husband This gives the father/husband a large degree of supremacy compared to that of the mother in relation to the marriage of their children.[165] Sec. 17 (ii) prescribes that only the consent of the mother or guardian is necessary, when the child is illegitimate, and it must be viewed in connection with sub-sec. (iii), authorizing the consent of the marriage officer in cases where the parents' consent cannot be obtained for reasons other than mere unwillingness to give it.

The question is, what happens in a situation where the mother has either been separated, divorced from, or deserted by the child's father, and to what degree is her consent only sufficient then. This issue is closely related to the general problem of women's guardianship over their children, an area where there are no statutes, but where the Roman-Dutch principles apply. According to these principles the father would have the guardianship and retain it in case of divorce, even though the mother or her guardian would have custody of the child.[166]

A combination of the formulation of the provisions of the Marriage Act sec. 17 and the principles stated above would lead to the conclusion that the consent of the mother alone to her children's marriage is not sufficient in cases where she is married, regardless of the actual location of the father or the status of the marriage, while no such limitation would be placed on the father. This leads to the inescapable conclusion that these provisions violate the constitutional provisions prohibiting discrimination on the basis of sex. They also violate AC's art. 18, as stated above.

Other relevant provisions include sec. 3 of the Affiliation Proceedings Act. (APA)[167] According to this provision a single woman who is with child or who has been delivered of an illegitimate child may apply, upon

---

164. Marriage Act, Law 42 of 1964.
165. Observe that the lack of consent of both parties involved in a cause for nullification of the marriage, according to the Matrimonial Causes Act, no. 1 1973, art. 22.3.f.
166. Armstrong ed., 1990, p. 27f.
167. Affiliations Proceedings Act, no. 50 1970, amended by Act 31, 1977.

complaint in writing, to a magistrate for a summons to be served on the man alleged by her to be the father of the child, thereby setting in motion procedures to determine the paternity.

Sec. 2 of the Act, defines the term "single woman" as applying also to a married woman who is "living apart" from her husband, without prescribing further the extent or nature of the separation. The important consequence of this provision is that it allows for a circumvention of the recognized principle of "*Pater est nuptiae demonstrant*", that the husband is always presumed to be the father of a child born during the marriage.[168] The woman may now initiate affiliation proceedings against a person other than her husband, when it can be proven and upheld that a state of separation existed between the spouses. Sec. 4 (1) of APA limits the time where such complaints can be presented to 12 months after the birth, unless undue influence by the man not to make the complaint has been exercised. Sec. 6 (1) provides that both the evidence of the woman and by or on behalf of the man must be heard, regardless of his consent to or denial of the paternity.

Sec. 6.3 authorizes the court to issue an order requiring the father to pay a sum of money, which may either be paid weekly or monthly, and limits the amount to 40 pula/month or the equivalent 10 pula/week, or a lump sum of money once and for all, the amount of which is to be determined by the court. The limitations upon the court may give rise to some disadvantage, since the Court cannot go beyond these rather low limits even in cases where it would seem appropriate, for instance if the father has a high financial status. In this case the Court will have to resort to the second solution, according to sec. 6.3 (c), and award a sum of money once and for all.

This would often put the woman and child in the most advantageous position, not only because of the size of the amount, but because there is a general problem of enforcement of such orders.[169] Since only a minority of those orders are fulfilled beyond 6 months, after which the payments, at best, become irregular, most women would be in a more advantageous position by accepting the lump sum of money, even though this may

---

168. See Armstrong ed., 1990, p. 28, which describes the prevalence of this concept, to the extent that the common law prescribed that no evidence with the effect of bastardizing such a child was admissible. The text mentions both the earlier case law confirming this, and the statute which has now changed the position and allowed it, the Evidence in Civil Proceeding (Amendment) Act (No. 26 of 1977).

169. Armstrong ed., 1990, opr. cit.

amount to a significantly smaller sum than that which is paid (ir-)regularly over a longer period of time.

These considerations, regarding enforcement of the payment order and lack of fulfilment hereof, apply in a similar way to the question of alimony in case of divorce or nullification of the marriage, regulated in the Matrimonial Causes Act (MCA) of 1973.[170] Sec. 25 of the Act states that a wife may be awarded alimony from her husband, supplemented by sec. 28 of the Act providing for the maintenance and custody of children.

Sec. 25.2 declares that such alimony may either be given in the form of a gross or annual sum of money for the rest of the woman's life, the amount of which is to be deemed reasonable by the court with due regards to her fortune, his ability and the conduct of the parties. It may also take the form of a periodical sum for her maintenance or support, as deemed reasonable by the Court, in addition to or instead of the amount mentioned above.

The sole ground for divorce is the irretrievable breakdown of the marriage, and sec. 15 of the Marriage Act (MA) specifies four factors which may be invoked: (i) the adultery of the defendant which has caused life to be intolerable for the plaintiff, (ii) such behaviour on the part of the defendant that the plaintiff cannot reasonably be expected to live with him or her, (iii) desertion by the defendant for a period of at least two years immediately preceding the action, and (iv) that the parties have lived apart for two years preceding the action, along with the consent of the defendant; a provision which is gender-neutral in formulation, if not always in effect.

The final provision to be dealt with here is another provision of the Matrimonial Causes Act (MCA) which distinguishes between men and women, sec. 22.3 (d), on nullification of marriage, which among a variety of otherwise gender-neutral provisions allows for, as a ground of nullification, "that the defendant was at the time of the marriage pregnant by some person other than the plaintiff". This provision must be seen in light of the lack of a corresponding provision giving the woman the option of having her marriage nullified in cases where proof existed that the husband was, at the time of the marriage, either already a father or expecting to be, or was burdened with obligations regarding child maintenance etc., without the consent or even knowledge of the woman.

Property Law Moving into the area of discrimination against women under property law, there are four Acts concerning the issues of married persons

---

170. Matrimonial Causes Act, no. 1, 1973.

property, deeds registration, succession, and administration of estates.

The first of these, the Married Persons Property Act (MPPA),[171] states in sec. 2 that the matrimonial domicile is that of the husband at the time of the marriage, without an opportunity for the spouses to choose that of the woman or a third party. The most significant provision of this Act is sec. 3, which states that the presumption of all marriages entered into since the commencement of this Act shall be out of community of property and community of profit and loss, shall apply. This stands, unless the parties have expressed their clear intention, in writing and before the authorities, that community of property shall apply.

Before the commencement of this Act, this was decided under Roman-Dutch law, according to which the reverse presumption was of the marriage being in community of property, unless the parties agreed otherwise. This latter principle still applies to marriage under customary law, according to the Married Persons Property Act art. 7. It is therefore no wonder that, in a great number of marriages, the status is not easily clarified, since it depends on the time of commencement of the marriage in combination with the chosen legal regime of common or customary law.

The effects on women are different and depending on their status and resources, as will be seen below, but, generally speaking, those women who have independent incomes and who make sure that immovable property is also registered in their name will benefit most from the provisions of the Act. Their status is fairly independent, while a housewife relying on her husband's income is in a more advantageous position with respect to recognition of her contributions to and participation in the family economy in a marriage registered in community of property.

Some of the more important consequences of the two versions are stated in the Deeds Registry Act (DRA).[172] Sec. 18 of the Act deals with transfer of property, and sub-sec. 3 hereof deals with the question of women married out of community of property, either as an effect of the MPPA, or because the parties have so agreed. The provision here states that a woman married out of community of property, who would otherwise have full legal capacity, shall be "assisted by her husband in executing any deed or other document" pertaining to her property, unless the marital power has been excluded or such assistance has been deemed necessary by the Registrar.

In relation to women married in community of property, even stricter

---

171. Married Persons Property Act, no. 69, 1970; latest amendment by Act 37, 1980.
172. Deeds Registry Act, Law 84, 1966.

rules apply according to sub-sec. 4, which states that immovable property shall not be transferred or ceded to her, except in cases where such property by law or clauses pertaining to a donation has been exempted from community of property, or in cases where the husband is a non-citizen of Botswana. Furthermore, sub-sec. 5 states that, in cases regarding immovable property belonging to a woman married in community of property before the commencement of this Act, her husband and he alone may deal with such property, unless the wife herself has been authorized to do so by an order of the court.

In contrast to these provisions stands sec. 90 of the same Act, which states that the competence to witness any document intended for registration or filing or production in the deeds registry shall be the same for male and female persons without distinction as to sex. This recognizes the legal competence of women in general, and makes the provisions stated above seem even more inappropriate.

Other limitations on a woman's legal competence are further illustrated in sec. 91.2 of the Administration of Estates Act,[173] which states that letters of confirmation shall not be granted to a woman married in community of property without the consent of her husband, or to a woman married out of community of property when the marital power of her husband is not excluded.

All these provisions effectively confirm the notion that women married in community of property have no independent power to acquire or dispose of immovable property, in contrast to their husbands' power to dispose both of his own share and her share of the joint estate. This would be the case if the legislation had placed husband and wife in the same position, but now it allows the husband to freely dispose of her share hereof without her consent or even qualifications with regards to her welfare or legitimate needs or interests. Therefore the legislation in this area must be deemed to be highly discriminatory and a violation of BC sec. 3 as well as the African Charter art. 18.

Furthermore, one might also argue that these provisions constitute a violation of BC art. 8.1 on freedom from compulsory interventions in one's interest in or right over property. Within this context it should be noted that the formulation of art. 14 of the African Charter guaranteeing the right to property allows for encroachment hereof in accordance with provisions of relevant laws, but only in the interest or public need or in the general

---

173. Administrations of Estates Act, No. 20/1972.

interest of the community. In such cases as those mentioned none of these requirements are fulfilled, and the right to property for the women should therefore stand uncontested.

Labour and Education Law On a formal level there are no limitations on the equal access of women to various fields of education or work, subject to those exceptions listed below.

One of two areas where women are subject to different treatment because of their sex is regulated through the Employment Act (EA),[174] where Part XII, sec. 114 through 124 contain a number of provisions on employment of females, one of the few examples in the legislation of Botswana where such particular provisions for women can be found. According to sec. 115, no woman is allowed to be employed for underground work in mines, except when she performs other tasks than manual labour such as management, health services, or works there during the course of her studies or on an occasional basis only and for reasons other than manual labour. The second restriction is found in sec. 116, according to which no female employee shall do industrial or agricultural work during the night, defining this, in sub-sec. 2, as the period between 10 p.m. and 6 a.m. and for a period of minimum 11 hours.

While these provisions were initially included in order to protect women against harsh working conditions, the women's groups of Botswana have objected to the provision, arguing that such protective measures are no longer needed in the light of women's changing roles. Instead they place women in a disadvantageous situation by excluding them from one of the major employment sectors, the mining industry.[175] Also, some women and in particular mothers of small children, might find it more convenient to work night hours. The provisions of sec. 115 and 155 of the EA are discriminatory, in accordance with the interpretation "offering different treatment on the basis of sex", and hereby constitute a violation of BC sec. 3 and AC art. 18. Furthermore, the provisions may also be in violation of AC art. 15, on the right for every individual to work under equitable and satisfactory conditions, insofar as they go against the interests of women by limiting their free choice of employment similar to that of the men.

Regarding maternity leave, women are not allowed to work for a period of 6 weeks before and 6 weeks after the delivery, according to sec.

---

174. Employment Act 29, 1982, S.I. 148, 1984.
175. Armstrong ed., 1990, p. 31.

117.1. of the EA, and her employer is obligated to pay her a minimum of 50t or 25 per cent of her basic pay, whichever is the greater amount, in accordance with sub-sec. 5 hereof. The maternity leave cannot be prolonged except in accordance with sec. 117.4, when the woman can provide medical evidence that she is unfit to return to work because of an illness arising from her confinement. Even in this case her leave can only be extended with two weeks to a period of 8 weeks after the confinement.

No provision regarding illness during the pregnancy and caused by it, which would make the woman unfit for work at an earlier stage of pregnancy, is included in the Act. Furthermore, a woman who fails to inform her employer of her knowledge or suspicion of pregnancy at the time of entering into the employment contract or at the beginning of her confinement, forfeits her right to maternity leave in accordance with sec. 119, unless she is able to show "good cause" for her failure. On the other hand sec. 123 of the Act provides a woman with the right to nurse in other ways feed her child for half-an-hour twice a day during her working hours, extending to a period of 6 months after her return to work. During this period her employer is obligated to pay her basic pay during that time.

Provisions relating to domestic workers, a field of employment mainly occupied by women, are contained in a separate set of regulations,[176] and are generally weaker than those applying to those working in other sectors. For instance, these individuals, who are mostly women, may be allowed to work up to 60 hours a week, in contrast to the maximum of 48 hours applying to other categories. They are entitled to four paid public holidays instead of eight, and, most important, they are not covered by the minimum wage regulations.[177]

With respect to women and education, the EA[178] contains no direct provisions giving different access for males and females to the educational system, and their respective position is therefore, technically speaking, identical. On the other hand, neither the Act nor other instruments seek to ensure that women are in reality given an equal access to various fields of education, by introducing measures of affirmative action in favour of women and girls.

A factor which would have the effect of hampering women and girls' full enjoyment of the right to education, is the attitude towards pregnancy

---

176. Employment Act (Domestic Employees) Regulations of 1987, S.I. 148, 1984.
177. Ibid.
178. Education Act Law No. 40, 1966, S.I. 4, 1975.

of schoolgirls, expressed in the various regulations under section 29 of the Education Act.

On the lower levels of education the provisions are the same, since both the Primary School Regulations (PSR)[179] sec. 14 and the Secondary Education Regulations (SER)[180] sec. 34 provide that if a pupil becomes pregnant, her guardian or parent shall withdraw her from school. She shall not be admitted to the same school again, and she may only be admitted to another school after at least one calendar year since the cessation of her pregnancy, and only upon written approval of the Permanent Secretary. Also, she is not allowed to write any examinations at any such type of school while she is pregnant or, with respect to Secondary Schools, before a minimum of six months have elapsed since the termination of her pregnancy.

Since abortion in Botswana is only permitted under very grave and particular circumstances, according to the Penal Code,[181] a girl or a young women would normally be required to go through with the pregnancy. As a consequence hereof she could be obliged to miss as long a period as more than a year of her secondary education, and more than two years of her primary school education, since she as a general rule must be admitted to the school no later than 9 days after the beginning of the term in accordance with sec. 5.1. of the PSR.

The Teacher Training College Regulations (TTCR)[182] contain similar provisions in art. 22, with the exception that the girl's return to school is not dependent on certain time-limits, but only on the approval of the Permanent Secretary. She is not allowed to write examinations at a college while

---

179. Education (Primary School) Regulations, under section 29 of the Education Act, 1980, S.I. 127, 1980.

180. Education (Government and Aided Secondary Schools) Regulations, under section 29 of the Education Act, 1978, S.I. 145, 1978.

181. The Penal Code, Law 2, 1964; sec. 160, 161 and 229. The absolute ban on abortion was modified through the Penal Code Amendment Act 1990, and a pregnancy may now be legitimately terminated within the first 16 weeks. However, the criteria to be fulfilled are that the pregnancy must result from rape, defilement or incest, that it presents an imminent danger to the life or health of the women, or that it has been established that the child, if born, would suffer from a serious physical or mental handicap. This means that abortion will only be an option to very few women in very distressing situations.

182. Teacher Training College Regulations under section 29 of the Education Act, 1978, S.I. 98, 1978.

she is pregnant and until at least 6 weeks after such pregnancy has ceased, with the exception of her second-year final examinations, and then only in cases where she has satisfied all the requirements of teaching practice.

Recently, however, the Botswana Court of Appeal ruled that similar provisions in the Molepolole College of Education Regulations were not, as claimed by the College and accepted by the High Court, protective measures to the mother and child and an encouragement of "a well planned maternity leave" but in reality were intended as a form of punishment for unmarried young mothers. This is particularly so since the occurrence of a second pregnancy would mean permanent expulsion, and married students would not be subjected to similar measures insofar as such instances would be regarded as "particular cases" in which the rules could be set aside. The Court of Appeal followed its progressive line laid down in the Unity Dow-case mentioned above, ruling that the provision was discriminatory against women and therefore a violation against BC sec. 3 and 15.[183]

It is not only the girls or young women, who have to bear the consequences of early pregnancy - all three instruments state, in the same articles as those mentioned above, that any student responsible for the pregnancy of a fellow student shall be withdrawn from school. He shall, without any of the time limits applying to the female students, only be allowed to return to or attend other schools at the discretion of the Permanent Secretary.

Regarding the writing of examinations, the rules applying to all three levels are different: At the primary level there are no provisions barring the male student from writing such examinations. At the secondary level, sec. 35 specifically declares that he shall not be allowed to write such examinations during that academic year, unless with the authorization of the Minister. The TTCR in contrast hereto are the most liberal, by stating in sec. 23 that a person responsible for the pregnancy of another student shall not be refused permission to write such examination in spite of his expulsion, unless the Permanent Secretary authorizes such refusal.

These rules allow for widespread differences in effect and consequences for boys and girls in the education system, a problem which is not insignificant in light of the substantive number of teenage pregnancies. Also it would appear problematic and give rise to some concern that the rules applying to girls are fixed and contrary to those applying to boys. Even

---

183. Student Representative Council, Molepolole College of Education vs. Attorney General of Botswana. Unreported, Civil Appeal No. 13, Misca No. 396 of 1993. Judgment was delivered on 31 January, 1995. Commentary, E. K. Quansah, 1995.

though there has been an increasing tendency to also hold the boys and men responsible in cases of schoolgirl pregnancies[184] and not just expel the girls, it seems clear that the rules applying are discriminatory in formulation as well as effect, and that they hereby constitute a violation of BC sec. 3 as well as AC art. 18.

Furthermore, one may add the view that it can be expected that a large number of the girls do not resume their studies or schooling after the termination of the pregnancy for a number of obvious reasons. Often it will not be neither possible nor practical to attend a different secondary school, as required by the provisions, due to problems relating to location, availability, child care etc. As such the provisions of, at least, the PSR are also in violation of AC art. 17.1 on the right to education. This seems a fair argument, even though the weakness of AC art. 17.1 is partly that it does not define any closer the term education in relation to various levels, freedom from school fees etc., and partly that it must be viewed in light of art. 17.3. This latter article states that "The promotion and protection of morals and traditional values recognized by the community shall be the duty of the State", and a clear example hereof are the regulations dealt with above, clearly designed to discourage teenage pregnancies and pre-marital sexual relations.

Conclusion The overall picture of the status of women in Botswana in relation to all the areas covered above, which in conjunction influence almost all aspects of life, is that the occurrence of discrimination on the basis of sex as prohibited by BC sec. 3 and AC art. 18, is widespread and needs to be taken seriously in view of Botswana's obligation to ensure the provisions of AC in national law.

Some of the areas listed above, and in particular those concerning family law, are governed by a large amount of provisions allowing for or directly prescribing different treatment for women and men. The underlying notion seems to reflect a perception of woman's subordination and dependency on the man. Hereby women are put in a position of direct disadvantage with respect to their independent life as an equal participant in the life of the community.

Combined with provisions such as those relating to education and employment of women, where the effect of the discrimination is of a more general and long-term detriment of women's position in society, as well as

---

184. Armstron ed., 1990, p. 32.

the individual's ability to maintain herself and her family, the overall picture of women's legal status in Botswana is one of inequality and disadvantage.

This suggests that several of the provisions of both AC and BC are being violated, and not just the prohibition of discrimination against women in AC art. 18 and BC sec. 3. It would be justified to conclude, for instance, that also the provisions in AC art. 3 on principles of equality before the law and equal protection by the law, provisions which have no counterpart in BC, are subject to violation by the provisions of the Botswana legislation listed above.

Also, some of the civil and political rights and freedoms protected by the provisions of AC and BC, such as freedom of movement and the right to property, would possibly be violated by the nature of the provisions, which has already been mentioned above.

Finally, the provisions could also be claimed as endangering the full enjoyment of the economic and social rights listed in AC art. 15 through 17, such as the right to education and health, for women and children endangered by the Citizenship and Education Acts as mentioned above. The consequences hereof are particularly serious, since those rights are not contained in the Constitution and, consequently, infringements hereof in various fields of legislation are not counter-balanced by constitutional provisions, contrary to most of the civil and political rights.

7 Other provisions

In the following is given a short overview of 3 distinctions of material provisions in the African Charter, the individual economic, social and cultural rights, the peoples' rights, and the catalogue of individual duties.

Different from the civil and political right analyzed above, these provisions have no counterparts in BC, which follows the model established by the ECHR. To a different extent, and with some variation, we find them reflected in both MAC and MOC.

In addition to giving a short analysis of each of these rights in AC in relation to national law, the following chapter will focus on their correspondence with principles and provisions already established by other general human rights instruments. This is done to determine whether the claim that many of these provisions are unique to the African Charter is valid, or if they can merely be seen as extensive elaborations of basic concepts found in the central international instruments and reflected at the national level as well.

Economic, social and cultural rights

Introduction

The African Charter does not distinguish sharply between the political and civil rights and freedoms on the one hand and the economic, social and cultural rights on the other hand. Still, some systematic presentation hereof is achieved, by placing the economic, social and cultural rights of the individual separately in art. 15 through 18, following the civil and political rights.

Another tendency recognized from the other human rights instruments, regional as well as international, is that the scope of articles concerning the economic, social and cultural rights is much more narrow than that of the civil and political rights. This taken into consideration, AC contains a fairly large number of these articles, consistent with the Preamble of the Charter, which state that "civil and political rights cannot be dissociated from economic, social and cultural rights in their conception as well as their universality", and "the satisfaction of economic, social and cultural rights is a guarantee for the enjoyment of civil and political rights".

At the regional level of regulation, neither ECHR nor AMCHR contain a catalogue of economic, social and cultural rights similar to that of AC.

The ECHR is entirely silent on this point, reflecting a traditional approach of distinguishing sharply between the civil and political rights and freedoms on the one hand and the economic, social and cultural rights on the other hand. All such concepts are therefore left to be dealt with in the relatively insignificant European Social Charter from 1961,[1] which shall not be discussed any further here.

The American Convention on Human Rights does mention, in art. 26, that the States Parties undertake to adopt measures of progressive development towards "the full realization of the rights implicit in the economic, social, educational, scientific, and cultural standards" set forth in the Charter of the OAS. In 1988 an Additional Protocol of San Salvador was added, which spells out in greater detail the various economic, social and cultural rights. These will also not be dealt with any further at this point.

This picture would indicate that the evolution has over time gone in the direction of greater integration between the different sets of rights.[2]

Rights and Freedoms

Work The first of the provisions on economic, social and cultural rights is AC art. 15, which states the right to work under equitable and satisfactory conditions. The article does not specify more closely the level and criteria of those standards, a feature which is enhanced by the other instruments' mentioning of a number of requirements related to working conditions. For instance, art. 23 of UD contains a provision similar to AC art. 15, but proceeds in art. 24 to declare also the right to rest and leisure, including reasonable limitation of working hours and periodic holidays with pay.

Art. 6 of the International Covenant on Economic, Social and Cultural Rights (ICESCR) also states the right to work, and includes an explicit provision on the corresponding duty of the state to provide technical and vocational training, social development and full employment. Furthermore,

---

1. Adopted by the European Council on 18 October, and entered into force on 26 February 1965.
2. Eide, in ed. Eide, Krause and Rosas, 1995, p. 23.

ICESCR art. 7 states the right to fair wages and enumeration, safe and healthy working conditions, to equal opportunity for everyone to be promoted, and to rest, leisure, limitation of working hours and periodic holiday with pay.

Given the elaborations in the other instruments, the African Charter shows up as a "frame", in which an implicit reference to the other instruments must be made, if the Charter shall have any effect at all. On the other hand it takes into account the present social and economic situation of the African countries today, where working conditions often are worsened by lack of information, equipment or knowledge and training.

The second part of art. 15 furthermore states the right to receive equal pay for equal work, the intention of which would be to support women as well as minority groups, and as such it should be viewed in conjunction with the general prohibition against discrimination of any kind in art. 2 dealt with in the previous chapter.

AC here differs from the ICESCR in its formulation, in the sense that the latter instrument directly mentions the right for women to receive equal pay. From a strictly legal perspective, one could be lead to interpret art. 15 as an exclusion of affirmative action, an interpretation supported by the extensive measures against discrimination of any kind whatsoever. Also, support for this interpretation can be found in the formulation of art. 18, which in sub-sec. 3 declares the protection of the right of women, but does not give the right "special measures" as for the aged and the disabled in sub-sec. 4. Still, from a more pragmatic point of view such an interpretation would be unnecessarily restrictive in cases where there is an opportunity for introducing a policy of appropriate and effective affirmative action for women and other groups.

Looking at the national Constitutions, we find that BC is silent, and that MAC and MOC both distinguish between the right to work in itself separate from provisions regulating labour practices.

With respect to the first, MAC sec. 29 states the right for every person to work and pursue a livelihood anywhere in Malawi as part of the right to engage in economic activities, an unequivocal declaration that the market economy will be dominant in the country.

Similarly, MOC declares in art. 88 sec. 1 and 2 that work shall be a right and a duty of all citizens regardless of sex, and that all citizens shall have the right to free choice of profession. The question of individual duties and their potentially negative implication is discussed more in detail below, but keeping in mind the problems in relation to women and work in

Botswana as outlined in the chapter on discrimination, this is a provision which would eliminate such questions arising in Mozambique. Furthermore, MOC art. 51 in relation to the general question of national economy, states that "labour shall merit respect and protection" and be the driving force of development, and that the State shall promote the just distribution of the proceeds of labour.

With respect to the second aspect, the actual labour rights falling more within the context of civil and political rights, both MAC and MOC contain provisions which correspond to, and even go far beyond, the rights found in AC art. 15.

Reflecting AC art. 15, MAC sec. 31.1 states the right to fair and safe labour practices and to fair remuneration, adding in sec. 31.3 the principle of non-discrimination particularly on the basis of gender, disability or race in relation to fair wages.

MOC art. 89 sec. 1 and 2 in a similar fashion declare that employees have the right to protection, safety and hygienic conditions at work, as well as the right to just payment in sec. 1.

In addition to these basic principles, MOC art. 91 grants to all employees the right to strike, but at the same time imposes the restriction that this right should be regulated by law, and states that some areas of essential services crucial to the "overriding needs" of society may be subject to particular limitations of this right. A similar provision, although briefer and less specific, is MAC sec.31.4 declaring that "the State shall take measures to ensure the right to withdraw labour".

Finally MOC art. 89 in sec. 1 goes beyond both AC and MAC in stating that all employees have the right to rest and to holidays, and adding in sec. 3 that employees may only be dismissed in accordance with the law. This instrument hereby comes closer than any of the other to a fulfilment of, for instance, UD art. 24 and ICESCR art. 7, even though several of the extensive provisions in the latter find no correspondence neither in AC nor in the African Constitutions of this study.

Health AC art. 16.1 states the right for every individual to enjoy "the best attainable state of physical and mental health".

This choice of formulation is a clear reflection of the fact that, in most cases, the economic and social rights cannot be defined as absolute rights, but rather as goals and ideals for the States to achieve in accordance with their own financial and administrative abilities. This provision is written from the recognition that most African states are rarely able to provide their peoples with a satisfactory standard of living.

The term is almost identical to the corresponding provision in ICESCR art. 12.1 ("the enjoyment of the highest attainable standard of physical and mental health"), and the UD art. 25 ("a standard of living adequate for the health and well-being of himself and his family").

Compare also the term "an adequate standard of living" and "the continuous improvement of living conditions" in the ICCPR art. 11.1, which has no counterpart provision in the African Charter.

UD art. 25 proceeds to elaborate on the conditions by mentioning the corresponding specific obligations for the state to provide food, housing, social security etc. In contrast hereto both of the legally binding instruments, AC and ICCPR, give more vague examples of areas in which states shall take steps to ensure the enjoyment of the right to health. As such, AC art. 16.2 states the obligations of the State to take "necessary measures" to protect the health of their people, and to ensure medical attention in case of sickness. Still, no provisions regarding social security or other special measures are included, in contrary to the provision of UD.

With respect to the national Constitutions, MAC has no direct provision stating the individual's right to physical or mental health, social benefits, adequate nutrition, health care etc. Still, looking to sec. 30 on the right to development, we find that this is formulated as an individual as well as a collective right, referring to "all persons and all peoples", and that this includes the right to social development. According to sec. 30.1 women, children and the disabled shall be give special consideration of this right, and the State shall take "all necessary measures" including equal opportunity to basic resources, health services, food and shelter among other things.

Finally, attention should be paid to MAC sec. 13 on "Principles of National Policy", according to which the State shall "actively promote the welfare and development of the people of Malawi by progressively adopting and implementing policies and legislation" aimed at gender equality, nutrition, health, the environment, rural life and education. Such policies should also be instituted and carried out for the benefit of such particular groups as the disabled, children, the family and the elderly. The importance between sec. 13 and the other sections on fundamental rights and freedoms in MAC is that while the latter constitute enforceable rights for the individual, sec. 13 is of a promotional nature, and should be viewed as a general declaration of intent supporting the rights and freedoms in chapter IV, rather than a legally enforceable obligation for the state.

It may very well be that the approach of Malawi in this respect is the most pragmatic, since it is evident that it would be very difficult for the State to fulfil even the most vaguely formulated rights of its citizens in this area due to its general level of poverty.[3] On the other hand it would have been an appropriate statement of intent to include, as a minimum, a formulation similar to that of AC art. 16, which entails a limited scope of State obligations as it stands.

According to MOC art. 94 all citizens shall have the right to medical and health care, within the terms of the law. This latter addition could accommodate differentiation with respect to level of income, age or special needs, or, if the right is extended to encompassing legally residing aliens as well, even restriction with respect to free health care etc. Attention must be paid, however, to the principle of non-discrimination, so that the dominant factor in the process of allocation of, often limited, resources is the actual needs of groups or individuals.

MOC art. 54 deals with the process related to art. 94, according to which a national health care service shall be organized with the procedures established by the law. It also states that the State shall promote the participation of citizens and institutions to raise the level of public health care and the system therefore seems to be structured in a way that the concerns mentioned in the preceding paragraph may well be avoided.

It should be noted that MOC art. 94 declares that not only do citizens have the right to health, they shall also have the duty to promote and preserve it. How such a duty would possibly be interpreted and implemented legally is unclear, and the danger is that it might be enforced too rigidly, and for instance used to deny medical care to persons with lung cancer or AIDS on the claim that they had brought it upon themselves by smoking or practising unsafe sex. In such cases it might very well be in conflict with the first part of art. 94 as well as other provisions in the Constitution, and it would therefore have to be applied in an empowering sense only.

Education In AC art. 17, section 1 states the right for every individual to education, again without further specifications on the conditions and criteria

---

3. Already in 1924 Malawi was described as "the poorest colony in Africa". It has been described as a Least Developed Country by the United Nations, has an Infant Mortality Rate of 178 and a life expectancy rate under 40, and less than one sixth of its estimated labour force is in recorded wage employment. CIIR Comment p. 7 and 18; CIA World Factbook, 1994.

to be fulfilled.

In contrast hereto stands the UD art. 26 and the ICESCR art. 13 sec. 1 and 2, which state that primary education shall be compulsory and available free to all, and that higher education should be generally accessible, with restrictions based solely on capacity, which should be expanded widely.

AC's art. 17.1 must be interpreted such that there is an obligation resting on the State to place education as one of the highest priorities, and to ensure as large a part as possible of its population access to free education without discrimination of any kind. On the other hand the formulation of AC art. is too vaguely formulated to serve as any effective guarantee hereof.

In the national Constitutions, MAC sec. 25 simply states that "all persons are entitled to education". This is perhaps an area where the general brevity of MAC's provisions is carried too far, even in light of the important addition that "primary education shall consist of at least 5 years of education" in sec. 2. The provision thus gives no right to free secondary, or for that matter even primary, education, and also does not apply the question of equal access and non-discrimination to this right beyond that which follows from the general provisions.

MOC art. 92 states that "In the Republic of Mozambique education shall be a right and a duty of all citizens", and adds in sec. 2 that the State shall promote greater and equal access to the enjoyment of this right by all citizens. Here, the same argument as presented above in relation to MAC sec. 25, that this provision only has limited effect because of its summaric formulation, is also valid. Also the physical aspect of education is contained in MOC art. 93, stating the citizens right to physical education and to sport as well as the State's obligation to promote these activities, a provision which has no correspondence in the other instruments. With respect to Mozambique's strategy for the fulfilment of this right, art. 52 sec. 1 and 2 state that a national educational system shall be developed, and an educational strategy promoted which aims towards national unity, eradication of illiteracy, mastering of science and technology, and at providing citizens "with moral and civic values". These are worthy aims, maybe a bit lofty, but nonetheless give a relatively clear and inspirational picture of Mozambique's visions in this area.

On the question of private schools and institutions of higher learning, MAC sec. 25.3 declares that they shall be permissible, provided that they are registered with a State department subject to legal regulations, and as long as it is ensured that the standard of learning is not inferior to that of State schools; one might add that the latter requirement in many cases is superfluous, since private schools may often provide a higher standard than those run, and more importantly financed, by the government. There is a close relationship between this right and for instance freedom of conscience and association, but in contrast to MOC, MAC is equally brief on these points and for instance does not address the right for religious communities to establish schools except in sec. 25.3.

A similar provision is MOC art. 52.3, according to which education provided by collective and other bodies shall operate in accordance with the law, and shall be subject to state supervision.

Culture AC art. 17.2. states the right for every individual to take part in the cultural life of his community. This principle is mentioned also in UD art. 27 and in ICCPR art. 15, where it has been supplemented in both cases by the right to enjoy the benefits of scientific progress and its applications. This latter right has not been included in the African Charter.

It is not absolutely clear what the scope and contents of art. 17.2 of the Charter are, but for instance the use of house arrest with the subsequent exclusion from social activities and association with others would constitute a breach with the intentions behind this article. Also, this right must be viewed in conjunction with the civil and political rights of expression, practice of religion and freedom of assembly, and with the obligation of the state in art. 17.3 to ensure the promotion and protection of morals and traditional values recognized by the community.

MAC sec. 26 states that every person shall have the right to participate in the cultural life. The corresponding provision in MOC is sec. 53, stating not the right but the general principle that the State shall promote the development of national culture and identity and shall guarantee free expression of the traditions and values of the society.

Additionally, MAC sec. 26 declares the right for a person to use the language of his or her choice, a provision which cannot be found in either AC and BC or in UD or ICESCR. The only exception is MOC art. 5, according to which Portuguese shall be the national language of Mozambique, adding the important sec. 2 according to which the State shall "esteem national languages", and promote their development as well as their increasing use as spoken languages and in the education of the people. Finally, MOC art. 53.2 obligates the State to "make Mozambican culture known internationally" and to take action to enable its people to benefit from the cultural achievements of other peoples. This provision is also unique to MOC, and the two young Constitutions of Mozambique and Malawi are herby far more progressive with respect to the protection of these rights than the other instruments used in this study.

The family AC art. 18 declares that "The family shall be the natural unit and basis of the society. It shall be protected by the state which shall take care of its physical health and moral". No corresponding provision is found in UD or ICESCR.

The same applies to AC art. 18 sec. 2, according to which the State shall have the duty to assist the family "which is the custodian of morals and traditional values recognized by the community". What form this "assistance" shall take is not defined, and critics could easily maintain that such a provision could be seen as legitimizing the State's interference in the individual's right to privacy. Interestingly enough, this latter right has not been included in its general form in the African Charter, similar to UD art. 12 and ICCPR art. 17 stating that "No one shall be subjected to arbitrary interference with his privacy, family, home or correspondence".[4] This is a clear expression of the characteristic African tradition of emphasizing the group rather than the individual, and is in line with the extensive catalogue of individual duties in AC sec. 27 through 29, which will be looked at below.

An interesting question relates to the definition of the term "family", which in the European context consists of parents and their children, and to some extent also the grandparents.[5] Possibly, the African Commission would decide that, in accordance with the custom and practices in most societies, the concept of family should also include other relatives, at least as long as some form of extended family unit can be defined.

Again, BC has no particular provision on the right of the family, in contrast to both MAC and MOC, where MAC sec. 22 reflects AC art. 18 by stating that "The family is the natural and fundamental group unit in society and is entitled to protection by society and the State". An addition, which goes beyond that of the other instruments is MAC sec. 22.2 declaring that "Each member of the family shall enjoy full and equal respect and shall be protected by law against all forms of neglect, cruelty and exploitation".

---

4. See ch. 6 on freedom of conscience for an overview of the national provisions on this right.
5. Marckx, ECourtHR decision 13 June 1979.

This section not only reflects the principle of equality, but also takes the responsibility of the State potentially far into the private domain, which is appropriate in relation to domestic violence against women and children.

Here, MOC is less expansive and merely declares in art. 55.1 that "The family is the basic unit of society", without attaching any particular individual rights to this principle. Protection hereof must therefore be found in the other more richly detailed provisions on women and children as well as social rights in general and the principle of non-discrimination.

The rights *of* the family are different from the right to *be* a family; even though AC in contrast to UD art. 16, ICESCR art. 10, and ECHR art. 12 does not specifically address this issue, both MAC and MOC contain provisions regulating various aspects hereof.

MAC sec. 22.3 declares the positive right to enter into marriage and to found a family, a right which belongs to all men and women over the age of eighteen according to sub-sec. 3 and 6 in conjunction.[6] The negative freedom from forced marriage is stated in MOC art. 55.3 as well as in MAC sec. 22.4, and closely related to this are the restrictions on marriage between persons under the age of eighteen. Here MAC sec. 22.7 stipulates that marriage for persons between the age of fifteen and eighteen shall only be entered into with the consent of their parents or guardians, and sec. 22.8 adds that the State shall actively encourage marriage between persons where either of them is under fifteen years.

Also MAC sec. 22.5 should be noted, according to which sub-sec. 3 and 4 shall apply to "all marriages at law, custom and marriages by repute or by permanent cohabitation". This provision is interesting, because this instrument does not in general take into account the existence of customary law, for instance in relation to women's rights and discrimination on the basis of gender as discussed above. Nonetheless, it has been recognized that a very liberal interpretation of the concept of marriage will have to be applied so that the protectional measures of MAC sec. 22 can be extended to cover customary law and traditional practices as well.

The extent of MOC art. 55 is more dubious in this respect, because apart from stating the general principle in sec. 1 that "The family is the basic unit of society", sec. 2 declares that "The State shall recognise and protect, in accordance with the law, marriage as the institution that secures

---

6. The linking of the rights of and the right to be a family may be very strong, thus "It is not unreasonable to conclude that the Constitution assumes that marriage is a condition for a family"; Kamchedzera, 1995.

the values of the family". If the definition of family follows that of MAC sec. 22.5, the protective measures in MOC art. 55.2 shall be viewed as beneficial to the individuals, since it means that rights to all forms of support can be derived from this. If, on the other hand, the law only accepts certain forms of marriage, such as that which is regulated by statute law only and excluding customary law, the provision may very well be not only in violation of the principle of non-discrimination and the right to cultural identity, but could also have unforeseen and potentially damaging consequences for persons married under one system or another.

Women AC art. 18.3 is an enhancement of art. 2, stating that all discrimination against women must be eliminated. This provision has been dealt with extensively in chapter 6, on freedom from discrimination, and will therefore not be looked at further in this context.

Children Closely related to the questions regarding the status of women and social issues in general is the welfare of children and the fulfilment of their special needs through protective legal provisions. This is expressed by AC art. 18.3, according to which the State shall protect the rights of the women and of the child "as stipulated in international declarations and conventions". The legal significance of such a reference has been discussed above,[7] insofar as both Botswana and Malawi, but not Mozambique, have ratified the main instrument in this area,[8] the International Convention on the Rights of the Child (ICRC) from 1992.[9] Similar to the area of refugee law, the OAU has adopted the African Convention on the Rights of the Child (ACRC), and it is hardly a coincidence that the references in AC art. 12.3 and 18.3 deal with these particular questions.

As mentioned before, the Constitution of Botswana does not contain any particular reference to children as a group or as individuals, in contrast to both MAC and MOC. This enhances the perspective that, although the UN Declaration of the Right of the Child (UNDRC) dates as far back as 1959,[10] the recognition that these rights needs to be given the highest

---

7. Look at the chapters on discrimination against women, AC art. 18, and freedom of movement, AC art. 12.
8. UN, 1995.
9. See ch. 3 on sources of universal human rights in relation to the particular status of this instrument due to its unique global recognition and support.
10. UN General Assembly Resolution 1386 (XIV) of 20 November 1959.

degree of legal protection is relatively new, expressed by the overwhelming number of ratifications which the ICRC has already received.[11]

Two provisions in MAC are designed specially for the protection of children, and the first hereof, sec. 42.2 (g) is part of the extensive complex regulating the area of fair trial and detention. These rights are meant to be an addition to, and not a replacement of, those pertaining to adults in the same situation, and recognize that children are vulnerable and thus shall have the right "to treatment consistent with (their) special needs".

Sub-sec. (i) through (v) all deal with children in some form of pre- or post-trial detention, and the first three of these sections are specific in nature. Sec. (i) states that children have the right not to be sentenced to life imprisonment without the possibility of release, and sec. (ii) declares that they shall be imprisoned "only as a last resort and for the shortest period of time". According to (iii) the main rule shall be that children are not imprisoned together with adults, with the possibility of making exceptions if this is deemed to be "in the best interest" of the child. Finally, this section states that the child shall have the right to maintain contact with his or her family through correspondence and visits, and with respect to the last right it cannot be certified that this right also implies the duty for the State to actively facilitate such contact, but merely must allow it to take place.

No similar clause of interpretation is added in sec. 42.2, similar to sec. 23.5 which defines children, for the purpose of that section, as being persons under sixteen years of age. Since sec. 23.5 is so specific, we cannot automatically assume that it should also apply to sec. 42.

The entire sec. 23 is devoted to the special protection of the rights and needs of children, echoing strongly the ICRC as mentioned above, since it reflects the rights and principles found in this instrument.

A general principle of non-discrimination and children's right to equal treatment before the law is stated in sec. 23.1, with the addition that this shall be accorded to them "regardless of the circumstances of their birth". This formulation should be interpreted liberally, so that it not only covers the question of paternity and social status, but also such criteria as mental or physical disability from birth, ethnic origin, parent's general status in society etc. Only in this way will it provide sufficient actual protection from, as well as be in conformity with the general and extensive section on, non-discrimination in sec. 20.

---

11. 190 states had ratified it and 3 signed it as of 31 December 1995, making it the largest human rights instrument of all; UN, 1995.

Sec. 23.2 declares the right for all children to a given name as well as a family name, without stipulating that it shall necessarily be that of one parent or the other. Children shall also have the right to a nationality, and a possible violation hereof could be in the area of citizenship as described in relation to discrimination against women, if the statues of Malawi had been similar to those of Botswana.[12]

Sec. 23.3 states that children shall have the right to know and to be raised by their parents, a formulation which would also have to be subject to legislative interpretation. Examples hereof would be rules on adoption and foster homes, and the use of modern fertility techniques such as sperm donors and surrogate mothers, although the latter in contrast to the first two is less relevant in an African than in a European context.

Finally, sec. 23.4 covers a wide scope of situations where children need special protection, encompassing economic exploitation in general as well as any treatment, work or punishment. Either one of three indications being violated is enough to invoke the protective measures, and those criteria are that such practices are either (a) hazardous, (b) an interference with their education, or (c) harmful to their health or to their physical, mental or spiritual or social development.

The very comprehensive formulation of these sections works for the extensive protection of children, since almost any situation could be seen as falling under this section. Also, the fact that this provision is found at the Constitutional level makes it difficult to abridge these principles through ordinary statutes and practices, and last but not least this indicates that Malawi would be one of the few African member states to ICRC to implement it to such an extent.

With respect to Mozambique, we find some of the same principles expressed, even though the formulations may be different, stemming from a general difference in formulation of the two instruments rather than differences in scope of protection. The sections of MOC, art. 56 and 58, are of a very different nature as will be seen below, particular since the former relates to children and the second to young people, without either of them defining where the line shall be drawn.

The first of these, art. 56, covers approximately the same area as MAC sec. 23, by stating in sec. 4 that "children may not be discriminated against on grounds of their birth, nor may they be subjected to ill treatment". In

---

12. See Unity Dow-case, in ch. 6 on citizenship and discrimination against women in Botswana.

addition, sec. 5 applies this to the current situation in Mozambique following the civil war, declaring that "State and society shall protect orphans and abandoned children".

That rights and duties in relation to children also involve that of other subjects entities is expressed in the three first sections of art. 56, where sec. 1 recognizes the mutual dependency between the well-being of women and children by announcing that "motherhood shall be afforded respect and protection". Without any explicit provisions in this area elsewhere in the Constitution, this may be translated into more specific duties for the State, such as providing pre- and post-natal care, adequate maternity leave etc.

Sec. 2 deals with the upbringing of children, stating explicitly that in this respect the bearer of the duties is both the State and the family. In fact, according to sec. 2 only the family has the responsibility of raising children "in a harmonious manner" and teaching them moral and social values. This latter aspect is in accordance with AC art. 18, where the duty of the State is not to fulfil this function directly but to assist the family in doing so, and the responsibility therefore stays with the family in both instruments.

In contrast hereto stands sec. 3, where the duty of education is held jointly by the State and the family, keeping in mind the individual duty to preserve and strengthen positive African cultural values in AC art. 29.7. While MOC sec. 52 and other provisions deal with the practical rights and implementation hereof in respect to education at all levels, art. 56.3 covers the ideological and visionary aspects, in the sense that children shall be brought up "in the values of national unity, love for the motherland, human equality, respect and social solidarity".

It is doubtful whether these last two sections will have much effect other than as a declaration of intent and policy, particularly since it is hard to imagine how the duties of family and individuals would actually be enforced as discussed below. On the other hand they contribute to the provisions regarding education by giving a more detailed perspective of what the aims hereof would be, and as such they are not without importance from a less rights-oriented perspective. MOC art. 58 is one of the provisions where the contextuality is highly visible, with sec. 1 praising the young people of Mozambique who "played a decisive role in the national liberation struggle", upholding the "patriotic traditions" and playing "a decisive role" in the national liberation struggle. Viewed independently from the other sections of this article, this provision may have some truth in it, but it is debatable whether such a statement without any legal significance, should have been included in the Constitution in this manner. This is particularly so in light of the fact that this was one of the areas where the world community criticized Mozambique as a violator of human rights by allowing children and teenagers to take part in the armed forces during the war.[13]

Looking to sec. 2 and 3 of the article, we find that sec. 1 provides a background for the rest of the provision, in stating the principles guiding State policy in this area, which among other things shall be to contribute to the "harmonious development of the character of young people". In addition, the aim shall be to help them develop a sense of serving their community, to provide "appropriate conditions" for their entering into active life, and to "acquire a taste for free and creative work". Seen in conjunction with sec. 1 of the article, the impression received is that these aims, with the possible exception of the third, are best promoted and fulfilled through young peoples's participation in some form of military activities. This notion is strengthened when looking at sec. 3, where the State shall promote, support and encourage young peoples' activities, not just in the reconstruction and development of the country, but also in the defence and in the consolidation of national unity.

This does give rise to concern from an outside, and more pacifist, perspective, and care should therefore be taken that this particular aspect does not dominate the implementation of MOC art. 58 entirely, but that other social and cultural activities are given the same or even a higher degree of promotion.

The aged and disabled AC art. 18.4 states that these groups have the right to "special measures of protection in keeping with their physical or moral needs", and this is a provision which cannot be found in neither UD and ICESCR nor in the other regional conventions.

The background for this article is the traditional reverence and respect in African culture for the elders on the one hand, and on the other hand the present and future situation on the continent, where larger and larger parts of the population are young, values are changing, and the elderly and the handicapped are likely victims in case of a crisis. In many such situations traditional structures of support may collapse, with dire consequences for the elder generation. Finally should be mentioned the rapid spread of AIDS on the continent, which has a natural tendency to affect most severely the

---

13. See, among other examples, the Annnual Reports of Amnesty International during the 1980s and 1990s.

sexually active, but also the most productive, part of the population, leaving both the older and younger generation to cope on their own.

The need for special measures for these groups is evident, given the sad reality that a very large percentage of the people in Africa are handicapped from war, disasters and, most of them, from hunger and malnutrition. An example of the latter is the fact that an estimated quarter of a million children go blind every year, simply because of lack of vitamin A.[14]

It is therefore suitable that the African Charter is the first general human rights instrument to include these provisions, without doubt under the inspiration of the UN Declaration on the Rights of Disabled Persons (1975), and the Declaration on the Rights of Mentally Retarded Persons (1971).[15]

Some indication that this is an area which has been developed and expanded over the last 10 years, may be that both MAC and MOC contain such a right. These provisions are MAC sec. 30.1 as outlined above, which is limited to the disabled along with women and children, and MOC art. 95 which states in sec. 1 that "All citizens have the right to assistance in the case of disability or old age" and in sec. 2 obligates the State to promote and encourage "the creation of conditions" for achieving this right. Finally, MOC art. 8 acknowledges the victims of the independence struggle, stating in sec. 2 that the State shall guarantee "the special care and protection" of those permanently injured as well as their orphans and other dependents.

Collective rights

Introduction

A feature of the African Charter which has gathered a fair amount of attention also among legal scholars is the catalogue of peoples' rights in sections 19 through 24.[16]

---

14. The Hunger Project, 1985, p. 12.
15. General Assembly Resolution 3447 (XXX) of 9 December 1975;
    General Assembly Resolution 2856 (XXVI) of 20 December 1971.
16. General comments to the African Charter including the concept of peoples' rights are ed. Crawford, 1988; Neff, 1983, p. 54-60; Bello, 1987, p. 169-170; Naldi, 1989, p. 124-127; D'sa, 1985, p. 77-78; 1987 p. 116-121; 1989 p. 109-114, Kunig, 1982, p. 156-159; and Kotey, 1982, p. 141-142. Articles dealing exclusively with the various

The important point to keep in mind here, however, is that to a large extent the African Charter only elaborates on a concept already recognized in international human rights law.

As such, art. 1 of the ICCPR and ICESCR state the right for all peoples to self-determination. By virtue hereof they freely determine their political status and pursue their economic, social and cultural development (sub-sec. 1). Furthermore, all peoples may, for their own ends, freely dispose of their natural wealth and resources, and in no case must a people be deprived of its own means of subsistence (sub-sec. 2).

These general human rights instruments are supplemented by the UN Declaration on the Granting of Independence to Colonial Countries and Peoples, stating the right of all peoples to self-determination and a peaceful existence, and General Assembly Resolution 1803 on a peoples' right to permanent sovereignty over natural resources.[17]

As such the principles of AC art. 19 through 24 do not lack predecessors with respect to the establishment of fundamental collective rights and freedoms.

The background for this extensive catalogue of peoples rights can be found in the Preamble of AC, which states that "Recognizing on the one hand, that fundamental rights stem from the attributes of human beings -, and on the other hand that the reality and respect of peoples' rights should necessarily guarantee human rights". The drafters of the Charter thereby adhered to the notion that respect for the rights of the group is a prerequisite for the rights and freedoms of the individual.

Another significant factor is the strong anti-colonial forces in Africa, which maintained that given the right to self-determination, declared in art. 1 of both the UN Covenants, there was the need for an elaboration on the context and substance of this right, so that not only political and formal but also economic and cultural independence could be a reality.

Finally, the basis for the emphasis on the peoples' rights can be found in the traditional importance which in African culture and history has been attributed to the nature of the local close-knit society. Often the extreme result hereof resulted in tribalism and wars, but it also produced a strong

---

aspects on the concept of peoples' rights in the African Charter are van Boven, 1986, p. 183-194; Addo, 1988, p. 182-193; Benedek, 1989, p. 1-17; Kiwanuka, 1988, p. 80-101; and Shepherd, 1985, p. 37-50.

17. General Assembly resolution 1514 (XV) of 14 December 1960; General Assembly resolution 1803 (XVII) of 14 December 1962.

social and racial identity which has led to the continuation and preservation of African culture up to the present time in spite of colonialism and other threats. This point of view is also expressed in the last article of the Preamble, where it is underscored that the states recognize their duty to promote and protect the human and peoples' rights and freedoms "taking into account the importance traditionally attached to these rights and freedoms in Africa".

Which ever one of these points of view is the most dominant, it remains a fact that the collective rights, which have been tentatively mentioned in the other instruments as stated earlier, here in the African Charter are fully elaborated on within the context of the more traditional human rights. This furthermore cements the notion that the international standards of human rights legitimately can be extended to include also the rights of peoples, stretching the concept beyond the individual as the sole bearer of rights.

Just as the economic, social and cultural rights have not been sharply divided from the civil and political rights, the peoples' rights have simply been gathered in the articles 19 to 24, and in art. 12.5.

AC art. 12.5 is probably closest to the individual civil and political rights and freedoms, as it states the prohibition against mass expulsion of non-nationals from a state, defining mass expulsion as directed at national, racial, ethnic or religious groups. Also, it should be viewed in conjunction with the rest of art. 12, stating the right for individuals to freedom of movement and residence, to asylum, and the freedom from individual expulsion without a decision made in accordance with the law.[18]

The AMCHR contains similar provisions in art. 22, where nr. 8 deals with individual deportation or involuntary return to a country in which he will be subject to violation of his right to life or personal freedom, due to race, nationality, religion, social status or political opinions. Art. 22.9 in the AMCHR further states that "the collective expulsion of aliens is prohibited", differing from AC on the point that the latter does not restrict itself to aliens, and as such covers also the mass expulsion of groups which have some affiliation with the state. ICCPR art. 13 prohibits unlawful expulsion, but deals only with that of the individual and not groups or peoples.

---

18. This concept has been further dealt with in chapter 6 on freedom of movement of the individual.

Definition

Before going further into this area, we must address one of the main problems in relation to the inclusion of these provisions in the African Charter. This arises from the use of the term "people", without any suggestion what the definition hereof should imply. This is particularly controversial in relation to the explicit right to self-determination and the right for a people to determine their political and economic status and development. This again should be seen in light of a peoples' right to free themselves from the bond of domination by resorting to any means recognized by the international community and to receive assistance in this battle from other State parties in AC art. 20.

The starting point is establishing which criteria shall be decisive when identifying which groups can legitimately claim the term "people". Some of the key features may be:[19]

1. an ethnic group united by a common heritage, and with a communal present time spirit and culture, or

2. a composition of the following criteria:
    a) a social unit, with a clear identity and characteristics.
    b) attachment to a geographical area, even though the people have been driven from it and artificially replaced by another.
    c) defined negatively, contradictory to an ethnic, religious or linguistic minority (which has its own rights, art. 27 of the Covenant on Civil and Political Rights).

Finally the subjective element can be emphasized, implying that people see themselves as a distinct group, one people, and in many ways this element probably covers most of the important conditions, at the same time as it in itself is totally inadequate as a definition.

On the basis of this, a liberal definition of the term "people" would be *a distinct group with a common identity, interests, and attached to a given territory*. This would include all people within the states, and in some cases also a specific group within that state.

If we look at international practice, the tendency is clear, given that

---

19. Kiwanuka, 1988; Addo, 1988; Benedek, 1989; van Boven 1986.

both the OAU, and the international community have maintained that the right to self-determination "stops" at the national territorial border and does not include parts of a state.[20] The importance hereof is underlined by art. 20.2 of the African Charter, which emphasizes that only "colonized or oppressed people shall have the right to free themselves from the bond of domination." This provision indicates that the initial aim of the OAU was to support states who were still dominated by forces outside of Africa to free themselves. The "internal" freedom fights and secessions were not acceptable to the OAU for various reasons, expressed clearly in the Charter of the OAU, prescribing the "respect for the sovereign and territorial integrity of each State and for its inalienable right to independent existence".[21]

Given art. 20 in the African Charter, which states "the unquestionable and inalienable right to self-determination", the crucial question is whether the African Charter here allows for the secession by tribes, minorities or other entities from a country. If one adopts the restrictive approach as outlined above, this could not be the case, and if one the other hand the more liberal approach is chosen this could be the case, but only under very distinctive circumstances.[22]

Rights and Freedoms

Looking at the national Constitutions, we find that also in this area do they differ in approach. BC, being the older and most heavily influenced by a European conception of rights, limits itself to dealing with individual rights, and has therefore no reference to collective rights in any form. Both MAC and MOC have provisions in some, but not all, of the areas found below, but it should be kept in mind that while AC's provisions on peoples right are of an external nature in relation to each state, the national Constitutions in contrast are internal and do not presume a conflict of interest between various "peoples". As such, it is mainly the three latter sections, on the right

---

20. In December 1985 a conference in Nairobi organized by the International Commission of Jurists adopted a particularly restrictive approach when it equated peoples with "*the national community as distinct from (the) ethnic, linguistic or tribal community*"; Benedek, 1989, p. 10.
21. Bello 1985, p. 169.
22. Examples hereof are Namibia and Eritrea, both of which have emerged as independent nations in later years.

to development, to peace and to a satisfactory environment, which have been reflected in MAC and MOC, since they may also be construed as individual rights.

Equality The actual peoples' rights begin with AC art. 19, which declares that all peoples shall be equal, entitled to the same respect and the same rights, and that nothing shall justify the domination of a people by another. This article takes more or less the form of a declaration of the very foundation for the co-existence between peoples, and as such it is consistent with art. 1 of the UN Covenants as well as the provisions of the Charter of the UN.[23] A similar principle is not directly expressed in any of the other instruments.

Existence AC art. 20.1 states the right for all peoples to existence, and their unquestionable and inalienable right to self-determination. They are free to determine political status, and to pursue their economic and social development in accordance with their freely chosen policy.

This article is similar to art. 1 in the two UN Covenants, as mentioned above, where art. 1.2 herein deals with the right to free disposal of wealth and resources. The term "foreign domination" should be enhanced, applying the word foreign to anything non-African or in conflict with the principles and politics of the OAU; only time will show how the provision will be interpreted by the African Commission and with what results. This provision is repeated in AC art. 21.1 and 21.3, which state that in no case shall a people be deprived of these rights. They shall be exercised exclusively in the interest of the people (in this sense the term "people" applies differently, in the sense of a group of individuals versus the State), and without prejudice to the promotion of international economic cooperation based on the principles of international law, mutual respect and equitable exchange.[24]

---

23. See for instance art. 1.2,"The Organisation is based on the principle of the sovereign equality of all its members", art. 2.4, "All members shall refrain from the threat or use of force against the territoril integrity or political independence of any state", and the purpose of the UN as stated in art. 1.2, "To develop friendly relations among nations based on respect for the principle of equal rights and self-determination of peoples".
24. See also art. 55 of the Charter of the UN, which emphasizes respect for the principle of equal rights and self-determination of peoples.

Natural resources Other provisions concerning natural resources are contained in AC art. 21.2, stating the right for dispossessed people to lawful recovery, as well as to adequate compensation. How such claims will be handled in practice is a question still open, given that the Commission or the OAU in general does not have the power to issue binding statements or judgments of such kind.[25]

Finally AC art. 21.4 declares the obligation for the states, individually and collectively, to exercise the right to free disposal of their wealth and natural resources "with a view to strengthening African unity and solidarity". This is an obligation which could be brought forward by the OAU or individual states against other states as political pressure, more or less appropriately.

This point also applies to art. 21.5, which declares the responsibility for the states to eliminate "all forms of foreign economic exploitation, particularly that which is practised by international monopolies". In this article the political and anti-colonial forces come through loud and clear, and apart from being a firm declaration on the intention of the OAU, it can hardly be considered a valid obligation legally enforceable in international law. From the point of view of Western Europe and USA, this article can be viewed as nothing less than a financial and political threat, however unlikely of actual success, and must be interpreted within the context of art. 21.1, stating that the rights should be exercised in the exclusive interest of the people.

It should be kept in mind that these obligations rest only on states, underlining the point of view by the drafters of the African Charter that the peoples' rights are intended to apply to states and as such all the collective obligations corresponding to the rights and freedoms also apply to states only and not to peoples, which is appropriate enough from the point of view that only actual states can be parties to the Charter.

Neither BC nor MAC has any reference to this right, but the issue of access to and distribution of land and natural resources is dealt with in several sections of MOC, such as art. 35, 36 and 46, 47 and 48, some of which have been discussed in relation to the right to property above. Of particular interest in relation to AC art. 21.5 is MOC art. 45, declaring in sec. 1 that "Foreign investment shall operate within the framework of state

---

25. Nowhere in the Charter of the OAU are contained provisions enabling the General Assembly, the Council of Ministers, the General Secretariat, or any of its Subcommissions to place such obligations on member states.

economic policy", and in sec. 2 that foreign ventures shall be permitted in all economic sectors excluding those which are exclusively reserved for state ownership or development. Rather than seeing it as direct contradiction to the provision in AC, this article serves to emphasize that AC's protective measures in this area should be applied only when appropriate for the general situation and the improvement of living conditions in the member State.

Development Art. 22.1 declares the right of all peoples to their economic, social and cultural development "with due regard to their freedom and identity and in the equal enjoyment of the common heritage of mankind".

This article in fact states the overall context for the African Charter, and must be viewed in conjunction with the other articles herein. Also ICESCR art. 11, which declares that the State Parties to the Covenant recognize the right of everyone to an adequate standard of living for himself and his family, and to the continuous improvement of living conditions, is relevant here. Still, this is a sum of individual rights and not the right for a community or a state as a whole to development, as in the AC. This step taken in the Charter has later been followed in the UN Declaration on the Right to Development from 1986.[26]

In art. 22.2 is stated a corresponding duty for the states, individually as well as collectively, to ensure the exercise of the right to development, and here it must be read as to imply a right for individuals and groups within the states, as well as other states within and outside of Africa too.

The obligation resting on the states must be interpreted as containing the duty to actively assisting other states, peoples and individuals appropriately in their exercise of the right to development, and a more passive obligation not to put any hindrance in the way of their exercise of this right.

This is the only area of collective rights where MAC has a corresponding provision, stating in sec. 30 the right for all persons and peoples to the enjoyment of economic, social, cultural and political development. Already here we see the strong attachment between this right and the general concept of economic and social rights, and this picture is strengthened when looking at sub-sec. 2, according to which the State shall take all necessary measures to ensure that the enjoyment of this right may become a reality for the people of Malawi. Such measures fall within the

---

26. Adopted by General Assembly Resolution 41/128 of 4 December 1986.

sphere of economic and social rights, including basic resources, education, health services, food, shelter, employment and infrastructure, but a reference is made to the general principle of non-discrimination in the term "equality of opportunity for all".

Sub-sec. 3 and 4 state more explicitly the duties of the State in relation to the implementation of the right to development, such as the introduction of reforms "aimed at eradicating social injustices and inequalities" and the justification of its policy in relation to respect for development. By stating what may or may not been inherent in relation to other rights, the importance of development in MAC stands out as a fundamental prerequisite for the realization of a society in which all aspect of human rights may be a living reality.

In relation to Mozambique the corresponding provision is MOC art. 38, which is not formulated as an individual or collective right but rather as the corresponding duty of the State. Also here we find that this principle is linked closely with economic rights and, in this case, national policy, since this shall be directed towards "laying the fundamental basis for development" and improving the living conditions of people, as well as strengthening State sovereignty and national unity. The further details of the economic policy are stated in art. 39 through 49, where art. 49 in particular should be noted, since sec. 2 herein declares that "State investment shall play a dynamising role in promoting development".

Peace Art. 23.1 states that all peoples shall have the right to national and international peace and security, and underlines the adherence to the principles of solidarity and friendly relations laid down by the Charter of the UN as well as by the OAU. This is hardly an obligation which can be directly enforced, but it serves as the governing principle for the co-existence of states and peoples, and as such is a declaration of the peaceful intentions and aspirations of Africa.

Also, it is in accordance with the Universal Declaration, which in art. 28 states that everyone is entitled to an international order in which the rights in that instrument can be fulfilled.

MOC adheres to this principle specifically, in contrast to BC and MAC, by stating in art. 65 that "The Republic of Mozambique shall pursue a policy of peace", expressed by only resorting to force in case of "legitimate" defence and supporting negotiated solutions to conflict and the principle of "general and universal disarmament of all states". As a further vehicle for such a policy on a more specific level, sec. 4 declares that

Mozambique shall advocate the transformation of the Indian Ocean into a nuclear zone of peace. This is a worthy goal, but it is, probably and unfortunately, also something which may not happen in the immediate future.

Environment Of the same basic character is art. 24, which declares the right for all peoples to a general satisfactory environment favourable to their development, without giving a further definition hereof.

Not surprisingly, in light of the strong emphasis being paid in later years to the environment in the sense of fighting pollution and the destruction of natural resources, the African Charter becomes the first convention to make this link between human rights and the preservation of the environment, and as such is playing a leading role in this area.[27]

Given the problems faced by the developing countries and the importance they attach to this issue, at least on an international level, there's no doubt that the Charter hereby establishes new paths in the field of human and peoples' rights, and hopefully this will also lead to an increase in the protective measures being applied by the states themselves.

Still, the provision would have to be tested and applied in practice in order to determine the extent to which actual rights for individual and groups hereof can be derived from it. If such attempts are successful, AC art. 24 will serve as a founding principle to be respected and upheld by its member States, but if not, the article will merely be a political statement without any real significance.

In contrast to the other two Constitutions, MOC has two provisions in this area, in addition to those regulating the use of natural resources as dealt with above.

MOC art. 72 states the right for all citizens "to live in a balanced natural environment", applying the individual approach characteristic of this instrument rather than the collective approach used in AC. Furthermore, the provision proceeds to state that this shall not just be a right, it shall also be a duty for each citizen to "defend" it, relating to the catalogue of individual duties in AC discussed below.

Supplementing art. 37, MOC art. 37 deals with the corresponding obligation for the State, which shall "promote efforts to guarantee the ecological balance and the conservation and preservation of the

---

27. The first major global resolution in this area is the final resolution of the United Nations Conference on Environment and Development, Rio de Janiero, June 1992.

environment", with the aim of improving the quality of life for its people. Here we see the implicit strong link between development and the environment, and this provision therefore responds accurately to Mozambique's duty to implement AC art. 24 according to art. 1.

Duties of the individual

Introduction

An extensive catalogue of individual duties is contained in AC art. 27 through 29, and has also given rise to critique because of the inherent danger that these duties could be used to limit or even nullify the rights and freedoms established by the African Charter.[28]

As a starting point it should be established that the idea of including provisions concerning individual responsibilities and duties in international human rights instruments is not unique to the African Charter. An example hereof is UD art. 29.1, which states that "Everyone has duties to the community", and art. 29.2, "everyone shall be subject only to such limitations as are determined by law solely for the purpose of securing due recognition and respect for the rights and freedoms of others - and of meeting the just requirements of morality, public order and the general welfare in a democratic society".

At the regional level we find the AMCHR art. 32, stating in section 1 that "Every person has responsibilities to his family, his community and mankind", and in sec. 2 that "The rights of each person are limited by the rights of others, by the security of all, and by the just demands of the general welfare in a democratic society".

Neither the two International Covenants ICESCR and ICCPR, nor ECHR contain such a provision.

Enforceable duties versus declarations

Before going into a discussion on the provisions of AC art. 27, we must make a distinction between two types of duties found in the provisions. The obligations resting on the individuals are directed against his or her state

---

28. Examples of sources discussing this subject are Neff, 1983, p. 60-61; Bello, 1987, p. 178-179; Naldi, 1989, p. 130-131; D'sa, 1985, p. 76-77; 1987, p. 115-116; 1989, p. 114-116); Kunig, 1982, p. 159-160; and Kotey, 1982-85, p. 142-143.

and individuals and entities within it, as well as towards Africa and the international community, as clearly stated in art. 27.1.

Still, those duties which are directly enforceable like the duty to contribute to the defence of one's country and the duty to pay taxes (art. 29.5 and 29.6) are duties towards the state, and therefore within the framework of domestic law. It should be kept in mind at this point that AC art. 1, according to which the states shall undertake to adopt the necessary measures to give effect to the rights and freedoms in the Charter, also includes the duties.

The other group of duties are directed towards the international and African community as a whole, as for example the duty to consider one's fellow being without discrimination (art. 28) and to preserve and strengthen positive African values (art. 29.7). They are, however, of such a nature that they impose a moral and political obligation rather than a directly enforceable duty, and so the conflict of how to deal with the upholding of individual obligations and responsibilities in an international forum to a large extent can be avoided.

Individual duties

The articles dealing with the duties of the individuals are contained in a separate chapter, Chapter II, art. 27 - 29, hereby indicating their distinction from the rights and freedoms of individuals and peoples and from the duties of states.

AC art. 27.1 deals with the duties towards family and society, the State, other legally recognized communities, and the international community, and hereby serves as the framework for the provisions enshrined in art. 28 and 29.

Supplementing this, AC art. 27.2 mentions the basic duty towards other individuals to exercise one's rights and freedoms with due regard to those of others. AC art. 27.2 limits the exercise of the rights and freedoms of the individual towards the community as a whole, giving due regard to "collective security, morality, and common interest". Similar provisions are found in art. 29.2 in UD, where the term used is "just requirements of morality, public order, and the general welfare in a democratic society", and basically covers the same spectre of interests.[29]

We find corresponding provisions in the national Constitutions of both Mozambique and Malawi, but not in that of Botswana. MAC sec. 15, introducing the chapter on Human Rights, states that its provisions shall be respected and upheld by all organs of government "and, where applicable to them, by all natural and legal persons in Malawi", and MOC art. 85 declares that "All citizens shall have the duty to respect the Constitutional order".

AC art. 28 is divided into two parts, where the first can be viewed as a supplement to the generally anti-discriminatory AC art. 2, hereby stating that not only the state and its agents such as teachers in public service and judges, but also an individual person, for instance a private employer, has a duty not to discriminate against other individuals for whatever reasons.

The second half of the article is much less concrete, declaring the duty for every individual to "maintain relations aimed at promoting, safeguarding, and reinforcing mutual respect and tolerance". Here we have an example of duties, which are of a moral and psychological nature, rather than directly enforceable, and therefore serve as a declaration instead of a specifically defined obligation.

AC art. 29 is by far the most extensive of the articles dealing with the duties of individuals, and can be viewed as the specific expression of the general principles established in the previous two articles.

The family AC art. 29.1 deals with the context closest to that of the individual, stating the individual's duty to work for the cohesion and respect of the family and to preserve its harmonious development. It is not clear to which extent this provision could be enforced, but it could easily be imagined that at some point this duty would clash with the rights and freedoms of the individual, particularly women, to pursue their own choice of way of life, right to education etc. Furthermore, the term "family" may appropriately be interpreted more expansively than in a European or American context, in order to accommodate the extended family, which is

---

29. See also ch. 4 on the introduction to the national Constitutions. Here the 1966 Republic Constitution of Malawi contained a similar clause, which was abused extensively in an attempt to legitimize the Government's systematic violations of human rights under the rule of Banda.

still a living concept in most African societies.[30] This, however, only increases the potential burden of this provision.

This conflict might also easily apply to the second part of the article, which states the duty for every individual to respect his or her parents and, especially, to maintain them in case of need. This is an aspect deeply rooted in traditional African culture, and is still very relevant given the lack of a social infrastructure in most African countries, which inevitably places the responsibility for the caretaking of the needs of the elders in the hands of the younger generation. Also here conflicts such as those mentioned above may arise, particularly in a society which in its development experiences wide gaps between values and ways of life of different generations.

The national community AC art. 29.2 obligates the individual "to serve his national community by placing his physical and intellectual abilities at its service", hereby opening up a legitimacy for the State to declare a kind of compulsory civil service for a given period. In the exercise hereof, AC art. 15 on working conditions should be kept in mind, particularly since none of the other provisions of AC contain a direct prohibition against the use of forced labour but only use the term "exploitation" in AC art. 5. Such measures could also, when used with restraint, to some degree make up for the prevalent problem of "brain drain" experienced by most African states.

Security and defence The three following articles, 29.3, 29.4, and 29.5, all deal with duties related to security- and defence issues.

AC art. 29.3 contains a prohibition against an individual compromising the security of a State, whose national or resident he is; this formulation leaves room for a very broad interpretation and can be used, as we have seen in so many cases around the world, to limit the exercise of individual rights and freedoms to a very wide extent, often far beyond any reasons except for the wish of a state to suppress critical points of view. Therefore this article should only be used in cases where it is evident from an objective point of view that there is a real threat to the security of the State and hereby to the well-being of the community as a whole.

AC art. 29.4 obligates the individual to preserve and strengthen social and national solidarity, particularly when the national solidarity (but not the social ditto) is threatened; also here a wide margin has been left open for

---

30. See the earlier part of this chapter and the economic and social rights of the family for a discussion on the definition of "family".

interpretations by the State, where an example could be compulsory membership of certain organizsations like unions or political institutions, or the banning of such organizations. In reality, this would contravene the provisions of art. 10.1 and 2, regarding freedom of association, and the question would then arise which of the two articles would take precedence over the other in practice.

The provision suggests that in the case of disturbances, riots, or political instability, which could be interpreted as a threat to national solidarity, the individual may be endowed with heavier duties and obligations, defying the full and free exercise of the rights and freedoms enshrined in the Charter.

AC art. 29.5 imposes on the individual the obligation to preserve and strengthen national independence and the territorial integrity of his country, a formulation which once more leaves the State with a wide margin for defining such duties of the individual. An example hereof could be for the individual to refrain from any actions which would support foreign troops in an invasion or guerilla raids, or even actively to take part in the defence of the country. This is specifically mentioned in the second half of the article, which states the duty for the individual to contribute to the defence of the territory in accordance with the law, i.e. by doing military service. No requirements for national law regarding length, age or form of service are mentioned in the Charter, and as such the other articles herein must serve as guidelines for the state. An example of this is the reference in art. 18.3 to international instruments protecting the welfare and specific needs of children, which would be violated if a state uses children in its armed forces.[31]

We do not find any such duty in the Constitutions of Malawi or Botswana, but MOC art. 84 states that it shall be a "sacred" duty, as well as an honour, for all Mozambican citizens to participate in the defence of the country's "independence, sovereignty and territorial integrity". How the concepts of honour and sanctity shall translate themselves legally, if at all, is not clear; also, the provision does not establish whether this duty pertains to both men, women and persons under a certain age, but merely states in sec. 2 that these terms shall be established by law. When doing so, the Government of Mozambique must ensure that none of the other provisions

---

31. See articles 38 and 39 of the International Convention on the Rights of the Child, according to which children under the age of fifteen must not be recruited into the armed forces of State Parties to the Convention.

of the Constitution are violated, such as those protecting the well-being of children as well as freedom of religion and organization. If, for instance, members of Jehovah's Witnesses refuse to do military service on conscientious grounds, the provisions of the Constitution in general should be weighed against art. 84. In addition, MOC art. 61 speaks about citizens' participation in civil defence units, but emphasizes that citizens shall be "encouraged" to join these, and no individual duty can therefore be derived from this article.

Work and payment of taxes In AC art. 29.6 the first part states the duty for the individual to work to the best of his abilities and competence, an article which supplements and partly overlaps art. 29.2 stating the duty of every person to serve his national community through the use of his physical and intellectual abilities. Interpretation of art. 29.6. could result in a general ban on vagrancy in national law, as well as different forms of labour duty, as long as it does not state a violation of art. 15, containing the right to work under equitable and satisfactory conditions and to receive equal pay to equal work. Again it should be noted here that the Charter contains no provisions against forced labour, similar to those established by the other international human rights instruments.[32]

The second part of art. 29.6. is one of the more specific articles in this chapter, stating the duty for the individual to pay taxes imposed by law in the interest of the society. This article must be interpreted so that it contains a corresponding duty on behalf of the State to include in domestic law precise provisions regarding taxes, and to administrate such regulations in order to prevent random or unjust collection hereof. In particular it must be seen to that the tax burden of the individual is not so heavy that he or she is unable to fulfil normal obligations or to sustain a living, conditions which must be interpreted as being contrary to the interests of society as well.

Again, it is only MOC which touches upon this issue, and even indirectly, by announcing the principle in art. 50 that "Taxes shall be imposed and altered by law, and shall be set according to criteria of social justice".

African values and African unity The last two articles in art. 29 are of a less restrictive and more positive nature; at the same time, they can hardly serve

---

32. See ch. 6 on civil and political rights, freedom from slavery and forced labour, for a discussion hereof.

as the basis for constituting enforceable duties of the individual, but serve as moral and cultural guidelines for the society and its members in their interactions.

AC art. 29.7 obligates the individual to preserve and strengthen positive cultural African values in his relations with other members of society, in the spirit of tolerance, dialogue, and consultation, and, in general, to contribute to the promotion of the moral well-being of society.

This article could be viewed as expressing the very essence of the Charter, in the sense that it aims at preserving distinct traditional African values, but also reflects a sense of conservatism directed against the foreign influence on the continent. The intention is to try to reverse a tendency among people, particularly in the cities, to turn their back to traditional ways of life and instead adopt more European norms and morals. Still, one may doubt the efficiency of a legal provision in contributing to a reversal of this process.

AC art. 29.8 rounds up this catalogue of individual obligations and duties by stating the duty for the individual to contribute to the best of his abilities, at all times and at all levels, to the promotion and achievement of African unity.

The broad formulation of this article leaves room for wide interpretations, such as the prohibition against membership or support of secessionist movements. It does not, however, leave any doubt as to the emphasis of African unity as the very basis of this Charter as well as the general well-being of African societies, and the key role of the individual herein.

Part IV
Conclusion

8 General conclusions and perspectives

The findings and conclusions of this study cover a wide span, from the concrete to the more abstract level, and distinctions must therefore be made between the various perspectives.

Starting with the national Constitutions of Botswana, Malawi and Mozambique in relation to the African Charter on Human and Peoples' Rights, the analysis shows that most of the provisions in the respective instruments correspond, ensuring a certain scope of rights and freedoms of the individual. The general conclusion is therefore that generally these states fulfil their obligation to ensure that the provisions of the African Charter are reflected appropriately in national law.

There are a few exceptions, however, where it can be concluded that the national law violates the African Charter. This is the case with respect to the question of discrimination against women on the basis of sex in Botswana, where a number of legislative provisions neither conform to the interpretation of the Bill of Rights in the Constitution in accordance with recent case law, nor to the provisions of the African Charter. Another area concerning Botswana's adherence to the African Charter is the question of the use of corporal punishment in the judicial and educational systems. If one adopts a strict universalistic approach to the African Charter, the conclusion will be that Botswana violates the provisions hereof. If, on the other hand, a more liberal approach is applied in the interpretation of the rights and freedoms of the African Charter, one may also reach the conclusion that the laws of Botswana comply with the African Charter on this point.

Still, it is evident that the nature and construction of the two instruments is very different; they are drawn up at different periods of time, with a difference of more than 20 years, and the results hereof show themselves in almost any aspect of the analysis. This is a general picture when looking at the constitutional model used by Botswana and Malawi as well as most of the other African Commonwealth states who gained independence in the early 1960s. Since they largely follow the model established by the European Convention on Human Rights, it also means that the scope of rights and freedoms in their national Bills of Rights is limited to the civil and political rights only. This means that the implementation of the economic, social and cultural rights as well as the peoples' rights will have to take place through other measures, for instance through the adoption of specific laws and acts in the various areas. Still, such measures do not have similar legal force and consistency, based simply on the fact that they are subordinate to the *lex superior* of constitutional provisions on, for instance, national security, and because they can easily be amended or terminated. In the end it will therefore have to be the individual member states who determine the degree to which the provisions of the African Charter shall become effective in a national context.

In contrast hereto one can look at the two other Constitutions from Malawi and Mozambique, which show a different picture. Here we find a much closer correspondence with the African Charter, shown most characteristically in the scope of rights and freedoms and the integration of economic, social and cultural rights, individual duties and collective rights along with individual civil and political rights and freedoms.

Both of these two latter instruments came into being after the entering into force of the African Charter, and a question which can still not be answered clearly is whether it actually did serve as the primary model for the drafters of the Constitutions. There is no clear documentation hereof for either of the Constitutions, but on the other hand it can also not be established that other international or regional conventions played such a role instead. What we can establish is that the Constitutions of Malawi and Mozambique at least reflect the same trend as the African Charter in including a more holistic and broader perspective of human rights. Therefore it might be interesting to keep this in mind when looking at other states' reformulation of their national Constitutions and to see if this is a general development, or if MAC and MOC are particular in this respect. If the case is the first, we can conclude that there is a demand for African states (like Botswana) to update their national human rights provisions in order to ensure that they comply with all aspects of the African Charter.

The Constitution of Malawi reflects a lot of consideration and legal expertise on behalf of its drafters, and in most areas fulfils or even goes beyond the scope of provisions in AC. An exception hereof is the use of the death penalty, which may still be applied in Malawi.

In contrast hereto stands the Constitution of Mozambique, which reveals itself as being a far more political document, both in its particular, and less effective, systematics and structure, and in the formulation of each provision. Many of these are formulated as declarations of policy and intent rather than as individual rights, and it will therefore be more difficult to use them as such before the national courts. On the other hand it also tailors MOC to the concrete situation in the country, adressing the needs of the people and their aspirations very specifically, while MAC, and BC even more so, are of a general nature. This speaks for their wide and long-term applicability, while MOC is of a more contextual nature and adresses the specific problems here and now.

One of the experiences to be gathered from the comparative study of the human rights provisions in the African Charter and the national constitutions, is that the implementation of the Charter in the national law of its member states does face some serious challenges.

The most obvious hereof would be the lack of commitment, or even willingness, on some State Parties, who do not regard with favour the outside interference in internal legal and political matters which the African Charter and the African Commission may represent effectively. Realizing that by not implementing of the Charter in national law, this would also in most cases mean that the citizens of that state are prevented from applying the Charter at national courts and other instances, one might fear that this policy might be deliberately chosen by some states. Hereby the success of the Charter and the Commission as effective measures of protection and promotion of human rights could be greatly endangered.

Not only does the comparative analysis give a clearer overview of the constitutional provisions on human rights in Botswana, Malawi and Mozambique, it also presents an enlightening picture of the more detailed aspects of the African Charter itself. One of the more problematic aspects hereof is the widespread use of liberal references to national law, the effect of which is the danger that the protective material provisions of the Charter in effect can be rendered without any legal effect.

In relation to other international human rights instruments, global as well as regional, the African Charter reveals two general features. The first hereof is that in a number of areas the provisions are formulated more broadly and with less substance than for instance the European Convention, the Universal Declaration, and the International Covenants on Civil and Political as well as Economic, Social and Cultural Rights. The positive aspect hereof is that this leaves room for the African Commission and other instances to adopt a dynamic mode of interpretation, allowing for a close adaption to concrete circumstances as well as a more general applicability. At the same time the negative aspect hereof is that the legal content of each article is limited, a problem which is further enhanced by the widespread references to national law as mentioned above.

The second feature is that the African Charter in broad terms confirms to a universally applicable framework of basic human rights concepts relating to life, personal integrity and security, judicial process, basic welfare and personal well-being, and the equality of all human beings, just to mention a few. The essence of all its material provisions can be found within those instruments, and principles herein, already recognized by international consensus as part of the international code of human rights.

On the basis hereof, we can attempt to answer the question posed by the title of this thesis, on the universality of human rights, with partly a "yes" and partly a "no". On the one hand we cannot maintain the existence of a culturally specific African conception of human rights, due to the lack of any historic or philosophical evidence hereof. On the other hand we must also reject the notion that human rights are constant regardless of their context, since an overview of the developments which have taken place in this area over the years have shown that this is not the case. Somewhere in between these two positions there exists a point, where we on the one hand recognize the existence of a set of principles relating to human welfare and survival which are universally applicable. On the other hand the definition hereof, resulting from the conceptualizing of these principles into concrete legal norms, must take place with some regard to their context of operation. This, then, is where the universality stops.

Finally, another significant effect of the African Charter is that it represents a broadening of the regional perspective in relation to human rights regulation. Particularly in relation to the African Commission on Human Rights, which has not been dealt with in this study, the African Charter is a valuable tool with respect to both the promotional as well as the protectional aspects of its functions. Through the establishment hereof, the African man or women now has direct access to an international body, where he or she can direct complaints against a State Party's violation of his or her human rights and freedoms.

Until recently we had only the European and the American systems, where particularly the former was closely related to the global conception of human rights, and so one tended to operate on the presumption that interpretations of various concepts did not vary greatly in the different systems and instruments. The African Charter now challenges this perceived unity by emphasizing regional regulation as separate from the global level of regulation. The regional level is characterized by ex- and implicit references to each instrument's cultural context, reflecting the political and legal agendas indigenous to each region. With the realization hereof, we may even take a fresh look at the European Convention on Human Rights, reaching the inevitable conclusion that while this instrument affords strong and substantial protection of the civil and political rights of the individual, it is also far more narrow in scope than the instruments of the other regions.

In some respects this added complexity of the picture of human rights regulation may seem to create problems which have so far been less significant. For instance the discussion on the linking of human rights with development aid becomes richer but also more complicated. This follows from the realization that human rights are not necessarily static, and that we cannot assume that the definition of the specific scope and implications of each right necessarily is the same in different cultures.

On the other hand it also contributes to a more diversified perception of the relationship between the various regions of the world, and of the problems, challenges and resources characteristic in each culture. In this respect the African Charter could serve as an important blockbuster for other regional human rights initiatives.

Appendix

AFRICAN CHARTER ON HUMAN AND PEOPLES' RIGHTS

PREAMBLE

African States members of the Organization of African Unity, parties to the present convention entitled "African Charter on Human and Peoples' Rights",

Recalling Decision 115 (XVI) of the Assembly of Heads of State and Government at its Sixteenth Ordinary Session held in Monrovia, Liberia, from 17 to 20 July 1979 on the preparation of a "preliminary draft on an African Charter on Human and Peoples' Rights providing inter alia for the establishment of bodies to promote and protect human and peoples' rights";

Considering the Charter of the Organization of African Unity, which stipulates that "freedom, equality, justice and dignity are essential objectives for the achievement of the legitimate aspirations of the African peoples";

Reaffirming the pledge they solemnly made in Article 2 of the said Charter to eradicate all forms of colonialism from Africa, to coordinate and intensify their cooperation and efforts to achieve a better life for the peoples of Africa and to promote international cooperation having due regard to the Charter of the United Nations and the Universal Declaration of Human Rights;

Taking into consideration the virtues of their historical tradition and the values of African civilization which should inspire and characterize their reflection on the concept of human and peoples' rights;

Recognizing on the one hand, that fundamental human rights stem from the attributes of human beings which justifies their national and international protection and on the other hand that the reality and respect of peoples rights should necessarily guarantee human rights;

Considering that the enjoyment of rights and freedoms also implies the performance of duties on the part of everyone;

Convinced that it is henceforth essential to pay a particular attention to the right to development and that civil and political rights cannot be dissociated from economic, social and cultural rights in their conception as well as universality and that the satisfaction of economic, social and cultural rights is a guarantee for the enjoyment of civil and political rights;

Conscious of their duty to achieve the total liberation of Africa, the peoples of which are still struggling for their dignity and genuine independence, and undertaking to eliminate colonialism, neo-colonialism, apartheid, zionism and to dismantle aggressive foreign military bases and all forms of discrimination, particularly those based on race, ethnic group, colour, sex. language, religion or political opinions;

Reaffirming their adherence to the principles of human and peoples' rights and freedoms contained in the declarations, conventions and other instrument adopted by the Organization of African Unity, the Movement of Non-Aligned Countries and the United Nations;

Firmly convinced of their duty to promote and protect human and people' rights and freedoms taking into account the importance traditionally attached to these rights and freedoms in Africa;

HAVE AGREED AS FOLLOWS;

PART 1 - RIGHTS AND DUTIES

CHAPTER I

HUMAN AND PEOPLES' RIGHTS

ARTICLE 1
The Member States of the Organization of African Unity parties to the present Charter shall recognize the rights, duties and freedoms enshrined in this Chapter and shall undertake to adopt legislative or other measures to give effect to them.

ARTICLE 2
Every individual shall be entitled to the enjoyment of the rights and freedoms recognized and guaranteed in the present Charter without distinction of any kind such as race, ethnic group, colour, sex, language, religion, political or any other opinion, national and social origin, fortune, birth or other status.

ARTICLE 3
1. Every individual shall be equal before the law.
2. Every individual shall be entitled to equal protection of the law.

ARTICLE 4
Human beings are inviolable. Every human being shall be entitled to respect for his life and the integrity of his person. No one may be arbitrarily deprived of this right.

ARTICLE 5
Every individual shall have the right to the respect of the dignity inherent in a human being and to the recognition of his legal status. All forms of exploitation and degradation of man particularly slavery, slave trade, torture, cruel, inhuman or degrading punishment and treatment shall be prohibited.

ARTICLE 6
Every individual shall have the right to liberty and to the security of his person. No one may be deprived of his freedom except for reasons and conditions previously laid down by law. In particular, no one may be arbitrarily arrested or detained.

ARTICLE 7
1. Every individual shall have the right to have his cause heard. This comprises:
(a) the right to an appeal to competent national organs against acts of violating his fundamental rights as recognized and guaranteed by conventions, laws, regulations and customs in force;
(b) the right to be presumed innocent until proved guilty by a competent court or tribunal;
(c) the right to defence, including the right to be defended by counsel of his choice;
(d) the right to be tried within a reasonable time by an impartial court or tribunal.
2. No one may be condemned for an act or omission which did not constitute a legally punishable offence at the time it was committed. No penalty may be inflicted for an offence for which no provision was made at the time it was committed. Punishment is personal and can be imposed only on the offender.

ARTICLE 8
Freedom of conscience, the profession and free practice of religion shall be guaranteed. No one may, subject to law and order, be submitted to measures restricting the exercise of these freedoms.

ARTICLE 9
1. Every individual shall have the right to receive information.
2. Every individual shall have the right to express and disseminate his opinions within

the law.

ARTICLE 10
1. Every individual shall have the right to free association provided that he abides by the law.
2. Subject to the obligation of solidarity provided for in Article 29 no one may be compelled to join an association.

ARTICLE 11
Every individual shall have the right to assemble freely with others. The exercise of this right shall be subject only to necessary restrictions provided for by law in particular those enacted in the interest of national security, the safety, health, ethics and rights and freedoms of others.

ARTICLE 12
1. Every individual shall have the right to freedom of movement and residence within the borders of a State provided he abides by the law.
2. Every individual shall have the right to leave any country including his own, and to return to his country. This right may only be subject to restrictions, provided for by law for the protection of national security, law and order, public health or morality.
3. Every individual shall have the right, when persecuted, to seek and obtain asylum in other countries in accordance with laws of those countries and international conventions.
4. A non-national legally admitted in a territory of a State Party to the present Charter, may only be expelled from it by virtue of a decision taken in accordance with the law.
5. The mass expulsion of non-nationals shall be prohibited. Mass expulsion shall be that which is aimed at national, racial, ethnic or religious groups.

ARTICLE 13
1. Every citizen shall have the right to participate freely in the government of his country, either directly or through freely chosen representatives in accordance with the provisions of the law.
2. Every citizen shall have the right of equal access to the public service of his country.
3. Every individual shall have the right of access to public property and services in strict equality of all persons before the law.

ARTICLE 14
The right to property shall be guaranteed. It may only be encroached upon in the interest of public need or in the general interest of the community and in accordance with the provisions of appropriate laws.

ARTICLE 15
Every individual shall have the right to work under equitable and satisfactory conditions, and shall receive equal pay for equal work.

ARTICLE 16
1. Every individual shall have the right to enjoy the best attainable state of physical and mental health.
2. States parties to the present Charter shall take the necessary measures to protect the health of their people and to ensure that they receive medical attention when they are sick.

ARTICLE 17
1. Every individual shall have the right to education.
2. Every individual may freely take part in the cultural life of his community.
3. The promotion and protection of morals and traditional values recognized by the community shall be the duty of the State.

ARTICLE 18
1. The family shall be the natural unit and basis of society. It shall be protected by the State which shall take care of its physical

health and morals.

2. The State shall have the duty to assist the family which is the custodian of morals and traditional values recognized by the community.

3. The State shall ensure the elimination of every discrimination against women and also ensure the protection of the rights of the woman and the child as stipulated in international declarations and conventions.

4. The aged and the disabled shall also have the right to special measures of protection in keeping with their physical or moral needs.

ARTICLE 19

All peoples shall be equal; they shall enjoy the same respect and shall have the same rights. Nothing shall justify the domination of a people by another.

ARTICLE 20

1. All peoples shall have the right to existence. They shall have the unquestionable and inalienable right to self-determination. They shall freely determine their political status and shall pursue their economic and social development according to the policy they have freely chosen.

2. Colonized or oppressed peoples shall have the right to free themselves from the bonds of domination by resorting to any means recognized by the international community.

3. All peoples shall have the right to the assistance of the States parties to the present Charter in their liberation struggle against foreign domination, be it political, economic or cultural.

ARTICLE 21

All peoples shall freely dispose of their wealth and natural resources. This right shall be exercised in the exclusive interest of the people. In no case shall a people be deprived of it.

2. In case of spoliation the dispossessed people shall have the right to the lawful recovery of its property as well as to an adequate compensation.

3. The free disposal of wealth and natural resources shall be exercised without prejudice to the obligation of promoting international economic cooperation based on mutual respect, equitable exchange and the principles of international law.

4. States parties to the present Charter shall individually and collectively exercise the right to free disposal of their wealth and natural resources with a view to strengthening African unity and solidarity.

5. States parties to the present Charter shall undertake to eliminate all forms of foreign economic exploitation particularly that practised by international monopolies so as to enable their peoples to fully benefit from the advantages derived from their national resources.

ARTICLE 22

1. All peoples shall have the right to their economic, social and cultural development with due regard to their freedom and identity and in the equal enjoyment of the common heritage of mankind.

2. States shall have the duty, individually or collectively, to ensure the exercise of the right to development.

ARTICLE 23

1. All peoples shall have the right to national and international peace and security. The principles of solidarity and friendly relations implicitly affirmed by the Charter of the United Nations and reaffirmed by that of the Organization of African Unity shall govern relations between States.

2. For the purpose of strengthening peace, solidarity and friendly relations, States parties to the present Charter shall ensure that:

(a) any individual enjoying the right of asylum under 12 of the present Charter shall not engage in subversive activities against his country of origin or any other State party to the present Charter;

(b) their territories shall not be used as bases for subversive or terrorist activities against the people of any other State party to the present Charter.

ARTICLE 24

All peoples shall have the right to a general satisfactory environment favourable to their development.

ARTICLE 25

States parties to the present Charter shall have the duty to promote and ensure through teaching, education and publication, the respect of the rights and freedoms contained in the present Charter and to see to it that these freedoms and rights as well as corresponding obligations and duties are understood.

ARTICLE 26

States parties to the present Charter shall have the duty to guarantee the independence of the Courts and shall allow the establishment and improvement of appropriate national institutions entrusted with the promotion and protection of the rights and freedoms guaranteed by the present Charter.

CHAPTER II

DUTIES

ARTICLE 27

1. Every individual shall have duties towards his family and society, the State and other legally recognized communities and the international community.

2. The rights and freedoms of each individual shall be exercised with due regard to the rights of others, collective security, morality and common interest.

ARTICLE 28

Every individual shall have the duty to respect and consider his fellow beings without discrimination, and to maintain relations aimed at promoting, safeguarding and reinforcing mutual respect and tolerance.

ARTICLE 29

The individual shall also have the duty:

1. to preserve the harmonious development of the family and to work for the cohesion and respect of the family; to respect his parents at all times, to maintain them in case of need;

2. To serve his national community by placing his physical and intellectual abilities at its service;

3. Not to compromise the security of the State whose national or resident he is;

4. To preserve and strengthen social and national solidarity, particularly when the latter is threatened;

5. To preserve and strengthen the national independence and the territorial integrity of his country and to contribute to its defence in accordance with the law;

6. To work to the best of his abilities and competence, and to pay taxes imposed by law in the interest of the society;

7. To preserve and strengthen positive African cultural values in his relations with other members of the society, in the spirit of tolerance, dialogue and consultation and, in general, to contribute to the promotion of the moral well-being of society;

8. To contribute to the best of his abilities, at all times and at all levels, to the promotion and achievement of African unity.

PART II - MEASURES OF SAFEGUARD

CHAPTER I

ESTABLISHMENT AND ORGANIZATION OF THE AFRICAN COMMISSION ON HUMAN AND PEOPLES' RIGHTS

ARTICLE 30

An African Commission on Human and Peoples' Rights, hereinafter called "the Commission", shall be established within the Organization of African Unity to promote human and peoples' rights and ensure their protection in Africa.

ARTICLE 31

1. The Commission shall consist of eleven members chosen from amongst African personalities of the highest reputation, known for their high morality, integrity, impartiality and competence in matters of human and peoples' rights; particular consideration being given to persons having legal experience.

2. The members of the Commission shall serve in their personal capacity.

ARTICLE 41

The Secretary General of the Organization of African Unity shall appoint the Secretary of the Commission. He shall also provide the staff and services necessary for the effective discharge of the duties of the Commission. The Organization of African Unity shall bear the costs of the staff and services.

CHAPTER II

MANDATE OF THE COMMISSION

ARTICLE 45

The functions of the Commission shall be:
1. To promote Human and Peoples' Rights and in particular:

(a) to collect documents, undertake studies and researches on African problems in the field of human and peoples' rights, organize seminars, symposia and conferences, disseminate information, encourage national and local institutions concerned with human and peoples' rights, and should the case arise, give its views or make recommendations to Governments.

(b) to formulate and lay down, principles and rules aimed at solving legal problems relating to human and peoples' rights and fundamental freedoms upon which African Governments may base their legislations.

(c) co-operate with other African and international institutions concerned with the promotion and protection of human and peoples' rights.

2. Ensure the protection of human and peoples' rights under conditions laid down by the present Charter.

3. Interpret all the provisions of the present Charter at the request of a State party, an institution of the OAU or an African Organization recognized by the OAU.

4. Perform any other tasks which may be entrusted to it by the Assembly of Heads of State and Government.

CHAPTER III

PROCEDURE OF THE COMMISSION

ARTICLE 46

The Commission may resort to any appropriate method of investigation; it may hear from the Secretary General of the Organization of African Unity or any other person capable of enlightening it.

COMMUNICATION FROM STATES

ARTICLE 47

If a State party to the present Charter has good reasons to believe that another State party to this Charter has violated the provisions of the Charter, it may draw, by written communication, the attention of that State to the matter. This communication shall also be addressed to the Secretary General of the OAU and to the Chairman of the Commission. Within three months of the receipt of the communication, the State to which the communication is addressed shall give the enquiring State, written explanation or statement elucidating the matter. This should include as much as possible relevant information relating to the laws and rules of procedure applied and applicable, and the redress already given or course of action available.

ARTICLE 48
If within three months from the date on which the original communication is received by the State to which it is addressed, the issue is not settled to the satisfaction of the two States involved through bilateral negotiation or by any other peaceful procedure, either State shall have the right to submit the matter to the Commission through the Chairman and shall notify the other States involved.

ARTICLE 49
Notwithstanding the provisions of art. 47, if a State party to the present Charter considers that another State party has violated the provisions of the Charter, it may refer the matter directly to the Commission by addressing a communication to the Chairman, to the Secretary General of the Organization of African Unity and the State concerned.

ARTICLE 50
The Commission can only deal with a matter submitted to it after making sure that all local remedies, if they exist, have been exhausted, unless it is obvious to the Commission that the procedure of achieving these remedies would be unduly prolonged.

ARTICLE 51
1. The Commission may ask the States concerned to provide it with all relevant information.

2. When the Commission is considering the matter, States concerned may be represented before it and submit written or oral representation.

ARTICLE 52
After having obtained from the States concerned and from other sources all the information it deems necessary and after having tried all appropriate means to reach an amicable solution based on the respect of Human and Peoples' Rights, the Commission shall prepare, within a reasonable period of time from the notification referred to in 48, a report stating the facts and its findings. This report shall be sent to the States concerned and communicated to the Assembly of Heads of State and Government.

ARTICLE 53
While transmitting its report, the Commission may make to the Assembly of Heads of State and Government such recommendations as it deems useful.

ARTICLE 54
The Commission shall submit to each ordinary Session of the Assembly of Heads of State and Government a report on its activities.

OTHER COMMUNICATIONS

ARTICLE 55
1. Before each Session, the Secretary of the Commission shall make a list of the communications other than those of States parties to the present Charter and transmit them to the members of the Commission, who shall indicate which communications should be considered by the Commission.

2. A communication shall be considered by the Commission if a simple majority of its members so decide.

ARTICLE 56
Communications relating to human and peoples' rights referred to in art. 55 received by the Commission, shall be considered if they:

1. Indicate their authors even if the latter request anonymity,

2. Are compatible with the Charter of the Organization of African Unity or with the present Charter,

3. Are not written in disparaging or insulting language directed against the State concerned and its institutions or to the Organization of African Unity,
4. Are not based exclusively on news discriminated through the mass media,
5. Are sent after exhausting local remedies, if any, unless it is obvious that this procedure is unduly prolonged,
6. Are submitted within a reasonable period from the time local remedies are exhausted or from the date the Commission is seized of the matter, and
7. Do not deal with cases which have been settled by these States involved in accordance with the principles of the Charter of the United Nations, or the Charter of the Organization of African Unity or the provisions of the present Charter.

ARTICLE 57
Prior to any substantive consideration, all communications shall be brought to the knowledge of the State concerned by the Chairman of the Commission.

ARTICLE 58
1. When it appears after deliberations of the Commission that one or more communications apparently relate to special cases which reveal the existence of a series of serious or massive violations of human and peoples' rights, the Commission shall draw the attention of the Assembly of Heads of State and Government to these special cases.
2. The Assembly of Heads of State and Government may then request the Commission to undertake an in-depth study of these cases and make a factual report, accompanied by its findings and recommendations.
3. A case of emergency duly noticed by the Commission shall be submitted by the latter to the Chairman of the Assembly of Heads of State and Government who may request an in-depth study.

ARTICLE 59
1. All measures taken within the provisions of the present Chapter shall remain confidential until such a time as the Assembly of Heads of State and Government shall otherwise decide.
2. However, the report shall be published by the Chairman of the Commission upon the decision of the Assembly of Heads of State and Government.
3. The report on the activities of the Commission shall be published by its Chairman after it has been considered by the Assembly of Heads of State and Government.

CHAPTER IV

APPLICABLE PRINCIPLES

ARTICLE 60
The Commission shall draw inspiration from international law on human and peoples' rights, particularly from the provisions of various African instruments on human and peoples' rights, the Charter of the United Nations, the Charter of the Organization of African Unity, the Universal Declaration of Human Rights, other instruments adopted by the United Nations and by African countries in the field of human and peoples' rights as well as from the provisions of various instruments adopted within the Specialized Agencies of the United Nations of which the parties to the present Charter are members.

ARTICLE 61
The Commission shall also take into consideration, as subsidiary measures to determine the principles of law, other general or special international conventions, laying down rules expressly recognized by member states of the Organization of African Unity, African practices consistent with international norms on human and people's rights, customs generally accepted as law, general principles of law recognized by African

states as well as legal precedents and doctrine.

ARTICLE 62
Each state party shall undertake to submit every two years, from the date the present Charter comes into force, a report on the legislative or other measures taken with a view to giving effect to the rights and freedoms recognized and guaranteed by the present Charter.

CONSTITUTION OF BOTSWANA

CHAPTER I

THE REPUBLIC

SECTION 1
Botswana is a sovereign Republic.

SECTION 2
The Public Seal of the Republic shall be such device as may be prescribed by or under an Act of Parliament.

CHAPTER II

PROTECTION OF FUNDAMENTAL RIGHTS AND FREEDOMS OF THE INDIVIDUAL

SECTION 3
Whereas every person in Botswana is entitled to the fundamental rights and freedoms of the individual, that is to say, the right, whatever his race, place of origin, political opinions, colour, creed or sex, but subject to respect for the rights and freedoms of others and for the public interest to each and all of the following, namely
a) life, liberty, security of the person and the protection of the law;
b) freedom of conscience, of expression and of assembly and association; and
c) protection for the privacy of his home and other property and from deprivation of property without compensation, the provisions of this Chapter shall have effect for the purpose of affording protection to those rights and freedoms subject to such limitations of that protection as are contained in those provisions, being limitations designed to ensure that the enjoyment of the said rights and freedoms by any individual does not prejudice the rights and freedoms of others or the public interest.

SECTION 4.
1. No person shall be deprived of his life intentionally save in execution of the sentence of a court in respect of an offence under the law in force in Botswana of which he has been convicted.
2. A person shall not be regarded as having been deprived of his life in contravention of subsection (1) of this section if he dies as the result of the use, to such extent and in such circumstances as are permitted by law, of such force as is reasonably justifiable -
a) for the defence of any person from violence or for the defence of property;
b) in order to effect a lawful arrest or to prevent the escape of a person lawfully detained;
c) for the purpose of suppressing a riot, insurrection or mutiny; or
d) in order to prevent the commission by that person of a criminal offence, or if he dies as the result of a lawful act of war.

SECTION 5
1. No person shall be deprived of his personal liberty save as may be authorized by law in any of the following cases, that is to say -
a) in execution of the sentence or order of a court, whether established for Botswana or some other country, in respect of a criminal offence of which he has been convicted;
b) in execution of the order of a court of record punishing him for contempt of that or another court;
c) in execution of the order of a court made to secure the fulfilment of any obligation imposed on him by law;
d) for the purpose of bringing him before a court in execution of the order of a court,
e) upon reasonable suspicion of his having committed, or being about to commit, a

criminal offence under the law in force in Botswana;

f) under the order of a court or with the consent of his parent or guardian, for his education or welfare during any period ending nor later than the date when he attains the age of eighteen years;

g) for the purpose of preventing the spread of an infectious or contagious disease;

h) in the case of a person who is, or is reasonably suspected to be, of unsound mind, addicted to drugs or alcohol, or a vagrant, for the purpose of his care or treatment or the protection of the community;

i) for the purpose of preventing the unlawful entry of that person into Botswana, or for the purpose of effecting the expulsion, extradition or other lawful removal of that person from Botswana or for the purpose of restricting that person while he is being conveyed through Botswana in the course of his extradition or removal as a convicted prisoner from one country to another;

j) to such extent as may be necessary in the execution of a lawful order requiring that person to remain within a specified area within Botswana or prohibiting him from being within such an area, or to such extent as may be reasonably justifiable for the taking of proceedings against that person relating to the making of any such order, or to such extent as may be reasonably justifiable for restraining that person during any visit that he is permitted to make to any part of Botswana in which, in consequence of any such order, his presence would otherwise be unlawful; or

k) for the purpose of ensuring the safety of aircraft in flight.

2. Any person who is arrested or detained shall be informed as soon as reasonably practicable, in a language that he understands, of the reasons for his arrest or detention.

3. Any person who is arrested or detained
a) for the purpose of bringing him before a court in execution of the order of a court; or
b) upon reasonable suspicion of his having committed, or being about to commit, a criminal offence under the law in force in Botswana, and who is not released, shall be brought as soon as is reasonably practicable before a court; and if any person arrested or detained as mentioned in paragraph (b) of this subsection is not tried within a reasonable time, then, without prejudice to any further proceedings that may be brought against him, he shall be released either unconditionally or upon reasonable conditions, including in particular such conditions as are reasonably necessary to ensure that he appears at a later date for trial or for proceedings preliminary to trial.

4. Any person who is unlawfully arrested or detained by any other person shall be entitled to compensation therefore from that other person.

SECTION 6

1. No person shall be held in slavery or servitude.

2. No person shall be required to perform forced labour.

3. For the purposes of this section, the expression "forced labour" does not include
a) any labour required in consequence of the sentence or order of a court;
b) labour required of any person while he is lawfully detained that, though not required in consequence of the sentence or order of a court, is reasonably necessary in the interests of hygiene or for the maintenance of the place at which he is detained;
c) any labour required of a member of a disciplined force in pursuance of his duties as such or, in the case of a person who has conscientious objections to service as a member of a naval, military or air force, any labour that that person is required by law to perform in place of such service;
d) any labour required during any period of public emergency or in the event of any other emergency or calamity that threatens the life and well-being of the community, to

the extent that the requiring of such labour is reasonably justifiable in the circumstances of any situation arising or existing during that period or as a result of that other emergency or calamity, for the purpose of dealing with that situation; or

e) any labour reasonably required as part of reasonable and normal communal or other civic obligations.

SECTION 7

1. No person shall be subjected to torture or to inhuman or degrading punishment or other treatment.

2. Nothing contained in or done under the authority of any law shall be held to be inconsistent with or in contravention of this section to the extent that the law in question authorizes the infliction of any description of punishment that was lawful in the former Protectorate of Bechuanaland immediately before the coming into operation of this Constitution.

SECTION 8

1. No property of any description shall be compulsorily taken possession of, and no interest in or right over property of any description shall be compulsorily acquired, except where the following conditions are satisfied, that is to say -

a) the taking of possession or acquisition is necessary or expedient -

i) in the interests of defence, public safety, public order, public morality, public health, town and country planning or land settlement;

ii) in order to secure the development or utilization of that, or other, property for a purpose beneficial to the community; or

iii) in order to secure the development or utilization of the mineral resources of Botswana; and

b) provision is made by a law applicable to that taking of possession or acquisition -

i) for the prompt payment of adequate compensation; and

ii) securing to any person having an interest in or right over the property a right of access to the High Court, either direct or on appeal from any other authority, for the determination of his interest or right, the legality of the taking of possession or acquisition of the property, interest or right, and the amount of any compensation to which he is entitled, and for the purpose of obtaining prompt payment of that compensation.

2. No person who is entitled to compensation under this section shall be prevented from remitting, within a reasonable time after he has received any amount of that compensation, the whole of that amount (free from any deduction, charge or tax made or levied in respect of its remission) to any country of his choice outside Botswana.

3. Subsection (1)(b)(i) of this section shall be deemed to be satisfied in relation to any law applicable to the taking of possession of minerals or the acquisition of rights to minerals that law makes provision for the payment at reasonable intervals of adequate royalties.

4. Nothing contained in or done under the authority of any law shall be held to be inconsistent with or in contravention of subsection (2) of this section to the extent that the law in question authorizes -

a) the attachment, by order of a court, of any amount of compensation to which a person is entitled in satisfaction of the judgment of a court or pending the determination of civil proceedings to which he is a party; or

b) the imposition of reasonable restrictions on the manner in which any amount of compensation is to be remitted.

5. Nothing contained in or done under the authority of any law shall be held to be inconsistent with or in contravention of subsection (1) of this section -

a) to the extent that the law in question makes provision for the taking of possession or acquisition of any property -

i) in satisfaction of any tax, rate or due;
ii) by way of penalty for breach of the law whether under civil process or after conviction of a criminal offence under the law in force in Botswana;
iii) as an incident of a lease, tenancy, mortgage, charge, bill of sale, pledge or contract;
iv) in the execution of judgments or orders of a court in proceedings for the determination of civil rights or obligations;
v) in circumstances where it is reasonably necessary so to do because the property is in a dangerous state or injurious to the health of human beings, animals or plants;
vi) in consequence of any law with respect to the limitation of actions; or
vii) for so long only as may be necessary for the purposes of any examination, investigation, trial or inquiry or, in the case of land, for the purposes of the carrying out thereon of work of soil conservation or the conservation of other natural resources or work relating to agricultural development or improvement (being work relating to such development or improvement that the owner or occupier of the land has been required, and has without reasonable excuse refused or failed, to carry out):
and except so far as that provision or, as the case may be, the thing done under the authority thereof is shown not to be reasonably justifiable in a democratic society; or
b) to the extent that the law in question makes provision for the taking of possession or acquisition of -
i) enemy property;
ii) property of a deceased person, a person of unsound mind, a person who has not attained the age of twenty one years, a prodigal, or a person who is absent from Botswana, for the purpose of its administration for the benefit of the persons entitled to the beneficial interest therein;
iii) property of a person declared to be insolvent or a body corporate in liquidation, for the purpose of its administration for the benefit of the creditors or the insolvent or body corporate and, subject thereto, for the benefit of other persons entitled to the beneficial interest in the property; or
iv) property subject to a trust, for the purpose of vesting the property in persons appointed as trustees under the instrument creating the trust or by a court, or by order of a court, for the purpose of giving effect to the trust.

6. Nothing contained in or done under the authority of any law shall be held to be inconsistent with or in contravention of subsection (1) of this section to the extent that the law in question makes provision for the compulsory taking of possession in the public interest of any property, or the compulsory acquisition in the public interest in or right over property, where that property, interest or right is held by a body corporate established by law for public purposes in which no moneys have been invested other than moneys provided by Parliament.

SECTION 9

1. Except with his own consent, no person shall be subjected to the search of his person or his property or the entry by others on his premises.

2. Nothing contained in or done under the authority of any law shall be held to be inconsistent with or in contravention of this section to the extent that the law in question makes provision -
a) that is reasonably required in the interests of defence, public safety, public order, public morality, public health, town and country planning, the development and utilization of mineral resources, for the purpose of any census or in order to secure the development or utilization of any property for a purpose beneficial to the community;
b) that is reasonably required for the purpose of protecting the rights or freedoms of other persons;

c) that authorizes an officer or agent of the Government of Botswana, a local government authority or a body corporate established by law for a public purpose to enter on the premises of any person in order to inspect those premises or anything thereon for the purpose of any tax, rate or duty or in order to carry out work connected with any property that is lawfully on those premises and that belongs to that Government, authority or body corporate, as the case may be; or

d) that authorizes, for the purpose of enforcing the judgment or order of a court in any civil proceedings, the search of any person or property by order of a court or entry upon any premises by such order, and except so far as that provision or, as the case may be, anything done under the authority thereof is shown not to be reasonably justifiable in a democratic society.

SECTION 10

1. If any person is charged with a criminal offence, then, unless the charge is withdrawn, the case shall be afforded a fair hearing within a reasonable time by an independent and impartial court established or recognized by law.

2. Every person who is charged with a criminal offence -

a) shall be presumed to be innocent until he is proved or has pleaded guilty;

b) shall be informed as soon as reasonably practicable, in a language that he understands and in detail, of the nature of the offence charged;

c) shall be given adequate time and facilities for the preparation of his defence;

d) shall be permitted to defend himself before the court in person or, at his own expense, by a legal representative of his own choice;

e) shall be afforded facilities to examine in person or by his legal representative the witnesses called by the prosecution before the court, and to obtain the attendance and carry out the examination of witnesses to testify on his behalf before the court on the same conditions as those applying to witnesses called by the prosecution; and

f) shall be permitted to have without payment the assistance of an interpreter if he cannot understand the language used at the trial of the charge, and except with his own consent the trial shall not take place in his absence unless he so conducts himself as to render the continuance of the proceedings in his presence impracticable and the court has ordered him to be removed and the trial to proceed in his absence.

3. When a person is tried for any criminal offence, the accused person or any person authorized by him in that behalf shall, if he so requires and subject to payment of such reasonable fee as may be prescribed by law, be given within a reasonable time after judgment a copy for the use of the accused person of any record of the proceedings made by or on behalf of the court.

4. No person shall be held to be guilty of a criminal offence on account of any act or omission that did not, at the time it took place, constitute such an offence, and no penalty shall be imposed for any criminal offence that is severer in degree or description than the maximum penalty that might have been imposed for that offence at the time when it was committed.

5. No person who shows that he has been tried by a competent court for a criminal offence and either convicted or acquitted shall again be tried for that offence or for any other criminal offence of which he could have been convicted at the trial for that offence, save upon the order of a superior court in the course of appeal or review proceedings relating to the conviction or acquittal.

6. No person shall be tried for a criminal offence if he shows that he has been pardoned for that offence.

7. No person who is tried for a criminal offence shall be compelled to give evidence at the trial.

8. No person shall be convicted of a criminal offence unless that offence is defined and the penalty therefore is prescribed in a written law:

Provided that nothing in this subsection shall prevent a court of record from punishing any person for contempt of itself notwithstanding that the act or omission constituting the contempt is not defined in a written law and the penalty therefore is not so prescribed.

9. Any court or other adjudicating authority prescribed by law for the determination of the existence or extent of any civil right or obligation shall be established or recognized by law and shall be independent and impartial; and where proceedings for such a determination are instituted by any person before such a court or other adjudicating authority, the case shall be given a fair hearing within a reasonable time.

10. Except with the agreement of all the parties thereto, all proceedings of every court and proceedings for the determination of the existence or extent of any civil right or obligation before any other adjudicating authority, including the announcement of the decision of the court or other authority, shall be held in public.

11. Nothing in the last foregoing subsection shall prevent the court or other adjudicating authority from excluding from the proceedings persons other than the parties thereto and their legal representatives to such extent as the court or other authority -

a) may consider necessary or expedient in circumstances where publicity would prejudice the interests of justice or in interlocutory proceedings; or

b) may be empowered by law to do so in the interests of defence, public safety, public order, public morality, the welfare of persons under the age of eighteen years or the protection of the private lives of persons concerned in the proceedings.

12. Nothing contained in or done under the authority of any law shall be held to be inconsistent with or in contravention of

a) subsection (2)(a) of this section to the extent that the law in question imposes upon any person charged with a criminal offence the burden of proving particular facts;

b) subsection (2)(d) or (2)(e) of this section to the extent that the law in question prohibits legal representation before a subordinate court in proceedings for an offence under African customary law (being proceedings against any person who, under that law, is subject to that law);

c) subsection (2)(c) of this section to the extent that the law in question imposes reasonable conditions that must be satisfied if witnesses called to testify on behalf of an accused person are to be paid their expenses out of public funds;

d) subsection (5) of this section to the extent that the law in question authorizes a court to try a member of a disciplined force for a criminal offence notwithstanding any trial and conviction or acquittal of that member under the disciplinary law of that force, so, however, that any court so trying such a member and convicting him shall in sentencing him to any punishment take into account any punishment awarded him under that disciplinary law;

e) subsection (8) of this section to the extent that the law in question authorizes a court to convict a person of a criminal offence under any African customary law to which, by virtue of that law, such person is subject.

13. In the case of any person who is held in lawful detention, the provisions of subsection (1), subsection (2)(d) and (e) and subsection (3) of this section shall not apply in relation to his trial for a criminal offence under the law regulating the discipline of persons held in such detention.

14. In this section "criminal offence" means a criminal offence under the law in force in Botswana.

SECTION 11

1. Except with his own consent, no person

shall be hindered in the enjoyment of his freedom of conscience, and for the purpose of this section the said freedom includes freedom of thought and of religion, freedom to change his religion or belief, and freedom, either alone or in community with others, and both in public and in private, to manifest and propagate his religion or belief in worship, teaching, practice and observance.

2. Every religious community shall be entitled, at its own expense, to establish and maintain places of education and to manage any place of education which it wholly maintains; and no such community shall be prevented from providing religious instruction for persons of that community in the course of any education provided at any place of education which it wholly maintains or in the course of any education which it otherwise provides.

3. Except with his own consent (or, if he is a minor, the consent of his guardian) no person attending any place of education shall be required to receive religious instruction or to take part in or attend any religious ceremony or observance if that instruction, ceremony or observance relates to a religion other than his own.

4. No person shall be compelled to take any oath which is contrary to his religion or belief or to take any oath in a manner which is contrary to his religion or belief.

5. Nothing contained in or done under the authority of any law shall be held to be inconsistent with or in contravention of this section to the extent that the law in question makes provision which is reasonably required -

a) in the interests of defence, public safety, public order. public morality or public health; or

b) for the purpose of protecting the rights and freedoms of other persons, including the right to observe and practice any religion without the unsolicited intervention of members of any other religion, and except so far as that provision or, as the case may be, the thing done under the authority thereof is shown to be reasonably justifiable in a democratic society.

SECTION 12

1. Except with his own consent, no person shall be hindered in the enjoyment of his freedom of expression, that is to say, freedom to hold opinions without interference, freedom to receive ideas and information without interference, freedom to communicate ideas and information without interference (whether the communication be to the public generally or to any person or class of persons) and freedom from interference with his correspondence.

2. Nothing contained in or done under the authority of any law shall be held to be inconsistent with or in contravention of this section to the extent that the law in question makes provision -

a) that is reasonably required in the interests of defence of public safety, public order, public morality or public health; or

b) that is reasonably required for the purpose of protecting the reputations, rights and freedoms of other persons or the private lives of persons concerned in legal proceedings, preventing the disclosure of information received in confidence, maintaining the authority and independence of the courts, regulating educational institutions in the interests of persons receiving instruction therein, or regulating the technical administration or the technical operation of telephony, telegraphy, posts, wireless, broadcasting or television; or

c) that imposes restrictions upon public officers, employees of local government bodies, or teachers, and except so far as that provision or, as the case may be, the thing done under the authority thereof is shown not to be reasonably justifiable in a democratic society.

SECTION 13

1. Except with his own consent, no person shall be hindered in the enjoyment of his freedom of assembly and association, that is to say, his right to assemble freely and associate with other persons and in particular to form or belong to trade unions or other associations for the protection of his interests.

2. Nothing contained in or done under the authority of any law shall be held to be inconsistent with or in contravention of this section to the extent that the law in question makes provision -

a) that is reasonably required in the interests of defence, public safety, public order, public morality or public health;

b) that is reasonably required for the purpose of protecting the rights or freedoms of other persons;

c) that imposes restrictions upon public officers, employees of local government bodies, or teachers; or

d) for the registration of trade unions and associations of trade unions in a register established by or under any law, and for imposing reasonable conditions relating to the requirements for entry on such a register (including conditions as to the minimum number of persons necessary to constitute a trade union qualified for registration, or of members necessary to constitute an association of trade unions qualified for registration, and conditions whereby registration may be refused on the grounds that any other trade union already registered, or association of trade unions already registered, as the case may be, is sufficiently representative of the whole or of a substantial proportion of the interests in respect of which registration of a trade union or associarion of trade unions is sought, and except so far as that provision or, as the case may be, the thing done under the authority thereof is shown not to be reasonably justifiable in a democratic society.

SECTION 14

1. No person shall be deprived of his freedom of movement, and for the purposes of this section the said freedom means the right to move freely throughout Botswana, the right to reside in any part of Botswana, the right to enter Botswana and immunity from expulsion from Botswana.

2. Any restriction on a person's freedom of movement that is involved in his lawful detention shall not be held to be inconsistent with or in contravention of this section.

3. Nothing contained in or done under the authority of any law shall be held to be inconsistent with or in contravention of this section to the extent that the law in question makes provision -

a) for the imposition of restrictions that are reasonably required in the interests of defence, public safety, public order, public morality or public health or the imposition of restrictions on the acquisition or use by any person of land or other property in Botswana and except so far as that provision or, as the case may be, the thing done under the authority thereof, is shown not to be reasonably justifiable in a democratic society;

b) for the imposition of restrictions on the freedom of movement of any person who is not a citizen of Botswana;

c) for the imposition of restrictions on the entry into or residence within defined areas of Botswana of persons who are not Bushmen to the extent that such restrictions are reasonably required for the protection or well-being of Bushmen;

d) for the imposition of restrictions upon the movement or residence within Botswana of public officers; or

e) for the removal of a person from Botswana to be tried outside Botswana for a criminal offence or to undergo imprisonment in some other country in execution of the sentence of a court in respect of a criminal offence under the law in force in Botswana of which he has been convicted.

4. If any person whose freedom of movement has been restricted by order under such

a provision as is referred to in subsection (3)(a) of this section (other than a restriction which is applicable to persons generally or to general classes of persons) so requests at any time during the period of that restriction not earlier than six months after the order was made or six months after he last made such request, as the case may be, his case shall be reviewed by an independent and impartial tribunal presided over by a person, qualified to be enrolled as an advocate in Botswana, appointed by the Chief Justice.

5. On any review by a tribunal in pursuance of this section of the case of a person whose freedom of movement has been restricted, the tribunal may make recommendations, concerning the necessity or expediency of continuing the restriction to the authority by which it was ordered but, unless it is otherwise provided by law, that authority shall not be obliged to act in accordance with any such recommendations.

SECTION 15

1. Subject to the provisions of subsections (4), (5) and (7) of this section, no law shall make any provision that is discriminatory either of itself or in its effect.
2. Subject to the provisions of subsections (6), (7) and (8) of this section, no person shall be treated in a discriminatory manner by any person acting by virtue of any written law or in the performance of the functions of any public office or any public authority.
3. In this section, the expression "discriminatory" means affording different treatment to different persons, attributable wholly or mainly to their respective descriptions by race, tribe, place of origin, political opinions, colour or creed whereby persons of one such description are subjected to disabilities or restrictions to which persons of another such description are not made subject or are accorded privileges or advantages which are not accorded to persons of another such description.
4. Subsection (1) of this section shall not apply to any law so far as that law makes provision -
a) for the appropriation of public revenue or other public funds;
b) with respect to persons who are not citizens of Botswana;
c) with respect to adoption, marriage, divorce, burial, devolution of property on death or other matters of personal law;
d) for the application in the case of members of a particular race, community or tribe or customary law with respect to any matter whether to the exclusion of any law in respect to that matter which is applicable in the case of other persons or not; or
e) whereby persons of any such description as is mentioned in subsection (3) of this section may be subjected to any disability or restriction or may be accorded any privilege or advantage which, having regard to its nature and to special circumstances pertaining to those persons or to persons of any other such description, is reasonably justifiable in a democratic society.
5. Nothing contained in any law shall be held to be inconsistent with or in contravention of subsection (1) of this section to the extent that it makes reasonable provision with respect to qualifications for service as a public officer or as a member of a disciplined force or for the service of a local government authority or a body corporate established directly by any law.
6. Subsection (2) of this section shall not apply to anything which is expressly or by necessary implication authorized to be done by any such provision of law as is referred to in subsection (4) or (5) of this section.
7. Nothing contained in or done under the authority of any law shall be held to be inconsistent with or in contravention of this section to the extent that the law in question makes provision whereby persons of any such description as is mentioned in subsection (3) of this section may be subjected to any restriction on the rights and freedoms

guaranteed by sections 9, 11, 12, 13 and 14 of this Constitution, being such a restriction as is authorized by section 9 (2), 11 (5), 12 (2) 13 (2), or 14 (3), as the case may be.

8. Nothing in subsection (2) of this section shall affect any discretion relating to the institution, conduct or discontinuance of civil or criminal proceedings in any court that is vested in any person by or under this Constitution or any other law.

9. Nothing contained in or done under the authority of any law shall be held to be inconsistent with the provisions of this section -

a) if that law was in force immediately before the coming into operation of this Constitution and has continued in force at all times since the coming into operation of this Constitution, or

b) to the extent that the law repeals and re-enacts any provision which has been contained in any written law at all times since immediately before the coming into operation of this Constitution.

SECTION 16

1. Nothing contained in or done under the authority of any law shall be held to be inconsistent with or in contravention of section 5 or 15 of this Constitution to the extent that the law authorizes the taking during any period when Botswana is at war or any period when a declaration under section 17 of this Constitution is in force, of measures that are reasonably justifiable for the purpose of dealing with the situation that exists during that period.

2. Where a person is detained by virtue of such an authorization as is referred to in subsection (1) of this section the following provisions shall apply -

a) he shall, as soon as reasonably practicable and in any case not more than five days after the commencement of his detention, be furnished with a statement in writing in a language that he understands specifying in detail the grounds upon which he is detained;

b) not more than fourteen days after the commencement of his detention, a notification shall be published in the Gazette stating that he has been detained and giving particulars of the provision of law under which his detention is authorized;

c) not more than one month after the commencement of his detention and thereafter during his detention at intervals of not more than six months, his case shall be reviewed by an independent and impartial tribunal established by law and presided over by a person, qualified to be enrolled as an advocate in Botswana, appointed by the Chief Justice; and

d) he shall be afforded reasonable facilities to consult and instruct, at his own expense, a legal representative and he and any such legal representative shall be permitted to make written or oral representations or both to the tribunal appointed for the review of his case.

3. On any review by a tribunal in pursuance of this section of the case of a detained person, the tribunal may make recommendations, concerning the necessity or expediency of continuing his detention, to the authority by which it was ordered but unless it is otherwise provided by law, that authority shall not be obliged to act in accordance with any such recommendations.

SECTION 17

1. The President may at any time, by Proclamation published in the Gazette, declare that a state of public emergency exists.

2. A declaration under subsection (1) of this section, if not sooner revoked, shall cease to have effect -

a) in the case of a declaration made when Parliament is sitting or has been summoned to meet within seven days, at the expiration of a period of seven days beginning with the date of publication of the declaration; or

b) in any other case, at the expiration of a period of twenty-one days beginning with the date of publication of the declaration, unless before the expiration of that period, it is approved by a resolution passed by the National Assembly, supported by the votes of a majority of all the voting members or the Assembly.

3. Subject to the provisions of subsection (4) of this section, a declaration approved by a resolution of the National Assembly under subsection (2) of this section shall continue in force until the expiration of a period of six months beginning with the date of its being so approved or until such earlier date as may be specified in the resolution: Provided that the National Assembly may, by resolution, supported by the votes or a majority of all the voting members of the Assembly, extend its approval of the declaration for periods of not more than six months at a time.

4. The National Assembly may by resolution at any time revoke a declaration approved by the Assembly under this section.

SECTION 18

1. Subject to the provisions of subsection (5) of this section, if any person alleges that any of the provisions of sections 3 to 16 (inclusive) of this Constitution has been, is being or is likely to be contravened in relation to him, then, without prejudice to any other action with respect to the same matter which is lawfully available, that person may apply to the High Court for redress.

2. The High Court shall have original jurisdiction -

a) to hear and determine any application made by any person in pursuance of subsection (1) of this section; or

b) to determine any question arising in the case of any person which is referred to it in pursuance of subsection (3) of this section, and may make such orders, issue such writs and give such direction as it may consider appropriate for the purpose of enforcing or securing the enforcement of any of the provisions of sections 3 to 16 inclusive of this Constitution.

3. If in any proceedings in any subordinate court any question arises as to the contravention of any of the provisions of sections 3 to 16 (inclusive) of this Constitution, the person presiding in that court may, and shall if any party to the proceedings so requests, refer the question to the High Court unless, in his opinion, the raising of the question is merely frivolous or vexatious.

4. Parliament may confer upon the High Court such powers in addition to those conferred by this section as may appear to be necessary or desirable for the purpose of enabling that court more effectively to exercise the jurisdiction conferred upon it by this section.

5. Rules of court making provision with respect to the practice and procedure of the High Court for the purpose of this section may be made by the person or authority for the time being having power to make rules of court with respect to the practice and procedure of that court generally.

SECTION 19

1. In this Chapter, unless the context otherwise requires -

"contravention", in relation to any requirement, includes a failure to comply with that requirement, and cognate expressions shall be construed accordingly;

"court" means any court of law having jurisdiction in Botswana other than a court established by a disciplinary law, and includes the Judicial Committee and in sections 4 and 6 of this Constitution a court established by a disciplinary law;

"disciplinary law" means a law regulating the discipline of any disciplined force ;

"disciplined force" means -

a) a naval, military or air force;

b) a police force; or

c) a prison service;

"legal representative" means a person entitled to practise in Botswana as an advocate or attorney;

"member", in relation to a disciplined force, includes any person who, under the law regulating the discipline of that force, is subject to that discipline.

2. In relation to any person who is a member of a disciplined force raised under an Act of Parliament, nothing contained in or done under the authority of the disciplinary law of that force shall be held to be inconsistent with or in contravention of any of the provisions of this Chapter other than sections 4, 6 and 7.

3. In relation to any Person who is a member of a disciplined force raised otherwise than as aforesaid and lawfully present in Botswana, nothing contained in or done under the authority or the disciplinary law of that force shall be held to be inconsistent with or in contravention of any of the provisions of this Chapter.

CONSTITUTION OF THE REPUBLIC OF MALAWI

CHAPTER IV:

HUMAN RIGHTS

SECTION 15
1. The human rights and freedoms enshrined in this Chapter shall be respected and upheld by the executive, legislature and judiciary and all organs of the Government and its agencies and, where applicable to them, by all natural and legal persons in Malawi and shall be enforceable in the manner prescribed in this Chapter.
2. Any person or group of persons with sufficient interest in the protection and enforcement of rights under this Chapter shall be entitled to the assistance of the courts, the Ombudsman, the Human Rights Commission and other organs of Governments to ensure the promotion, protection and redress of grievance in respect of those rights.

SECTION 16
Every person has the right to life and no person shall be arbitrarily deprived of his or her life: Provided that the execution of the death sentence imposed by a competent court on a person in respect of a criminal offence under the laws of Malawi of which he or she has been convicted shall not be regarded as arbitrary deprivation of his or her right to life.

SECTION 17
Acts of genocide are prohibited and shall be prevented and punished.

SECTION 18
Every person has the right to personal liberty.

SECTION 19
1. The dignity of all persons shall be inviolable.
2. In any judicial proceedings or in any other proceedings before any organ of the State, and during the enforcement of a penalty, respect for human dignity shall be guaranteed.
3. No person shall be subject to torture of any kind or to cruel, inhuman or degrading treatment or punishment.
4. No person shall be subject to corporal punishment in connexion with any judicial proceedings or in any other proceedings before any organ of the State.
5. No person shall be subjected to medical or scientific experimentation without his or her consent.
6. Subject to this Constitution, every person shall have the right to freedom and security of person, which shall include the right not to be -
a) detained without trial;
b) detained solely by reason of his or her political or other opinions; or
c) imprisoned for inability to fulfil contractual obligations.

SECTION 20
1. Discrimination of persons in any form is prohibited and all persons are, under any law, guaranteed equal and effective protection against discrimination on grounds of race, colour, sex, language, religion, political or other opinion, nationality, ethnic or social origin, disability, property, birth or other status.
2. Legislation may be passed addressing inequalities in society and prohibiting discriminatory practices and the propagation of such practices and may render such practices criminally punishable by the courts.

SECTION 21

1. Every person shall have the right to personal privacy, which shall include the right not to be subject to -
   a) searches of his or her person, home or property;
   b) the seizure of private possessions; or
   c) interference with private communications, including mail and all forms of telecommunications.

SECTION 22

1. The family is the natural and fundamental group unit of society and is entitled to protection by society and the State.
2. Each member of the family shall enjoy full and equal respect and shall be protected by law against all forms of neglect, cruelty or exploitation.
3. All men and women have the right to marry and found a family.
4. No person shall be forced to enter into marriage.
5. Sub-sections (3) and (4) shall apply to all marriages at law, custom and marriages by repute or by permanent cohabitation.
6. No person over the age of eighteen years shall be prevented from entering into marriage.
7. For persons between the age of fifteen and eighteen years a marriage shall only be entered into with the consent of their parents or guardians.
8. The State shall actually discourage marriage between persons where either of them is under the age of fifteen years.

SECTION 23

1. All children, regardless of the circumstances of their child birth, are entitled to equal treatment before the law.
2. All children shall have the right to a given name and a family name and the right to a nationality.
3. Children have the right to know, and to be raised by, their parents.
4. Children are entitled to be protected from economic exploitation or any treatment, work or punishment that is, or is likely to -
   a) be hazardous;
   b) interfere with their education; or
   c) be harmful to their health or to their physical, mental or spiritual or social development.
5. For purposes of this section, children shall be persons under sixteen years of age.

SECTION 24

1. Women have the right to full and equal protection by the law, and have the right not to be discriminated against on the basis of their gender or marital status which includes the right -
   a) to be accorded the same rights as men in civil law, including equal capacity -
      i) to enter into contracts;
      ii) to acquire and maintain rights in property, independently or in association with others, regardless of their marital status;
      iii) to acquire and retain custody, guardianship and care of children and to have an equal right in the making of decisions that affect their upbringing; and
      iv) to acquire and retain citizenship and nationality.
   b) on the dissolution of marriage -
      i) to a fair disposition of property that is held jointly with a husband; and
      ii) to fair maintenance, taking into consideration all the circumstances and, in particular, the means of the former husband and the needs of any children.
2. Any law that discriminates against women on the basis of gender or marital status shall be invalid and legislation shall be passed to eliminate customs and practices that discriminate against women, particularly practices such as -
   a) sexual abuse, harassment and violence;
   b) discrimination in work, business and public affairs, and
   c) deprivation of property, including property obtained by inheritance.

SECTION 25

1. All persons are entitled to education.
2. Primary education shall consist of at least five years of education.
3. Private schools and other private institutions of higher learning shall be permissible, provided that -
a) such schools or institutions are registered with a State department in accordance with the law;
b) the standards maintained by such schools or institutions are not inferior to official standards in State schools.

SECTION 26

Every person shall have the right to use the language and to participate in the cultural life of his or her choice.

SECTION 27

1. No person shall be held in slavery or servitude.
2. Slavery and the slave trade are prohibited.
3. No person shall be subject to forced labour.
4. No person shall be subject to tied labour that amounts to servitude.

SECTION 28

1. Every person shall be able to acquire property alone or in association with others.
2. No person shall be arbitrarily deprived of property.

SECTION 29

Every person shall have the right freely to engage in economic activity, to work and to pursue a livelihood anywhere in Malawi.

SECTION 30

1. All persons and peoples have a right to development and therefore to the enjoyment of economic, social, cultural and political development and women, children and the disabled in particular shall be given special consideration in the application of this right.
2. The State shall take all necessary measures for the realization of the right to development. Such measures shall include, amongst other things, equality of opportunity for all in their access to basic resources, education, health services, food, shelter, employment and infrastructure.
3. The State shall take measures to introduce reforms aimed at eradicating social injustices and inequalities.
4. The State has a responsibility to respect the right to development and to justify its policies in accordance with this responsibility.

SECTION 31

1. Every person shall have the right to fair and safe labour practices and to fair remuneration.
2. All persons shall have the right to form and join trade unions or not to form or join trade unions.
3. Every person shall be entitled to fair wages and equal remuneration for work of equal value without distinction or discrimination of any kind, in particular on basis of gender, disability or race.
4. The State shall take measures to ensure the right to withdraw labour.

SECTION 32

1. Every person shall have the right to freedom of association, which shall include the freedom to form associations.
2. No person may be compelled to belong to an association.

SECTION 33

Every person has the right to freedom of conscience, religion, belief and thought, and to academic freedom.

SECTION 34

Every person shall have the right to freedom of opinion, including the right to hold opinions without interference to hold receive and impart opinions.

SECTION 35
Every person shall have the right to freedom of expression.

SECTION 36
The press shall have the right to report and publish freely, within Malawi and abroad, and to be accorded the fullest possible facilities for access to public information.

SECTION 37
Subject to any Act of Parliament, every person shall have the right of access to all information held by the State or any of its organs at any level of Government in so far as such information is required for the exercise of his rights.

SECTION 38
Every person shall have the right to assemble and demonstrate with others peacefully and unarmed.

SECTION 39
1. Every person shall have the right of freedom of movement and residence within the borders of Malawi.
2. Every person shall have the right to leave the Republic and to return to it.

SECTION 40
1. Subject to this Constitution, every person shall have the right -
a) to form, to join, to participate in the activities of, and to recruit members for, a political party;
b) to campaign for a political party or cause;
c) to participate in peaceful political activity intended to influence the composition and policies of the Government;and
d) freely to make political choices.
2. The State shall, where necessary, provide funds so as to ensure that, during the life of any Parliament, any political party which has secured more than one-tenth of the national vote in elections to that Parliament has sufficient funds to continue to represent its constituency.
3. Save as otherwise provided in this Constitution, every person shall have the right to vote, to do so in secret and to stand for election for public office.

SECTION 41
1. Every person shall have a right to recognition as a person before the law.
2. Every person shall have access to any court of law or any other tribunal with jurisdiction for final settlement of legal issues.
3. Every person shall have the right to an effective remedy by a court of law or tribunal for acts violating the rights and freedoms granted to him by this Constitution or any other law.

SECTION 42
1. Every person who is detained, including every sentenced prisoner, shall have the right -
a) to be informed of the reason for his or her detention promptly, and in a language which he or she understands;
b) to be detained under conditions consistent with human dignity, which shall include at least the provision of reading and writing materials, adequate nutrition and medical treatment at the expense of the State;
c) to consult confidentially with a legal practitioner of his or her choice, to be informed of this right promptly and, where the interests of justice so require, to be provided with the services of a legal practitioner by the State;
d) to be given the means and opportunity to communicate with, and to be visited by, his or her spouse, partner, next-of kin, relative, religion counsellor and a medical practitioner of his or her choice;
e) to challenge the lawfulness of his or her detention in person or through a legal practitioner before a court of law; and
f), to be released if such detention is

unlawful.

2. Every person arrested for, or accused of, the alleged commission of an offence shall, in addition to the rights which he or she has as a detained person, have the right -

a) promptly to be informed, in a language which he or she understands, that he or she has the right to remain silent and to be warned of the consequences of making any statement;

b) as soon as it is reasonably possible, but not later than 48 hours after the arrest, or if the period of 48 hours expires outside ordinary court hours or on a day which is not a court day, the first court day after such expiry, to be brought before an independent and impartial court of law and to be charged or to be informed of the reason for his or her further detention, failing which he or she shall be released;

c) not to be compelled to make a confession or admission which could be used in evidence against him or her;

d) save in exceptional circumstances, to be segregated from convicted persons and to be subject to separate treatment appropriate to his or her status as an unconvicted person;

e) to be released from detention, with or without bail unless the interests of justice require otherwise,

f), as an accused person, to a fair trial, which shall include the right -

i) to public trial before an independent and impartial court of law within a reasonable time after having been charged;
ii) to be informed with sufficient particularity of the charge;
iii) to be presumed innocent and to remain silent during plea proceedings or trial and not to testify during trial;
iv) to adduce and challenge evidence, and not to be a compellable witness against himself or herself;
v) to be represented by a legal practitioner of his or her choice or, where it is required in the interests of justice, to be provided with legal representation at the expense of the State, and to be informed of these rights;
vi) not to be convicted of an offence in respect of any act or omission which was not an offence at the time when the act was committed or omitted to be done, and not to be sentenced to a more severe punishment than that which was applicable when the offence was committed;
vii) not to be prosecuted again for a criminal act or omission of which he or she has previously been convicted or acquitted;
viii) to have recourse by way of appeal or review to a higher court than the court of first instance;
ix) to be tried in a language which he or she understands or, failing this, to have the proceedings interpreted to him or her, at the expense of the State, into a language which he or she understands; and
x) to be sentenced within a reasonable time after conviction;

g) in addition, if that person is a child, to treatment consistent with the special needs of children, which shall include the right -

i) not to be sentenced to life imprisonment without possibility of release;
ii) to be imprisoned only as a last resort and for the shortest period of time;
iii) to be separated from adults when imprisoned, unless it is considered to be in his or her best interest not to do so, and to maintain contact with his or her family through correspondence and visits;
iv) to be treated in a manner consistent with the promotion of his or her sense of dignity and worth, which reinforces respect for the rights and freedoms of others;
v) to be treated in a manner which takes into account his or her age and the desirability of promoting his or her reintegration into society to assume a constructive role; and
vi) to be dealt with in a form of legal proceedings that reflects the vulnerability

of children while fully respecting human rights and legal safeguards.

SECTION 43
Every person shall have the right to -
a) lawful and procedurally fair administrative action, which is justifiable in relation to reasons given where his or her rights, freedoms, legitimate expectations or interests are affected or threatened; and
b) be furnished with reasons in writing for administrative action where his or her rights, freedoms, legitimate expectations or interests if those interests are known.

SECTION 44
1. There shall be no derogation, restrictions or limitation with regard to -
a) the right to life;
b) the prohibition of torture and cruel, inhuman or degrading treatment or punishment;
c) the prohibition of genocide;
d) the prohibition of slavery, the slave trade and slave-like practices;
e) the prohibition of imprisonment for failure to meet contractual obligations;
f), the prohibition on retrospective criminalization and the retrospective imposition of greater penalties for criminal acts;
g) the right to equality and recognition before the law;
h) the right to freedom of conscience, belief, thought and religion and to academic freedom; or
i) the right to habeas corpus.
2. Without prejudice to subsection (1), no restrictions or limitations may be placed on the exercise of any rights and freedoms provided for in this Constitution other than those prescribed by law, which are reasonable, recognized by international human rights standards and necessary in an open and democratic society.
3. Laws prescribing restrictions or limitations shall not negate the essential content of the right or freedom in question, shall be of general application.
4. Expropriation of property shall be permissible only when done for public utility and only when there has been adequate notification and appropriate compensation, provided that there shall always be a right to appeal to a court of law.
5. Wherever it is stated in this Constitution that a person has the right to the services of a legal practitioner or medical practitioner of his or her own choice, that right shall be without limitation, save where the State is obliged to provide such services of a legal practitioner or medical practitioner, in which case an Act of Parliament may prescribe that the choice of the legal practitioner or medical practitioner should be limited to those in Government service or employment.

SECTION 45
1. No derogation from rights contained in this Chapter shall be permissible save to the extent provided for by this section and no such derogation shall be made unless there has been a declaration of a state of emergency, within the meaning of this section.
2. The President may declare a state of emergency -
a) only to the extent that it is provided for in this section;
b) only with the approval of the Defence and Security Committee of the National Assembly;
c) only in times of war, threat of war, civil war or widespread natural disaster;
d) only with regard to the specific location where that emergency exists, and that any declaration of a state of emergency shall be publicly announced; and
e) only after the state of emergency has been publicly announced.
3. Derogation shall only be permissible during a state of emergency -
a) with respect to freedom of expression, freedom of information, freedom of movement, freedom of assembly and rights under section 19 (6) (a) and section 42 (2) (b);

b) to the extent that such derogation is not inconsistent with the obligations of Malawi under International Law; and
c) to the extent that -
  i) in the case of war or threat of war, it is strictly required to prevent the lives of defensive combatants and legitimate military objectives from being placed in direct jeopardy; or
  ii) in the case of a widespread natural disaster, it is strictly required for the protection and relief of those people in the disaster area.

4. The declaration of a state of emergency and any action taken in consequence thereof shall be in force for a period of not more than twenty-one days, unless it is extended for a period of not longer than three months, or consecutive periods of not longer than three months at a time, by resolution of the National Assembly adopted by a majority of at least two-thirds of all its members.

5. The High Court shall be competent to hear applications challenging the validity of a declaration of a state of emergency, any extension thereof, and any action taken, including any regulation enacted, under such declaration.

6. Where a person is detained under a state of emergency such detention shall be subject to the following conditions -
a) an adult family member or friend of the detainee shall be notified of the detention as soon as is reasonably possible and in any case not later than forty-eight hours of detention;
b) the name of every detainee and a reference to the measures in terms of which he or she is being detained shall be published in the Gazette within five days of his or her detention;
c) when rights entrenched in section 19 (6) (a) or section 42 (2) (b) have been suspended -
  i) the detention of a person shall, as soon as it is reasonably possible but not later than ten days after his or her detention, be reviewed by a court, and the court shall order the release of the detainee if it is satisfied that the detention is not necessary to restore peace or order;
  ii) a detainee shall at any stage after the expiry of a period of five days after a review under of subparagraph (i) be entitled to apply to a court of law for a further review of his or her detention, and the court shall order the release of the detainee if it is satisfied that the detention is no longer necessary to restore peace or order;
d) the State shall for the purpose of a review referred to in paragraph (c) submit written reasons to justify the detention or further detention of the detainee to the court, and shall furnish the detainee with such reasons not later than two days before the review.

7. If a court finds the grounds for the detention of a person to be unjustified or illegal it shall order his or her release and that person shall not be detained again on the same grounds unless the State shows good cause to a court prior to such re-detention.

8. Under no circumstance shall it be possible to suspend this Constitution or any part thereof or dissolve any of its organs, save as is consistent with the provisions of this Constitution.

SECTION 46

1. Save in so far as it may be authorized to do so by this Constitution, the National Assembly or any subordinate legislative authority shall not make any law, and the executive and the agencies of Government shall not take any action which abolishes or abridges the fundamental rights and freedoms conferred by this Chapter, and any law or action in contravention thereof shall, to the extent of the contravention, be invalid.

2. Any person who claims that a fundamental right or freedom guaranteed by this

Constitution has been infringed or threatened shall be entitled -
 a) to make application to a competent court to enforce or protect such a right or freedom; and
 b) to make application to the Ombudsman or the Human Rights Commission in order to secure such assistance or advice as he or she may reasonably require.

3. Where a court referred to in subsection (2) (a) finds that rights or freedoms conferred by this Constitution have been unlawfully denied or violated, it shall have the power to make any orders that are necessary and appropriate to secure the enjoyment of those rights and freedoms and where a court finds that a threat exists to such rights or freedoms, it shall have the power to make any orders necessary and appropriate to prevent those rights and freedoms from being unlawfully denied or violated.

4. A court referred to in subsection (2) (a) shall have the power to award compensation to any person whose rights or freedoms have been unlawfully denied or violated where it considers it to be appropriate in the circumstances of a particular case.

5. The law shall prescribe criminal penalties for violations of those non-derogable rights listed in subsection 44 (1).

CONSTITUTION OF THE REPUBLIC OF MOZAMBIQUE

PREAMBLE

At zero hours on 25 June 1975, the Central Committee of the Mozambique Liberation Front (FRELIMO) solemnly proclaimed the total and complete Independence of Mozambique and its Constitution as the People's Republic of Mozambique.

This was the culmination of a centuries long process of resistance to colonial rule. It was the unforgettable victory of the armed national liberation struggle, led by FRELIMO, which brought together all the patriotic sectors of Mozambican society in the same ideals of freedom, unity, justice and progress.

The Constitution then proclaimed attributed a determinant role to FRELIMO as the legitimate representative of the Mozambican people. Under its leadership, the uplifting process of the exercise of state power as an expression of the people's will was begun.

The state that we have created has made it possible for the Mozambican people to deepen democracy and, for the first time in their history, to exercise political power and organise and direct social and economic life at a national level.

The way in which state institutions have functioned and the democratic practice of citizens impose new definitions and developments.

After 15 years of independence, the Mozambican people, using their inalienable right to sovereignty, determined to consolidate the nation's unity and to respect the dignity of Mozambicans, adopts and proclaims this Constitution, which shall be the basic law for all political and social organisation in the Republic of Mozambique.

The fundamental rights and freedoms enshrined in the Constitution are gains of the Mozambican people in their struggle to build a society of social justice, where the equality of citizens and the imperatives of the law are the pillars of democracy.

We, the Mozambican people, determined to deepen the arrangement of political life in our country, in a spirit of responsibility and pluralism of opinion, are decided to organise society in such a way that the will of the citizens may be the greatest value of our sovereignty.

PART 1

BASIC PRINCIPLES

CHAPTER 1

THE REPUBLIC

ARTICLE 1
The Republic of Mozambique is an independent, sovereign, unitary and democratic state of social justice.

ARTICLE 2
1. Sovereignty is vested in the people.
2. The Mozambican people shall exercise their sovereignty in the manner provided for in the Constitution.

ARTICLE 3
1. The territory of the Republic of Mozambique is a single whole, indivisible and inalienable, comprising the entire land surface, territorial waters and air space delimited by the national boundaries.
2. The breadth, limits and legal order of Mozambique's territorial waters, the exclusive economic zone, the contiguous zone and seabed rights shall be fixed by law.

ARTICLE 4

1. The territory of the Republic of Mozambique shall be subdivided into provinces, districts, administrative posts and localities.
2. Urban zones shall be classified as either cities or towns.
3. The definition of administrative divisions, the creation of any new units. as well as the power to decide on politico-administrative organisation shall be fixed by law.

ARTICLE 5

1. In the Republic of Mozambique, Portuguese shall be the official language.
2. The State shall esteem national languages and promote their development and increasing use as spoken languages and in the education of citizens.

ARTICLE 6

The fundamental aims of the Republic of Mozambique shall be:
a) The defence of independence and sovereignty;
b) The consolidation of national unity;
c) The building of a society of social justice. and the achievement of material and spiritual well-being for its citizens:
d) The defence and promotion of human rights and of the equality of citizens before the law:
e) The strengthening of democracy, of freedom and of societal and individual stability;
f) The development of the economy, and scientific and technological progress:
g) The affirmation of the Mozambican personality, of its traditions and other social and cultural values;
h) The establishment and development of relations of friendship and cooperation with other peoples and states.

ARTICLE 7

1. The Republic of Mozambique shall uphold the values of the heroic struggle and centuries of resistance by the Mozambican people against foreign rule.
2. In the building of the Mozambican nation, in the strengthening of national unity, and in the promotion of the democratic participation of citizens, the State shall retain as a national heritage the decisive role played by the Mozambique Liberation Front (FRELIMO) in the victory over colonialism and In the winning of national independence.

ARTICLE 8

1. The Republic of Mozambique shall acknowledge and esteem the sacrifices made by those who gave their lives to the national liberation struggle and to the defence of the country's sovereignty.
2. The state shall guarantee the special care and protection of those who suffered permanent injury in the national liberation struggle, in the defence of independence, sovereignty and territorial integrity, as well, as the orphans and other dependents of those who died in this cause.

ARTICLE 9

1. The Republic of Mozambique shall be a lay state.
2. The activity of religious institutions shall be subject to the law.
3. The State shall respect the activities of religious denominations in order to promote a climate of social understanding and strengthen national unity.

CHAPTER 3

PARTICIPATION IN THE POLITICAL LIFE OF THE STATE

ARTICLE 30

The Mozambican people shall exercise political power through elections of their representatives by universal, direct, secret and periodic suffrage, through referenda on major national issues, and through permanent democratic participation by citizens in the affairs of the nation.

ARTICLE 31

1. Parties are expressions of political pluralism. They shall compete to form and proclaim the will of the people, and shall work as fundamental instruments for the democratic participation of citizens in the government of the country.
2. The internal structure and the operation of political parties must be democratic.

ARTICLE 32

1. In profound respect for national unity, political parties shall be bound by the principles enshrined in the Constitution and In the law.
2. The formation and operations of political parties are subject to the following conditions, Political parties shall:
a) be national in scope;
b) defend national interests;
c) contribute to the formation of public opinion, particularly on major national issues;
d) strengthen the patriotic spirit of citizens and the consolidation of the Mozambican nation.
3. Parties shall contribute, through the political and civic education of citizens, towards peace and stability in the country.
4. The formation, structure and operation of parties shall be regulated by law.

ARTICLE 33

Political parties shall be prohibited from advocating or resorting to violence in order to change the political and social order of the country.

ARTICLE 34

1. Social organisations, as associations of citizens having joint interests and affinities, play an important role in promoting democracy, and in the participation of citizens in political life.
2. Social organisations contribute to achieving the rights and freedoms of citizens, as well as towards raising individual and collective consciousnessin the fulfilment of civic duties.

CHAPTER 4

ECONOMIC AND SOCIAL ORGANISATION

ARTICLE 35

1. Natural resources located in the soil and subsoil, in interior waters, in territorial waters, on the continental shelf, and in the exclusive economic zone shall be property vested in the state.
2. The public domain of the State shall also include:
a) the maritime zone:
b) the airspace;
c) archaeological heritage;
d) nature conservancy zones;
e) hydraulic power resources;
f) energy resources:
g) other goods and assets classified as such by law.

ARTICLE 36

The State shall promote knowledge, surveys and evaluation of natural resources, and shall determine the conditions under which they may be used and developed, in the national interest.

ARTICLE 37

The State shall promote efforts to guarantee the ecological balance, and the conservation and preservation of the environment, seeking to improve the quality of life for citizens.

ARTICLE 38

State economic policy shall be directed towards laying the fundamental bases for development, improving the living conditions of the people, strengthening the sovereignty of the State, and consolidating national unity, through the participation of citizens and the efficient use of human and material resources.

ARTICLE 39
1. The Republic of Mozambique shall treat agriculture as the basis for national development.
2. The State shall guarantee and promote rural development in order to satisfy the growing and diverse needs of the people, and for the economic and social progress of the country.

ARTICLE 40
The Republic of Mozambique shall treat industry as a dynamising factor for the national economy.
1. The economic order of the Republic of Mozambique shall be based on the value of labour, on market forces, on the initiatives of economic agents, on the contributions by all types of ownership, and on the role of the State in regulating and promoting economic and social growth and development, in order to satisfy the basic needs of the people, and to promote social well-being.
2. The national economy shall consist of the following types of ownership, which shall complement each other:
a) State ownership:
b) cooperative ownership:
c) joint ownership;
d) private ownership.
3. The State shall ensure that economic activities conform with the interests provided for in the Constitution and in the law.

ARTICLE 42
1. In satisfying the basic needs of the people, the family farming sector plays a fundamental role.
2. The State shall support and provide incentives for family sector production, and shall encourage peasants as well as individual labourers to organise themselves into more advanced forms of production.

ARTICLE 43
The State shall promote and support the active participation of the national business sector in the development and consolidation of the country's economy.

ARTICLE 44
The State shall recognise the contribution made by small scale production to the national economy, and shall support its development as a way of making good use of the capacities and creativity of the people.

ARTICLE 45
1. Foreign investment shall operate within the framework of state economic policy.
2. Foreign ventures shall be permitted in all economic sectors, except those that are exclusively reserved for State ownership or development by the State.

ARTICLE 46
1. All property in land shall vest in the State.
2. Land may not be sold, or mortgaged, encumbered or otherwise alienated.
3. As a universal means for the creation of wealth and of social well-being, the use and enjoyment of land shall be the right of all the Mozambican people.

ARTICLE 47
1. The State shall determine the conditions under which land may be used and enjoyed.
2. The right to use land shall be granted to individual or collective persons, taking into account its social purpose.
3. The terms for the establishment of rights in respect of land shall be governed by law and shall prioritise direct users and producers. The law shall not permit such rights to be used to favour situations of economic domination or privilege to the detriment of the majority of citizens.

ARTICLE 48
In granting titles for the use of land, the

State shall recognise and protect rights acquired through inheritance or occupation, unless there is a legal reservation, or the land has been legally granted to another person or entity.

ARTICLE 49
1. The State shall promote and coordinate economic activity, acting directly or indirectly to resolve the basic problems of the people and to reduce social and regional inequalities.
2. State investment shall play a dynamising role in promoting development.

ARTICLE 50
Taxes shall be imposed and altered by law, and shall be set according to criteria of social justice.

ARTICLE 51
1. Labour shall merit respect and protection, and it shall be the driving force of development.
2. The State shall promote the just distribution of the proceeds of labour.

ARTICLE 52
1. The Republic of Mozambique shall promote an educational strategy that aims at national unity, at wiping out illiteracy, at mastering science and technology, and at providing citizens with moral and civic values.
2. The State shall organise and develop education through a national educational system.
3. Education provided by collective and other bodies shall operate in accordance with the law, and shall be subject to state supervision.

ARTICLE 53
1. The State shall promote the development of national culture and identity, and shall guarantee free expression of the traditions and values of Mozambican society.
2. The State shall make Mozambican culture known internationally, and shall take action to enable the Mozambican people to benefit from the cultural achievements of other peoples.

ARTICLE 54
1. Medical and health care for citizens shall be organised through a national health service which shall benefit all Mozambicans.
2. To achieve the goals of the national health system, the law shall establish the way in which medical and health care is delivered.
3. The State shall promote the participation of citizens and institutions in order to raise the level of public health care.

ARTICLE 55
1. The family is the basic unit of society.
2. The State shall recognise and protect, in accordance with the law, marriage as the institution that secures the values of the family.
3. In the context of developing social relations based on respect for human dignity, the State shall guarantee the principle that marriage is based on free consent.

ARTICLE 56
1. Motherhood shall be afforded respect and protection
2. The family shall be responsible for raising children in a harmonious manner, and shall teach the new generations moral and social values.
3. The family and the State shall ensure an allround education of children, bringing them up in the values of national unity, love for the motherland, human equality, respect and social solidarity.
4. Children may not be discriminated against on grounds of their birth, nor may they be subjected to ill treatment.
5. State and society shall protect orphans and abandoned children.

ARTICLE 57

1. The State shall promote and support the emancipation of women, and shall act to increase the role of women in society.
2. The State shall recognise and hold in high esteem the participation of Mozambican women in the national liberation process.
3. The State shall encourage and hold in high esteem the participation of women in the defence of the motherland, and in all spheres of the country's political, economic, social and cultural activity.

ARTICLE 58

1. Young people, bravely upholding the patriotic traditions of the Mozambican people, played a decisive role in the national liberation struggle, and constitute a force for the renewal of Mozambican society.
2. State policy shall be directed particularly towards ensuring the harmonious development of the character of young people, to helping them acquire a taste for free and creative work, to developing their sense of serving the community, and to providing appropriate conditions for their entering into active life.
3. The State shall promote, support and encourage young people's initiatives In consolidating national unity, and in the reconstruction, development and defence of the country.

CHAPTER 5

NATIONAL DEFENCE

ARTICLE 59

The State's defence and security policy shall seek to defend national independence, preserve the country's sovereignty and integrity, and guarantee the normal functioning of institutions and the security of citizens against any armed aggression.

ARTICLE 60

1. The defence and security forces shall be subordinate to national defence and security policy, and owe allegiance to the Constitution and to the Nation.
2. The oath taken by members of the defence and security forces shall, establish their duty to respect the Constitution.

ARTICLE 61

Citizens shall be encouraged to join civil defence units, particularly for the protection of economic, social and production infrastructures.

CHAPTER 6

FOREIGN POLICY

ARTICLE 62

1. The Republic of Mozambique, as a non-aligned country, shall establish relations of friendship and cooperation with other states on the basis of principles of mutual respect for sovereignty and territorial integrity, equality, non-interference in internal matters and reciprocity of benefits.
2. The Republic of Mozambique shall accept, observe and apply the principles of the United Nations Charter, and of the Charter of the Organisation of African Unity.

ARTICLE 63

1. The Republic of Mozambique shall be in solidarity with the struggle for the unity of the peoples and states of Africa in respect of their freedom, dignity, and right to economic and social progress.
2. The Republic of Mozambique shall seek to strengthen relations with countries undertaking the consolidation of their national independence and the recovery of the use and control of their natural resources for their respective peoples.
3. The Republic of Mozambique shall join with all states struggling for the establishment of a just and equitable international economic order.

ARTICLE 64

1. The Republic of Mozambique shall support and be in solidarity with the struggles of peoples for their national liberation.
2. The Republic of Mozambique shall grant asylum to foreigners persecuted because of their fight for peace, democracy, national and social liberation, and for the defence of human rights.

ARTICLE 65

1. The Republic of Mozambique shall pursue a policy of peace, and shall only resort to force in the case of legitimate defence.
2. The Republic of Mozambique shall support the primacy of a negotiated solution to conflicts.
3. The Republic of Mozambique shall support the principle of general and universal disarmament of all states.
4. The Republic of Mozambique shall advocate the transformation of the Indian Ocean into a nuclear free zone of peace.

PART 2

FUNDAMENTAL RIGHTS, DUTIES AND FREEDOMS

CHAPTER 1

GENERAL PRINCIPLES

ARTICLE 66

All citizens are equal before the law, They shall enjoy the same rights, and shall be subject to the same duties regardless of colour, race, sex, ethnic origin, place of birth, religion, educational level, social position, the legal status of their parents, or their profession.

ARTICLE 67

Men and women shall be equal before the law in all spheres of political, economic, social and cultural life.

ARTICLE 68

Disabled citizens shall enjoy fully the rights enshrined in the Constitution, and shall be subject to the same duties, except those rights and duties which their disability prevents them from undertaking.

ARTICLE 69

All acts intended to undermine national unity, to disturb social harmony, or to create divisions or situations of privilege or discrimination based on colour, race, sex, ethnic origin, place of birth, religion, educational level, social position, physical or mental ability, the legal status of one's parents, or profession, shall be punished according to law.

ARTICLE 70

1. All citizens shall have the right to life. All shall have the right to physical integrity, and may not be subjected to torture or to cruel or inhuman treatment.
2. In the Republic of Mozambique there shall be no death penalty.

ARTICLE 71

All citizens shall have the right to their honour, good name and reputation, as well as the right to privacy and to defend their public image.

ARTICLE 72

All citizens shall have the right to live in a balanced natural environment and shall have the duty to defend the same.

CHAPTER 2

RIGHTS, DUTIES AND FREEDOMS

ARTICLE 73

1. All citizens shall have the right and the duty to participate in the process of extending and consolidating democracy at all

levels of State and society.

2. Citizens 18 years of age and over shall have the right to vote and to be elected, with the exception of those legally deprived of this right.

3. The right to vote shall be personal and shall constitute a civic duty.

ARTICLE 74

1. All citizens shall have the right to freedom of expression and to freedom of the press, as well as the right to information.

2. The exercise of freedom of expression, which consists in the ability to make known one's opinions by all legal means, and the exercise of the right to information, shall not be limited by censorship.

3. Freedom of the press shall include in particular the freedom of journalistic expression and creativity, access to sources of information, protection of professional independence and confidentiality, and the right to establish newspapers and other publications.

4. The exercise of the rights and freedoms referred to in this article shall be regulated by law based on the necessary respect for the Constitution, for the dignity of the human person, and for the mandates of foreign policy and national defence.

ARTICLE 75

All citizens shall have the right to freedom of assembly within the terms of the law.

ARTICLE 76

1. All citizens shall enjoy freedom of association.

2. Social organisations and associations shall have the right to pursue their aims, to create institutions designed to achieve their specific objectives, and to own assets in order to carry out their activities, in accordance with the terms of the law.

ARTICLE 77

1. All citizens shall have the freedom to form or to participate in political parties.

2. Party membership shall be voluntary, and shall derive from the freedom of citizens to associate on the basis of the same political ideals.

ARTICLE 78

1. All citizens shall have the freedom to practise or not to practise a religion.

2. Religious denominations shall have the right to pursue their religious aims freely, and to own and acquire assets for realising those aims.

ARTICLE 79

1. All citizens shall have the right to freedom of scientific, technical, literary and artistic creativity.

2. The State shall protect rights related to intellectual property, including copyright, and shall promote the practice and dissemination of literature and art.

ARTICLE 80

1. All citizens shall have the right to present petitions, complaints and claims before the relevant authority to obtain the restoration of rights that have been violated, or in defence of the public interest.

2. All citizens shall have the right not to comply with orders that are illegal or which infringe upon their rights.

ARTICLE 81

All citizens may contest acts that violate their rights recognised under the Constitution and other laws.

ARTICLE 82

All citizens shall have the right of recourse to the courts against any act which violates their rights recognised by the Constitution and the law.

Article 83

1. All citizens shall have the right to take up residence in any part of the national

territory.

2. All citizens shall be free to travel inside the national territory and abroad, except those legally deprived of this right by the courts.

ARTICLE 84

1. It shall be a sacred duty and honour for all Mozambican citizens to participate in the defence of the country's independence, sovereignty and territorial integrity.

2. Military service shall be rendered according to terms established by law.

ARTICLE 85

1. All citizens shall have the duty to respect the Constitutional order.

2. Acts contrary to the Constitution shall be subject to sanction in accordance with the law.

CHAPTER 3

ECONOMIC AND SOCIAL RIGHTS AND DUTIES

ARTICLE 86

1. The State shall recognise and guarantee the right to ownership of property.

2. Expropriation may only take place on grounds of public need, usefulness or interest, as defined by law, and there shall be just compensation.

ARTICLE 87

The State shall recognise and guarantee, within the terms of the law, the right of inheritance.

ARTICLE 88

1. Work shall be a right and a duty of all citizens, regardless of sex.

2. All citizens shall have the right to a free choice of profession.

3. Forced labour shall be forbidden, with the exception of work performed in the context of penal law.

ARTICLE 89

1. All employees shall have the right to just payment, to rest and to holidays.

2. Employees shall have the right to protection, safety and hygienic conditions at work

3. Employees may only be dismissed in accordance with the law.

ARTICLE 90

1. All employees shall have the freedom to organise professional associations or trade unions.

2. The exercise of trade union activity shall be regulated by law.

ARTICLE 91

1. Employees shall have the right to strike. The exercise of this right shall be regulated by law.

2. The law shall limit the exercise of the right to strike in essential services and activities, in the interests of the overriding needs of society.

3. Lockouts shall be prohibited.

ARTICLE 92

1. In the Republic of Mozambique education shall be a right and duty of all citizens.

2. The State shall promote greater and equal access to the enjoyment of this right by all citizens.

ARTICLE 93

1. Citizens shall have the right to physical education and to sport.

2. The State shall promote, through sporting and educational institutions, the practise and dissemination of physical education and sport.

ARTICLE 94

All citizens shall have the right to medical and health care, within the terms of the law, and shall have the duty to promote and preserve health.

ARTICLE 95

1. All citizens shall have the right to assistance in the case of disability or old age.
2. The State shall promote and encourage the creation of conditions for achieving this right.

CHAPTER 4

GUARANTEES OF RIGHTS AND FREEDOMS

ARTICLE 96

1. Individual rights and freedoms shall be guaranteed by the State, and shall be exercised within the framework of the Constitution and the laws.
2. The exercise of rights and freedoms may only be limited if public order or individual rights, freedoms or guarantees are endangered, or if the use of force is implied or threatened.

ARTICLE 97

The State shall be liable for damages caused by illegal acts of its agents, committed in the exercise of their functions, without prejudice to the right of appeal in accordance with the law.

ARTICLE 98

1. In the Republic of Mozambique no-one may be arrested and put on trial except within the terms of the law.
2. Persons charged with an offence shall enjoy the presumption of innocence until final judgement has been passed.

ARTICLE 99

1. No-one may be punished for an act that was not considered a crime at the time it was committed.
2. Criminal laws may be applied retroactively only in favour of the accused.

ARTICLE 100

1. The State shall guarantee the access of citizens to the courts. It shall guarantee to persons charged with an offence the right to defence and the right to legal assistance and aid.
2. The State shall make provision to ensure that justice is not denied for lack of resources.

ARTICLE 101

1. Preventive imprisonment shall only be permitted in cases provided for by the law, which shall limit the duration of such imprisonment.
2. Citizens held in preventive imprisonment shall be brought within the period fixed by law before the judicial authorities who alone shall have the power to decide on the validity and continuation of imprisonment.

ARTICLE 102

1. In case of illegal imprisonment or detention, citizens shall have the right to interpose a writ of habeas corpus.
2. The writ of habeas corpus shall be interposed before a court, and the procedures shall be fixed by law.

ARTICLE 103

1. Extradition may only take place by court decision.
2. Extradition for political motives shall not be authorised.
3. No Mozambican citizen may be expelled or extradited from the national territory.

ARTICLE 104

The home and the correspondence or other forms of private communication of citizens shall be inviolable, except in such cases as specifically stipulated by law.

ARTICLE 105

1. The right to information, the freedom of the press, and the independence of the media, as well as broadcasting rights and the right of reply, shall be guaranteed by the Supreme Council for Mass Communication.

2. The law shall regulate the jurisdiction, composition and operation of the Supreme Council for Mass Communication.

ARTICLE 106

1. Individual freedoms and guarantees may only be temporarily suspended or limited in the event of the declaration of a state of war, a state of siege, or a state of emergency.

2. A state of siege or a state of emergency may not exceed six months, and any extension must be made in the terms of the law.

3. The law shall define rules for a state of war, a state of siege and a state of emergency, and shall establish judicial guarantees to protect the rights of citizens that are to be safeguarded.

PART 3

ORGANS OF STATE

CHAPTER 1

GENERAL PRINCIPLES

ARTICLE 107

1. Public elective officers shall be chosen through elections in which all citizens shall have the right to participate.

2. The election of public officers shall take place through universal, direct, secret, personal and periodic vote.

3. Results of elections shall be established according to the system of majority vote.

4. The electoral process shall be regulated by law.

ARTICLE 108

1. Legally constituted political parties may compete in elections.

2. Political parties shall hold public office in accordance with the results of the elections.

ARTICLE 109

The sovereign public offices are the President of the Republic, the Assembly of the Republic, the Council of Ministers, the Courts and the Constitutional Council.

ARTICLE 110

Central State offices are the sovereign public offices, governmental bodies as a whole, and such central institutions as are responsible for guaranteeing the precedence of national interests and the realisation of a unitary state policy.

ARTICLE 111

1. Central offices shall, in general, have power to act in exercise of sovereignty, to regulate matters in accordance with the law, and to define national policies.

2. The central offices shall have exclusive powers in the following matters: representation of the State, definition and organisation of the territory, national defence, public order, supervision of borders, issuing currency, and diplomatic relations.

ARTICLE 112

1. Central offices shall take action directly, or through appointed heads or agents of the administration who shall supervise central activities within a particular territorial area.

2. The law shall determine the form, organisation and powers for the exercise of public administration.

ARTICLE 113

The representative of central authority at the provincial level is the Provincial Governor.

ARTICLE 114

1. The Provincial Government is the body charged with ensuring the implementation, at provincial level, of centrally defined government policies.

2. The Provincial Government shall be directed by the Provincial Governor.

3. Members of Provincial Governments shall be appointed centrally.
4. The composition, powers and operation of Provincial Governments shall be defined by law.

ARTICLE 115
1. Democratically elective bodies may be set up at provincial level.
2. The law shall regulate the organisation, composition, powers and operation of the bodies mentioned in the previous clause.

ARTICLE 116
At the various territorial levels, local State bodies shall guarantee that citizens may participate and decide on matters of interest to their respective communities.

ARTICLE 161
1. It shall be the function of the courts to guarantee and strengthen the rule of law as an instrument of legal stability, to guarantee respect for the laws, to safeguard the rights and freedoms of citizens, as well as the vested interests of the other entities with legal capacity.
2. The courts shall educate citizens in the voluntary and conscious observance of laws, thus establishing a just and harmonious social community.
3. The courts shall punish violations of the legal order and shall adjudicate disputes in accordance with the law.

ARTICLE 162
Under no circumstances may the courts apply laws or principles which are contrary to the Constitution.

ARTICLE 163
It shall be obligatory for all citizens and other legal entities to obey court decisions. The decisions of the courts take precedence over the decisions of other authorities.

ARTICLE 164
1. In the exercise of their functions, judges shall be independent, and shall owe obedience only to the law.
2. Judges shall likewise be impartial and disinterested.

ARTICLE 165
1. Judges may be held responsible in civil, criminal and disciplinary proceedings for acts committed in the discharge of their duties only in cases specified by law.
2. The removal of a professional judge from the bench may only take place under legally established terms.

ARTICLE 166
Professional judges may not undertake any other public or private activity, except teaching or research.

ARTICLE 167
1. In the Republic of Mozambique there shall be the following courts:
a) the Supreme Court and other courts of justice;
b) the Administrative Court;
c) courts-martial;
d) customs courts;
e) fiscal courts;
f) maritime courts;
g) labour courts.
2. Other than the courts specified in the Constitution, no other court may be established with jurisdiction over specific categories of crimes.

A "doughnut"-model for regulation of human rights

Global, regional and local/national levels of human rights regulation

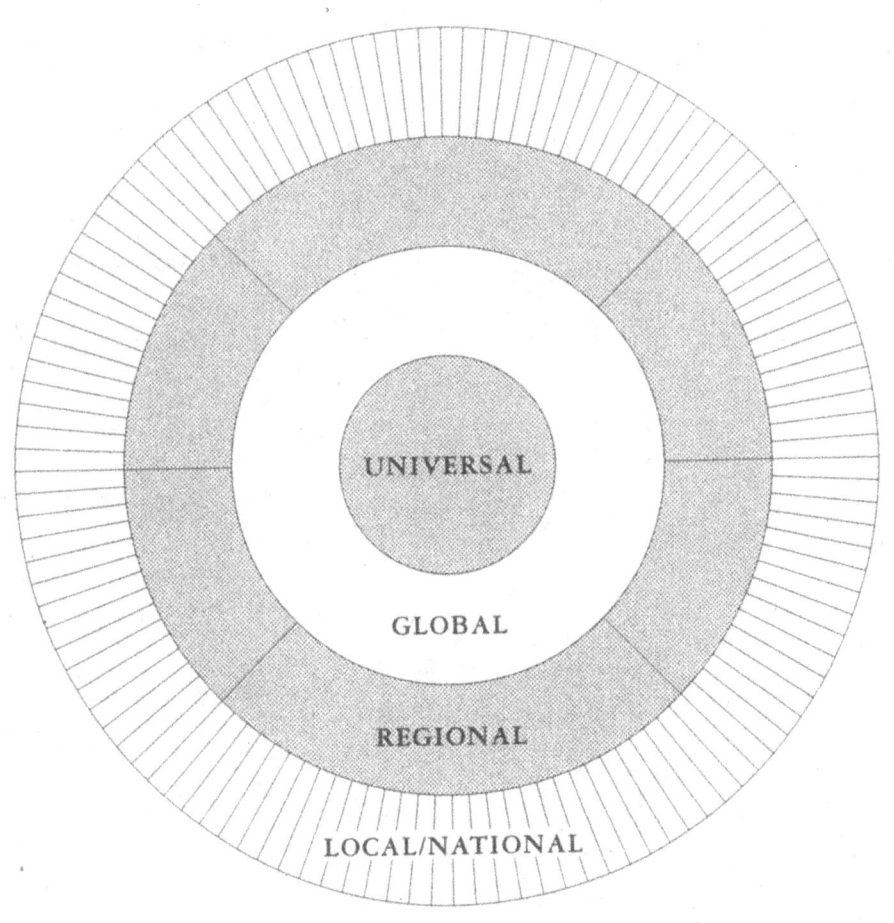

Bibliography

1. Books, articles and papers
2. Reports
3. Instruments

1. Books, articles and papers

Addo, Michael K. (1988),"Political Self Determination within the Context of The African Charter on Human and Peoples' Rights", *Journal of African Law,* Vol. 32, No.2, 1988, pp. 182-192.

Aluko, Olajide (1981),"The Organisation of African Unity and Human Rights. *The Commonwealth Journal of International Affairs,* pp. 234-242.

Amate (1986), *Inside the Organization of African Unity (OAU). Pan-Africanism in Practice.* McMillan Publishers.

An-Na'im, Abdullahi Ahmed (1992), *Human Rights in Cross-Cultural Perspectives.* University of Pensylvania Press.

Arat, Zehra F. (1991), *Democracy and Human Rights in Developing Countries,* Lynne Rienner Publishers.

Armstrong, Alice and Stewart, Julie (eds) (1990), "The Legal Situation of Women in Southern Africa", *Women and Law in Southern Africa, vol.II.* University of Zimbabwe Publications, Print Brokers (Pvt) Ltd., Harare, Zimbabwe.

Armstrong, Alice (1993), "Uncovering Reality: Excavating Women's Rights in African Family Law", *Women and Law in Southern Africa, Working Paper No.7,* WLSA, P.O. Box UA171, Union Ave., Harare, Zimbabwe.

"Bangkok Governmental Declaration, The" (1 May 1993), *Law & Society Trust Review,* Vol. III, No. 57, pp. 1-31.

Bello, Emmanuel G. (1985), "Human Rights, African Developments", *Encyclopedia of Public International Law.* Max Planck Institute for Comparative Public Law and International Law, Elsevier Science Publishers, Amsterdam.

Bello, Emmanuel G. (1987), *The African Charter on Human and Peoples' Rights.* Martinus Nijhoff Publishers, Dordrecht/Boston/Lancaster.

Benedek, Wolfgang and K. Ginther (eds) (1983), "New Perspectives and Conceptions of International Law. An Afro-European Dialogue", *Austrian Journal of Public and International Law.* Springer-Verlag Wien.

Benedek, Wolfgang (1989), "Reflections on the Concept of Peoples' Rights in the African Charter", *African Association of International Law, Seminar on "The Judiciary and Human Rights in Africa,* Banjul 13-17 November, 1989, paper.

Benedek, Wolfgang and Heinz, Wolfgang (eds) (1992), *Regional systems of human rights protection in Africa, America and Europe: Third Afro-Americo-European Conference, Strasbourg, June 1992.* Friedrich-Naumann-Stiftung, Nomos Verlagsgesellschaft, Baden-Baden.

Blackburn, Robert and John Tayler (eds) (1991), *Human Rights for the 1990's - Legal, Political and Ethical Issues.* British Institute of Human Rights.

van Boven, Theo (1986), "The Relations between Peoples' Rights and Human Rights in the African Charter", *Human Rights Law Journal,* Vol. 7, N.P. Engel Publisher, Kehl am Rhein/Strasbourg/Arlington, pp. 183-194.

Brownlie, Ian (1966), *Principles of Public International Law.* Clarendon Press, Oxford.

Cassese, Antonio (1990), *Human Rights in a Changing World.* Polity Press (Basil Blackwell).

Crawford, James (ed) (1988), *The Rights of Peoples.* Clarendon Press, Oxford.

Dixon, Martin (1990), *Textbook on International Law.* Blackstone Press Limited.

Dokali, Emillias (1993), "Can Malawi Pay a Bill of Rights ?" *Paper delivered to Political Leaders Seminar,* 26-27 November.

Donnelly, Jack (1984), "Cultural Relativism and Universal Human Rights", *Human Rights Quarterly,* Vol. 6, pp. 400-419.

Donnelly, Jack (1989), *Universal Human Rights in Theory and Practice.* Cornell University Press, second printing, 1989.

D'Sa, Rose (1985), "Human and Peoples' Rights: Distinctive Features of the African Charter", *Journal of African Law,* Vol. 29, No.1, pp. 72-81.

D'Sa, Rose (1987), "The African Charter on Human and Peoples' Rights: Problems and Prospects for Regional Action", *Australian Year Book of International Law,* Australian National University, pp. 101-130.

Appendix - Bibliography

D'Sa, Rose (1989),"The Domestic Application of the African Charter on Human and Peoples' Rights", *Developing Human Rights Jurisprudence*, Vol. 2, Judicial Colloquium in Harare 19-22 April, pp. 101-124.

Eide, Asbjørn; Catarina Krause and Allan Rosas (1995), *Economic, Social and Cultural Rights, A Textbook*. Martinus Nijhoff Publishers, Dordrecht/Boston/London.

Eide, Asbjørn; Gudmundur Alfredsson, Göran Melander, Lars Adam Rehof and Allan Rosas with the collaboration of Theresa Swinehart (1992), *The Universal Declaration of Human Rights. A Commentary*. Scandinavian University Press, Universitetsforlaget AS 1992, Norway. Oxford University Press, Walton Street.

Eide, Asbjørn and Jan Helgesen (1991), *The Future of Human Rights in a Changing World. Fifty Years since the Four Freedoms Address. Essays in honour of Torkel Opsahl*. Norwegian University Press, Oslo, Norway.

Eide, Asbjørn (1989), "Realization of Social and Economic Rights and the Minimum Threshold Approach", *Human Rights Law Journal*, Vol. 10, No. 1-2, pp. 35-51.

Espiell, Prof. H. Gros (1979), *The Evolving Concept of Human Rights: Western, Socialist and Third World approaches. In Human Rights: Thirty Years after the Universal Declaration*, Dr. B.G. Ramcharan (eds). Martinus Nijhoff, The Hague/Boston/London.

Granberg, Per and J.R. Parkinson (1988), *Botswana. Country Study and Norwegian Aid Review*, Chr. Michelsen Institute, Department of Social Science and Development, Bergen. A/S Repro-Trykk, Bergen.

Hall, M. and Young, T. (1991), "Recent Constitutional Changes in Mozambique", *Journal of African Law*, Vol. 35, Nos. 1 and 2.

Henkin, Louis (eds) (1981), *The International Bill of Rights: The Covenant on Civil and Political Rights*, Columbia University Press, New York.

Hopkinson, Nicholas (1992), *Good Government in Africa*, Wilton Park Paper 54, University of London, Institute of Advanced Legal Studies, London.

Howard, Rhoda E. (1986), *Human Rights in Commonwealth Africa*, Rowman and Littlefield, New Jersey.

The Hunger Project (1985), *Ending Hunger: An Idea Whose Time Has Come*, Praeger Publishers International Offices, Europe, the Middle East & Africa, Holt Saunders, Ltd.

Jensen, Marianne og Karin Poulsen (1983), *Human Rights and Cultural Change*, Det Danske Center for Menneskerettigheder, Copenhagen.

Kalaile, J.B. (1995), *Comments on the Provisional Constitution*, submission to the National Constitutional Committee.

Kamchedzera, Garton (1985), *Malawi: The New Constitution and the Family*, submission to the National Constitutional Committee.

Kamminga, Menno T. (1992), *Inter-State Accountability for Violations of Human Rights*. University of Pensylvania Press.

Kaunda, Desmond Mudala (1994), *Malawi: From Human Wrongs to Human Rights. Some Consideration on Constitutional, Institutional and Political Reform*, LL.B dissertation, Faculty of Law, University of Malawi, Chancellor College, Zomba.

Kiwanuka, Richard N. (1988), "The Meaning of "People" in the African Charter on Human and Peoples' Rights", *American Journal of International Law*, Vol. 82, No.1, pp. 80-101.

Kobia, Samuel (1993), *The Quest for Democracy in Africa*, National Council of Churches of Kenya, Nairobi.

Kotey, E.N.A. (1989), "The African Charter on Human and Peoples' Rights : an Exposition, Analysis and Critique", *University of Ghana Law Journal*, Vol. XVI, 1982-85, pp. 130-152.

Kpundeh, Sahr John (ed) (1992), Panel on Issues in Democratization, *Democratization in Africa: African Views, African Voices*. National Academy Press, Washington, D.C.

Kunig, Philip (1982), "The Protection of Human Rights by International Law in Africa", *German Yearbook of International Law*, Vol. 25, Duncker & Humblot, Berlin, pp. 138-168.

Lindholt, Lone (1995), *Derogationsforbudi internationalemenneskerettigheds-instrumenter*, Retsvidenskabeligt Institut B, Studier nr. 59, Københavns Universitet.

Mair, Lucy (1962), *The Nyasaland Elections of 1961*, University of London. The Athlone Press.

Maope, K.A. (1986), *Human Rights in Botswana, Lesotho and Swaziland*, survey, Human Rights Project (1983), National University of Lesotho, paper.

McMaster, Carolyn (1974), *Malawi - Foreign Policy and Development*. Julian Friedmann Publishers Ltd.

Morton, Fred and Ramsay, Jeff (ed.) (1987), *The Birth of Botswana*. Longman Botswana, Gaborone.

Naldi, Gino J. (1989), *The Organization of African Unity*. Mansell Publishing Limited.

Neff, Steven (1983), "Human Rights in Africa. Thoughts on the African Charter on Human and Peoples' Rights in the Light of Case Law from Botswana, Lesotho and Swaziland", *International and Comparative Law Quarterly*, Vol. 33, 1984, pp. 331-347.

Neff, Steven (1986), *Human Rights in Botswana, Lesotho and Swaziland Implications of Adherence to International Human Rights Treaties*, Human Rights Project (1983), National University of Lesotho, paper.

Nguema, Isaac (Nov.-Dec. 1989), "Universality and Specificity in Human Rights in Africa", *The Courier*, no. 118, pp. 16-17.

Nguema, Isaac (1990), "Human Rights Perspectives in Africa. The Roots of a Constant Challenge", *Human Rights Law Journal*, Vol. 11, No. 3-4, pp. 261-283.

Nickel, James W.(1987), *Making Sense of Human Rights*. University of California Press, Berkeley; Los Angeles; London.

Nordskov Nielsen, Lars; Claus Gulmann og Lars Adam Rehof (eds) (1987), *Menneskerettigheder - viden og handling*. G.E.C. Gad, København.

Nowak, Manfred (1993), *U.N. Covenant on Civil and Political Rights*, CCPR Commentary. N.P. Engel, Kehl am Rhein; Strasbourg; Arlington.

Nsereko, Daniel D. Ntanda (1988), "The Right to Legal Representation in Botswana", *Israel Yearbook on Human Rights*, 1988, pp. 211-227.

Nsereko, Daniel D. Ntanda (1995), "The Poisoned Tree: Responses to Involuntary Confessions in Criminal Proceedings in Botswana, Uganda and Zambia", Bassiouni, Cherif M and Ziyad Motala (eds) (1995), *The Protection of Human Rights in African Criminal Proceedings*. Martinus Nijhoff Publishers.

Okere, B. Obinna (1984), "The Protection of Human Rights in Africa and the African Charter on Human and Peoples' Rights : A Comparative Analysis with the European and American Systems", *Human Rights Quarterly*, Vol. 6, No.2, pp. 141-159.

Oxford Advanced Learners Dictionary of Current English (1989). Oxford University Press, Oxford.

Pachai, Bridglal (1972), *The Early History of Malawi*. Northwestern University Press.

Pachai, Bridglal (1973), *Malawi: The History of the Nation*. Longman Group Limited, London.

Quansah, E.K. (1995), "Is the right to get pregnant a fundamental right in Botswana ?: Case Note", *Journal of African Law,* Vol. 39 no. 1, p. 97-102.

Quashigah, Kofi (1992), "The Philosophical Basis of Human Rights and its Relation to Africa", *Journal of Human Rights Law and Practice,* Vol. 1 no. 3 / Vol. 2 nos. 1&2, Nigeria.

Rehof, Lars Adam and Claus Gulmann (1989), *Human Rights in Domestic Law and Development Assistance Policies of the Nordic Countries,* Publications from the Danish Center of Human Rights No. 2. Martinus Nijhoff Publishers.

Rehof, Lars Adam og Tyge Trier (1990), *Menneskeret.* Jurist- og Økonomforbundets Forlag, København.

Robertson, A.H. and J.G. Merrills (1989), *Human Rights in the World. An introduction to the study of the international protection of human rights.* Manchester University Press, Manchester and New York.

Roche, Mgr. John (1993), *Options for Church and State: Now and Post Referendum,* Occasional papers, No 47, Centre of African Studies, Edinburgh University.

Sachs, Albie (1991), *South Africa and Human Rights in Africa,* University of London, Institute of Commonwealth Studies, Banjul.

Sachs, Albie (1988), "Building a New Legal System", *Mozambique Briefing,* no. 8. 1988.

Schapera, Isaac (1938, rev. ed. 1984), *A handbook of Tswana Law and Custom.* Frank Cass and Company Ltd., Gainsborough House, London.

Shepherd, George W. Jr. (1985), "The Tributary State and "People's Rights" in Africa: The Banjul Charter and Self-Reliance", *Africa Today,* Vol. 32, 1st and 2nd Quarters, pp. 37-50.

Shivji, Issa G. (1989), *The Concepts of Human Rights in Africa,* CODESRIA BOOK SERIES, London.

Shivji, Issa G. (1991), *State and Constitutionalism: An African Debate on Democracy,* Southern Africa Political Economy Series (SAPES) Trust. Harare, Zimbabwe.

Sieghart, P. (1983), *The International Law of Human Rights".* Clarendon Press, Oxford.

Sieghart, P. (1991), "International human rights law: some current problems", Blackburn, Robert and John Taylor (eds) (1991), *Human Rights for the 1990's - Legal, Political and Ethical Issues.* British Institute of Human Rights.

Sinha, Surya Prakash (1981),"Human Rights: A Non-Western Viewpoint", *Archiv für Rechts- Und Sozialphilosophie*, Vol. 19, 1, pp. 76-91.

Sinha, Surya Prakash (1984), "Freeing Human Rights from Natural Rights", *Archiv für Rechts- Und Sozialphilosophie*, Vol. 3, 1984, pp. 342-383.

Sinha, Surya Prakash (1989),"Why has it not been possible to define Law?", *Archiv für Rechts- Und Sozialphilosophie*, Vol. 1, 1989.

Singh, Nagendra (1986), *Enforcement of Human Rights, in Peace & War and the Future of Humanity*. Martinus Nijhoff Publishers, Eastern Law House Private Ltd.

Solo, Kholisano (1995), "Police Training and Human Rights in Botswana", Bassiouni, Cherif M and Ziyad Motala (eds), *The Protection of Human Rights in African Criminal Proceedings*. Martinus Nijhoff Publishers.

Spence, C. F. (1963), *Mocambique*, Howard Timmins, Cape Town.

Steen Preis, Ann-Belinda (1996),"Human Rights as Cultural Practice: An Anthropological Critique", *Human Rights Quarterly*, Vol. 18, 1996, pp.286-315.

Steiner, Henry J. and Philip Alston (eds) (1996), *International Human Rights in Context*, Clarendon Press, Oxford.

Tévoédjré, Albert (1986), "Human Rights and Democracy in Africa", *Annual Lecture Series:2*, The United Nations University.

Tomasevki, Katarina (1994) "Human Rights", in Childers, *Challenges to the United Nations*, CIIR, London.

Vaenerberg, Ann-Marie (1990), *Mänskliga rättigheter i Afrika : den fackliga förenings friheten i Botswana, Kenya och Senegal*, Avhandling pro gradu i folkrätt, Åbo Akademi, Åbo.

Vincent, R.J. (1986), *Human Rights and International Relations*, The Royal Institute of International Affairs. Cambridge University Press.

Welch, Claude E. (1981), "The OAU and Human Rights: Towards a New Definition", *The Journal of Modern African Studies*, 19, 3 (1981), pp. 401-420.

Welch, Claude E. and Ronald I. Meltzer (1984), *Human Rights and Development in Africa*, State University of New York Press, New York.

Wills, A. J. (1985), *An Introduction to the History of Central Africa, Zambia, Malawi, Zimbabwe*, Fourth Edition, Oxford University Press.

Women's World Banking Malawi Affiliate (Ms. N. Nyandovi-Kerr) (1994), *Women Empowerment in Malawi*, paper presented to Cabinet Ministers, Blantyre, Malawi.

Zetterqvist, Jenny (1990), "Refugees in Botswana in the Light of International Law." *Research report no. 87*, The Scandinavian Institute of African Studies, Uppsala, Motala Grafiska, Motala.

2. Reports

African Conference on the Rule of Law: A report on the proceedings of the conference, Lagos, Nigeria, 3-7 Jan., 1961. International Commission of Jurists, Geneve, 1961.

Amnesty International (1991), *Amnesty International Report, 1991*. Amnesty International Publications, London.

Amnesty International (1993), *Malawi, Preserving the one-party state - human rights violations and the referendum*, Amnesty International Publications, London.

Amnesty International (1993), *Malawi, recommendations for permanent protection of basic human rights following the pro-democracy vote*, London.

Amnesty International (1994), *Malawi, A new future for human rights*, London.

Botswana Chronology, the Constitution of Botswana (1986), *Constitutions of the Countries of the World*. Oceana Publications.

CIIR Comment: Malawi, School of Oriental and African Studies, University of London, 1993/1994.

Constitutional Change in Malawi: Report of a delegation of the council of the bar of England and the Wales and the Scottish Faculty of Advocates, 7 - 17 October 1993.

The Constitution of the Bechuanaland Protectorate (1961), An account prepared by the Information Branch of the Bechuanaland Protectorate Government. Botswana Book Centre, Lobatsi.

Declaration on Human Rights, EEC Bulletin no. 7/8, 1989.

Det Danske Center for Menneskerettigheder (1988), *Menneskerettigheder. En tekstsamling, I + II*. København.

Eight Annual Activity Report of the African Commission on Human and Peoples' Rights: 1994-1995.

Fifth Annual Activity Report of the African Commission on Human and Peoples' Rights: 1991-1992. *Human Rights Watch World Report 1993: Events of 1992,* New York, Washington, Los Angeles.

Mozambique - Draft Amended Constitution, (1990), Dossier No. 3, Mozambique Information Office.

Report of the Law Reform Committee: on (i) Marriage Act, (ii) Law of Inheritance, (iii) Electoral Law and (iv) Citizenship Law. Botswana, June to December, 1986. The Government Printer, Gaborone, Botswana.

Report of the United Nations Conference on Environment and the Development: Principle 20, Chapter 24, Rio de Janeiro, 3 - 14 June 1992.

UNHCR, Branch Office Malawi: *Voluntary Repatriation of Mozambican Refugees from Malawi,* Update No. 3. June 15, 1994.

United Nations: *International Instruments, Chart of Ratifications as at 31 December 1995,* New York and Geneva 1995.

CIA, World Factbook 1994: *Malawi,* The University of Missouri-St. Louis.

World Population Data Sheet 1993: of the Population Reference Bureau, Inc., Washington D.C.

3. Instruments

A Compilation of International Instruments: U.N., New York, 1988.

African Charter on Human and Peoples' Rights.

Basic Documents in International Law: Ed. Ian Brownlie. Oxford University Press, 1972.

Draft Ombudsman Bill: Ministry of Justice, February 1996, Malawi.

Den Europæiske Menneskerettighedskonvention: G.E.C.Gads Forlag, 1985.

The International Bill of Rights: The Covenant on Civil and Political Rights, see Henkin, Louis.

The Vienna Convention on the Law of Treaties, see Sinclair, I.M.

Vienna Declaration and Programme of Action, 25 June 1993